D1062064

LONG
ISLAND
AND THE SEA

LONG ISLAND AND THE SEA

ISLAND

AND THE SEA

· A Maritime History ·

BILL BLEYER

Foreword by Billy Joel

THE
History
PRESS

Published by The History Press
Charleston, SC
www.historypress.com

Copyright © 2019 by Bill Bleyer
All rights reserved

Front cover: B.J. Phillips painting *The HMS Sylph & HMS Maidstone Attacking off Horton Point, Southold, New York, June 1814*. Courtesy of the Southold Historical Society, Southold, New York.
Back cover, top: Nathaniel Currier lithograph of the fire that destroyed the *Lexington* on Long Island Sound in 1840. *Author's collection.*
Back cover, inset: Republic Engine and Airplane Corporation's experimental *X-1* submarine built for the U.S. Navy after its launch at Jakobson Shipyard in Oyster Bay in 1955. *U.S. Navy–Submarine Force Museum.*

First published 2019

Manufactured in the United States

ISBN 978-1-5402-3840-5

Library of Congress Control Number: 2018966260

Notice: The information in this book is true and complete to the best of our knowledge. It is offered without guarantee on the part of the author or The History Press. The author and The History Press disclaim all liability in connection with the use of this book.

All rights reserved. No part of this book may be reproduced or transmitted in any form whatsoever without prior written permission from the publisher except in the case of brief quotations embodied in critical articles and reviews.

PORT JEFFERSON FREE LIBRARY
100 THOMPSON STREET
PORT JEFFERSON, NY, 11777

For my mother, Adele, a lover of all things nautical who introduced me to life on the water by taking me paddling on Long Island Sound as an infant.

CONTENTS

CONTENTS

FOREWORD

I was always fascinated with boats and the water. I was very aware at an early age that I was an islander, and I wanted to be part of the "boating thing."

Having grown up in Hicksville, if you didn't have a car, you were pretty far from the water. So I used to ride my bike up to the North Shore to Oyster Bay and Bayville just to look at the boats and be near the water. And my mom used to drive me and my friends, because she was in love with Long Island, too.

Right now the boats I have are *Alexa*, which is a thirty-six-foot BHM fiberglass swordfish boat built on Shelter Island in 1992 and named for my elder daughter; *Della Rose*, named after my second daughter, a thirty-foot Rybovich that's a cold-molded wood sportfishing boat built in Palm Beach in 1960; *Argos*, a thirty-six-foot Ellis fiberglass lobster boat with a marlin tower built in Maine in 2009; and a twenty-eight-foot aluminum landing craft built in Washington State. I also gave my wife a little twenty-one-foot fiberglass lobster boat built by a company called Atlas. That one's named *Oyster Babe*.

Alexa I designed pretty much from the hull up. I went up to Maine to pick out the BHM hull. I wanted a swordfish boat, so I was pretty specific about how I wanted that boat fitted out. *Argos* I designed as well. I went up to Maine to the Ellis boat company and picked out a thirty-six-foot hull and had it fitted out pretty much as a sportfishing boat.

I'm kind of a history nut. I was always fascinated with the history of Long Island. And a lot of the history of Long Island is commercial fishing,

boatbuilding and pleasure boating. It goes back to colonial times.

I was always interested when I got up to places on the North Shore or the South Shore in the history of the area. Why there were marinas or why there was sportfishing going on or commercial fishing going on. I always wanted to know why. Why is this place here? What did it used to be?

To learn the answers, I talked to as many people as I could. To people at the marinas, to other boat owners, or I would go to a library and get books on the history of the area. It made me feel like more of an islander. I wanted to have an identity. And that's how I defined myself: as an islander from a place with a maritime history.

It's important for other people to understand the region's maritime history. It lets people realize how precious the resources that they have are, that they might lose them. Once they realize how much of what they love about Long Island is from its history, it would make them more conscious of not losing it. All of the marinas and harbors are really a lot of what makes Long Island the place that it is. Even people who are not from Long Island but are visiting may not know about commercial fishing and the maritime history but they like the way things look. They like the villages, the waterfront areas. I think it's important for people to understand that it looks that way because it was that way for a long, long time.

I think this new book on the maritime history of Long Island will be essential reading in schools.

—Billy Joel, Centre Island, New York

ACKNOWLEDGMENTS

J oshua Stoff, whose 1994 Long Island maritime history book for young readers was an inspiration and a valuable resource for this volume.

For help with research and photographs: Joshua Stoff of the Cradle of Aviation Museum; Tim Harrison of *Lighthouse Digest*; Smithtown Town Historian Brad Harris; Natalie Naylor; Oyster Bay Town Historian John Hammond; Captain Dan Berg; Richard Barons, Stacy Myers and Lucia Akard of the East Hampton Historical Society; Gina Piastuck of the East Hampton Library; Ronna Dixson of the New York State Office of Parks, Recreation and Historic Preservation; Yale University Library; Jennifer Gaudio of the U.S. Coast Guard Museum; Rob Damroth of the Connecticut Office of Tourism; Bob Gundersen of the Madison (Connecticut) Historical Society; Litchfield (Connecticut) Historical Society; Amy Folk of the Southold Historical Society and Oysterponds Historical Society and Southold town historian; Caren Zatyk at the Smithtown Public Library; Torkel Knutson; Jeff Schock of the Billy Joel Archives; Huntington Town Historian Robert Hughes; Asharoken Village Historian Ed Carr; Alexandra Wolff and Lauren Brincat of Preservation Long Island; Joshua Ruff of the Long Island Museum; Arthur Mattson; Adam Grohman; Heather A. Hales of the Eskenazi Museum of Art at Indiana University; Port Jefferson Village Historian Chris Ryon and graphics designer Susan Orifici; Jason Bischoff-Wurstle of the New Haven Museum; Mary Cummings of the Southampton Historical Museum; Kristen J. Nyitray of Special

Collections at Stony Brook University; Sara Reres of the Sea Cliff Village Museum; Harriet Gerard Clark of the Raynham Hall Museum; Bev Tyler and Karen Martin of the Three Village Historical Society; Vicki Aspinwall and Barbara Guzowski of the Long Island Studies Institute at Hofstra University; Joshua M. Smith of the American Merchant Marine Museum; Bob Doxsee Jr.; artist Frank Litter; Laura Warren, Kathleen Cash and Lawrence Mirsky of the Historical Society of Greater Port Jefferson; Iris Levin of the Nassau County Photo Archives Center; Lisa Nordstrom of the Garvies Point Museum-Preserve; Joshua Voda of the National Museum of the American Indian; Tracy Pfaff and Kathy Fitzpatrick of the Northport Historical Society; North Hempstead Town Historian Howard Kroplick; Maura Feeney of the Montauk Public Library; *Newsday* reporter Mark Harrington; Steven King; Robert MacKay; FBI historian John F. Fox; Kerri Allegretta and Jay Carson of Webb Institute; Susan Sarna and Elizabeth DeMaria of Sagamore Hill National Historic Site; Regina Feeney of the Freeport Memorial Library; Cynthia Krieg of the Freeport Historical Society; Christine Edwins, Kim Barteau and Barbara Compono at the Bayville Public Library; John Strong; Melisa Andruski of the Southold Free Library; Kate Igoe of the National Air and Space Museum Library; Dianne Baumert-Moyik and John Eagan of Northrup Grumman Corporation; Jack Youngs and Barbara Schwartz of the Sag Harbor Historical Society; Mark Procknik of the New Bedford Whaling Museum; Dana Howell of the Monmouth County (New Jersey) Historical Association; Deborah Boudreau of the Ward Melville Heritage Organization; Pierce Rafferty of the Henry L. Ferguson Museum; Mark Berhow and Bolling Smith of the Coast Defense Study Group; Mark Spring of Bowling Green (Kentucky) State University; Wendy Gulley of the Submarine Force Museum; Stan Mickus of Cross Sound Ferry Services; Fred Hall of Bridgeport & Port Jefferson Steamboat Company; Bridg Hunt of North Ferry Company; Bill Clark of South Ferry Company; Luke Kaufman of Fire Island Ferries; Richard Welch; Nomi Dayan of the Whaling Museum & Education Center in Cold Spring Harbor; Richard Doctorow of the Sag Harbor Whaling Museum; Arlene Stephani and Barbara Forde of the Long Island Maritime Museum; and especially Nancy Solomon of Long Island Traditions for extensive information on bay houses and boatyards.

Audrey C. Tiernan for her photographs in the color center insert.

Acknowledgments

My advance readers for some chapters—Nomi Dayan, Amy Folk, Robert MacKay, Susan Sarna, Nancy Solomon, Joshua Stoff and Beverly Tyler—and those who reviewed the entire manuscript: Joe Catalano and especially the exacting and knowledgeable Natalie Naylor.

My helpful editors at The History Press: J. Banks Smither and Abigail Fleming.

My friend Joe Catalano for advice and general support.

And special thanks to Billy Joel for his insightful foreword.

INTRODUCTION

From its first Native American inhabitants to the tens of thousands of current-day commercial mariners and recreational boaters, those living and working near the shores of Long Island have always had a strong connection to the sea. And with its nearly 120-mile-long fish shape and 1,100 miles of shoreline, no one on the island is ever more than 10 miles from the water.

It was the waterways that allowed Long Island to be settled and then fueled its economic development over the succeeding two centuries. The first Europeans came to Long Island in the seventeenth century via the sea. In the eighteenth and early nineteenth centuries, it was the water that provided the fastest and most reliable transportation as well as livelihoods and food. It was the water that employed fishermen, baymen, mariners and shipbuilders. And even those working ashore as farmers relied on the sea for fertilizer.

Over the last three centuries, the Atlantic Ocean, Long Island Sound and the bays connected to them increasingly provided recreational outlets as well as hundreds of jobs supporting pleasure boating.

The same waterways that provided transportation and employment for residents also provided a pathway for the nation's enemies in wartime. From the British blockade and skirmishes during the American Revolution to the landing of saboteurs and sinking of merchant vessels by Germany in World War II, the waters around the Island were the scene of international conflict. Shipwrecks from those wars remain to remind us of the struggles and provide recreation and an economic boost from visits by scuba divers and fishermen.

A 1776 map of Long Island. *Courtesy of Natalie A. Naylor.*

Today, Long Island geographically consists of four counties—Suffolk, Nassau, Queens and Kings. Because the last two are boroughs of New York City, which has its own unique history, this volume will only deal with Nassau and Suffolk, which for most of those living there constitutes Long Island.

While officially designated a peninsula by the Supreme Court in 1985, Long Island has always been an island. That was proven in the Age of Discovery, when Captain Adriaen Block was the first European to explore Long Island Sound. And the current residents are reminded of it every time they leave by bridge, tunnel or ferry.

The island has been the setting for a rich and varied maritime history. But some aspects are little-known: the connection to slave ships; the Pan-American flying boats landing in Manhasset Bay in the early days of commercial transatlantic flight; the development of submarines and torpedoes on the East End; and the high-speed commuter yachts used by Gold Coast millionaires to get to their offices in Manhattan. This book tells those stories and many more.

As for the person telling the stories, I've loved the water and history as far back as I can remember. I was privileged to grow up spending my summers from age one on the shore of Long Island Sound. That meant that over the years I was lucky enough to have first a dinghy with an outboard motor, then two speedboats (one after the other) in high school, then a beach catamaran purchased the day *Newsday* hired me in 1981 so I could escape being landlocked in New Jersey and finally a kayak and my current sailboat, *Adele B.* I've had it for thirty-three years, and it's named for my mother, a water rat like me, who made everything described above possible. And scuba diving on shipwrecks off the South Shore since the early 1980s has only intensified my interest in maritime history.

My twin passions came together during my thirty-three-year career as a *Newsday* staff writer. I was already writing about history part-time when in 1992 the paper's editor, Anthony Marro, decided someone—me—should be covering Long Island as an island, with all of the nautical activity that entailed. That dream job provided me with the background to draw on and build on to compile this book—the most comprehensive on the subject to date.

NATIVE AMERICANS

F ishing is the oldest maritime activity on Long Island, first done by the region's earliest inhabitants.

The Native Americans who gave Long Island so many place names, from Aquebogue to Wantagh, lived in small villages by the water. The Indians are believed to have gathered shellfish on the bays along Long Island Sound as early as AD 700. Before European settlers began to exploit the resource, the waterways teemed with more than two hundred types of fish and many kinds of shellfish.[1]

Excavations at Native American village sites show the inhabitants hunted deer, wild turkey and other game with arrowheads chipped from stones of chert and quartz found on the beach. They planted beans, squash and corn. But their primary source of protein was marine life.

Archaeological digs indicate that small fish were caught in nets cast by hand. This conclusion is based on the discovery of grooved stones that were likely used as net sinkers. The Indians also likely used fish weirs fashioned from woven brush suspended between stakes. "The fishermen made ingenious use of the tide as part of the trapping mechanism," writes John Strong, a historian who has written extensively about Long Island's Native American population. "The wall of stakes and brush was stretched across the mouth of a tidal pond at low tide level. The incoming tide rose over the barrier carrying the fish into the trap and the outgoing tide left them helpless in the shallow water where the women scooped them into baskets."[2]

Native Americans also towed traps made from branches behind their dugout canoes and fished with hooks made from bone and antler. Sea turtles, sturgeon and other fish would be dried on scaffolds or smoked to help the population survive the winter. Small silver fish known as menhaden were used to fertilize fields of corn—a technique passed on to the white settlers.

The abundance of shells found at excavations in Mount Sinai, Lloyd Neck, Shelter Island and other locations indicated that shellfish—clams, oysters, scallops, mussels and whelks—were harvested year-round. The Native Americans also showed the European settlers how to harvest shellfish. The Indians used the shells as tools. Shells were the raw material for wampum, which was strung together or sewn onto belts for decoration of clothing or trading. The shells of whelk and large clams known as quahogs were thicker and more durable and could be drilled and shaped into beads for artwork and trade. The beads could be white but also purple if they came from the area where the muscle held the two halves of a shell together. The purple beads were rare and more valuable. The arrival of the Europeans meant there were tools to make it easier to make the wampum. The beads were about one-eighth of an inch in diameter and from one-quarter of an inch to one-half of an inch long. The Native Americans strung them together to make them easier to carry. The wampum was traded with other bands, especially inland Indians with no access to shells and who had never developed the skills to make wampum.

For fishing and travel, Long Island's coastal Algonquians relied mostly on dugout canoes made from hollowed-out logs. They also used the bark of elm trees for lighter canoes built over frames, but these were reserved for protected waterways. The dugouts were made from large fallen trees, usually pine, oak, chestnut or tulip. They were hollowed out with fire and then stone tools. One man could construct a dugout in ten to twelve days. The largest of these canoes were forty to fifty feet long and could carry up to forty men. One early white settler claimed he observed a sea canoe with eighty people aboard plowing easily through the waves on Long Island Sound. The earliest colonists also reported that the Native Americans often raised poles rigged with small sails on their dugouts.

While the Native vessels were simple compared to sailing vessels that brought the Europeans across the ocean, the newcomers were astonished by what the Indians could do with dugouts that were heavy and seemingly unwieldy. One wrote that the Indians "will venture to Seas, when an English Shallope dare not bear a knot of sayle; scudding over the overgrown waves as fast as a winde-driven ship." As the Europeans established communities,

Painting of Native American encampment along the Long Island shoreline with birch bark canoes. *Courtesy of Nassau County Photo Archives Center.*

they appreciated the dugouts even more as an efficient and fast means of transportation. Some colonists were afraid to ride in the tippy boats, where "the edge was not more than a hand's-breadth above the water." But one wrote that taking a canoe instead of walking from one village to another "made full three hours difference." During the seventeenth century, the English and Dutch would hire Algonquians to carry their correspondence in the dugouts. One of these messengers regularly traveled fifty miles along Long Island Sound, even in the middle of winter. The colonists realized that the canoes were so useful that some began building their own dugouts to transport people and goods.[3]

The canoes allowed trading with other bands as far away as upstate New York and the Great Lakes. This trading explains why flint tools have been found in Indian sites on Long Island when the raw material came from up along the Hudson River and copper jewelry when copper could not be found closer than the Great Lakes.[4]

Whales that died and washed up on the beach—"drift whales"—were an important source of food for the Native Americans. The frequent appearance of these whales was seen as a gift from the gods. They were so critical to the lives of the Indians and economy of the settlers that rights to harvest them were frequently mentioned in early deeds. A 1661 deed between Southampton officials and Montaukett Indians specified that Lion Gardiner and Thomas James would divide the first whale that washed up on the shore and subsequent whales would be divided between the two men and the inhabitants of East Hampton.[5]

Besides facilitating trading with other bands, the Long Island Native Americans' dugout canoes allowed them to pursue whales that were still alive and swimming along the shore. This technique would give rise to Long Island's second industry, a story told in chapter 3.

2

THE AGE OF EXPLORATION

I f a fire hadn't destroyed his ship, Adriaen Block might never have set foot on Long Island and proved that it was, in fact, an island.

Four years after Henry Hudson sighted the island that would be named Manhattan and explored the river that now bears his name, Block—in the summer of 1613—sailed to that same island on his third voyage to the region. While Hudson was seeking a passage to the Orient, Block, a Dutch lawyer-turned-adventurer, was looking to get rich on furs. He arrived in New York after a two-month voyage to New England and then down the Atlantic coast, along the south shore of Long Island and into the harbor, where he filled the hold of his ship *Tiger* with beaver and otter pelts.

While Block and his men were camped on the southern tip of Manhattan in preparation for returning to the Netherlands, they watched in horror as the *Tiger* caught fire and burned to the waterline. With no other means of salvation to return to their homes 3,600 miles away, the men spent a long hard winter constructing a new forty-four-foot ship, the *Onrust—Restless* in English. By late spring, they were able to launch the first ship built in what would become New York State.

As an explorer as well as a fur trader, Block wanted to investigate nearby landmasses and bodies of water. He considered *Onrust* too small to cross the Atlantic, so he sailed up the East River and through the treacherous rock-strewn passage named *Hellegat* in Dutch—"Hell Gate" in English—and into Long Island Sound. He was the first European to see it. Block sailed up the Connecticut River before landing at what he

Right: Portrait of Adriaen Block at the former U.S. Customs House in lower Manhattan, now the National Museum of the American Indian. *Reginald Marsh (1898–1954), Adriaen Block, circa 1936–37. Photo by Joshua Voda/NMAI.*

Below: A 1914 postcard depicting Adriaen Block and his men building the *Restless* on lower Manhattan prior to sailing it down Long Island Sound. *Author's collection.*

named Point of the Fishers, now Montauk Point, a reference to Native Americans he saw fishing there. As the first European to set foot on eastern Long Island, Block was able to conclude that the landmass he had been following to his south was, in fact, an island. After claiming it all for the Netherlands, the captain apparently hoped to spot a larger Dutch ship sailing to or from today's New York Harbor as a means of getting home. But when none materialized, he continued on and came upon an island fifteen miles to the east that had been discovered and mapped by Giovanni da Verrazzano. Block named it Adriaen Blocks Eylandt—Block Island.

He then sailed on to Cape Cod, where fortuitously he spotted another Dutch ship, the *Fortune*, under the command of his friend Hendrick Christiaenzen. Block hitched a ride back to Holland on the larger vessel. What became of the *Restless* is not recorded. Some accounts have the vessel being turned over to Block's subordinate, Captain Cornelius Hendricksen, and returning home in 1616 after further exploration in the region.

Block's discoveries led to a 1614 map titled *Adriaen Block's Chart*. The original, housed in the Dutch National Archives, depicts Long Island and the sound with surprising accuracy. After government officials questioned the captain, they named the area he had explored New Netherland.

Five years later, English captain Thomas Dermer traveled the sound in the reverse direction on a trip to Virginia. He was told about the body of water and the very long island to its south that formed it by a well-traveled Indian during a stop in New England. The Native leader even helpfully drew him a chalk map.

The Dutch West India Company acquired Manhattan Island from the Indians by 1626, and it became New Amsterdam. The Dutch soon spread out across the East River to western Long Island. English colonists came across the sound from Connecticut to establish towns on eastern Long Island and in Dutch territory such as Hempstead in the 1640s.[6]

3

THE WHALERS

I n the seventeenth century, whaling would become Long Island's second industry, after farming. And in both, the European colonists learned a great deal from the Native Americans who preceded them.

It was a natural progression for the Algonquian communities to move from harvesting beached whales for food, oil and bones that became tools to using canoes to hunt them close to shore. This probably occurred before the appearance of the first Europeans. The discovery of two deer-bone harpoons at an archaeological site in Mount Sinai demonstrates that the Indians targeted larger sea life, probably sea sturgeon, seals and small whales that became trapped in shallow tidal bays.[7]

The early Native American whalers would use several canoes to drive the whales toward the beach and then stab them with stone-tipped spears. The Basque fishermen who hunted whales off the Atlantic coast in the 1500s may have provided an example for the Native Americans on hunting techniques. The first written account of Indians whaling from shore on the East Coast dates from 1605. It describes how a sachem and a party of men in several canoes surrounded a small whale and attacked it with harpoons, spears and bows and arrows. Ropes were attached to the harpoons so the men could pull their craft close enough to the wounded whale for the archers to finish it off.[8]

The early English settlers on eastern Long Island saw how the Indians took advantage of beached whales and hunted those feeding along the shore. They quickly grasped the potential profit from whale oil, as it provided illumination that was much brighter and cleaner than other lighting sources, and later realized that it was also useful for lubricating tools. The baleen that some whales used to filter nutrients from the ocean made excellent corset stays, buggy whips and other products that needed to be strong but flexible.

For settlers interested in capturing whales, it worked out fortuitously that farming and whaling took place in different seasons. While farming took place mostly in the spring, summer and fall, whaling from the shore occurred mostly in winter. So in the early years, many settlers, especially on the East End, worked as both farmers and whalers.

The Europeans upgraded the hunting methods, substituting iron for the Indians' stone and bone implements. Having little experience with harpoons and lances, Southampton's settlers left their use to the Indians. But fearing an uprising, the English didn't want the Natives to actually possess the iron tools. So in 1643, three years after their arrival in Southampton, the white leaders prohibited blacksmiths from providing harpoons and lances, "which are known to be dangerous weapons to offend the English," to the Indians. But within a decade, the desire for profit outweighed that caution and the prohibition was lifted.[9]

A Shinnecock whaling crew depicted by David Martine. *Courtesy of David Martine and John Strong.*

The next year, Southampton's leaders divided the town into four districts in which residents could harvest whale carcasses that washed ashore. The local Indians were allocated the tail and fins for religious ceremonies. David Gardiner, a descendant of Lion Gardiner, the first English settler on Long Island, wrote that the Montaukett Indians would hold a celebration when they harvested a whale. They roasted the flesh and sacrificed the tails and fins to gain the favor of Cawhlutoowut, their most powerful deity.[10]

Most of the farmers had little experience on the sea and generally could not swim. So they were happy to hire the Native Americans, who were already proficient at chasing and killing whales, and let them risk their lives and endure the harsh conditions encountered in hunting along the coast in the winter. That practice began with Southampton entrepreneurs John Ogden and John Cooper around 1650. That year, Ogden asked the town for a license to "kill whales upon the south sea," while whales that washed ashore would still be community property shared by the inhabitants of each section of beach. The town fathers granted Ogden the first whaling license in America.[11]

Other English settlers followed the example of Ogden and Cooper in organizing companies to kill the North Atlantic right whales that swam close to shore from November to March. Even Southold, also founded in 1640, established a whaling company early on, although whales were less common around the North Fork.[12]

The right whale got its name because it was the "right" or best whale to hunt. It swims slowly in shallow water, scooping up meals of tiny copepods and filtering them through the plates of baleen made of keratin, similar in texture to human fingernails. Right whales also have thicker blubber than other species and so produced the most oil. And, conveniently, they floated when killed.

To make it easier to spot the prey from shore, the whaling groups set up wigwams along the beach for lookouts who would raise a flag when they saw a whale, or they erected posts similar to a ship's mast every three miles along the beach so lookouts could stand on them and look for spouts. Whales were so plentiful along the South Shore that Samuel Maverick wrote in 1669 that thirteen were killed that winter and twenty more in the spring.[13]

Dutchman James Loper established the first whaling station in East Hampton with his stepfather around 1668. They employed many Native Americans in the operation. Loper's success spurred the leaders of the Massachusetts island of Nantucket in 1672 to offer him land if he would come north and teach them how to "carry on a designe of whale fishing."

Loper accepted the arrangement. The island and the Massachusetts town of New Bedford came to dominate the industry in America.[14]

Early Long Island whaling from shore took place not just in today's Suffolk County. It was also carried out from what became East Rockaway and Jones Beach in Nassau County. Major Thomas Jones, who previously had been a privateer and enjoyed other adventures, was granted a license in 1705 "to take drift whales" found along the southern shore of central Long Island. He obtained a second colonial patent from Governor Robert Hunter in 1710 that gave him the right to any whale, shipwreck or fish found between Gravesend Bay in Brooklyn and western Suffolk County. The whaling crews would move into shacks along the beach during the fall and remain through the winter.[15]

By 1687, Southampton was home to fourteen whaling companies that produced 2,148 barrels of oil that year. Whales were so prevalent that a young woman on horseback who rode from East Hampton to the hamlet of Mecox in Southampton in 1702 counted thirteen carcasses along the beach, with great numbers of living whales spouting offshore.[16]

The hunt or "whale design" farther from shore that could be safely accomplished in a canoe was undertaken from two small boats from twenty-seven to thirty feet in length. Each would be manned by six Indians: a boatheader, who was in charge and steered from the stern; a boatsteerer, who would row from the front and then wield the harpoon when they got close to the prey; and four rowers. The harpoon was attached to more than one thousand feet of rope coiled in a wooden tub. The harpooned whale would pull out the rope and then tow the boat—in what would later became known as a "Nantucket Sleighride"—until it was exhausted. With the quarry motionless on the surface, boatsteerer and boatheader changed places so the man in charge could plunge lances into the whale to finish it off. If the harpoon or lance hit a vital spot, the chase could be over quickly. Otherwise, it would drag on for hours and prove to be extremely dangerous for the hunters as the huge creature thrashed or whipped its tail.

The carcass would be dragged ashore and processed over several days of hard around-the-clock labor because dead whales spoil quickly. The foot-thick blubber was peeled off, sliced into chunks and then "rendered," or boiled in cauldrons called "tryworks" to convert it into oil. The final product would be scooped into wooden barrels for shipping. Early on, a temporary tryworks would be set up on the beach near the dead whale. In later years, the blubber would be carted to larger permanent and malodorous tryworks that by law had to be far from and downwind of residential areas. An adult right whale could yield up to sixty barrels of oil, generating enough profit to pay for a medium-sized East End farm.[17]

Whale oil was not only sold or traded—it also functioned as a barter currency. John Thomas of Setauket purchased a slave named Samboe from Isack Rainer of Southampton for "19 barrels of good whale oyle." Communities often paid ministers, schoolteachers and other employees in oil.[18]

The company owners competed to get the Native American hunters to sign exclusive contracts. They offered exploitative small shares of the profit, usually in manufactured goods but also in food and sometimes rum and other liquor. In a 1667 agreement with Tobacus, the sachem of the Unkechaug Indians living at what is now Mastic, the Southampton leaders agreed to pay five pounds of wampum for each whale captured.[19] Even though these contracts were entered into official town records to keep affairs orderly, the company owners continually tried to raid their competitors and sign up their Native whalers.

As the companies gained more control over the fishery, they began to squeeze the Native Americans on compensation. In 1672, the Southampton magistrates, who included whaling company owners Joseph Raynor and John Jessup, approved a payment system that lowered the shares of profits for the Indians. The new rules also stipulated that the companies did not have to pay the Natives anything if they returned empty-handed. Some of the Indian whalers tried to push back by forming their own company, with limited success.

At the same time, the European settlers were pushing the Indians off their land and keeping them in debt by providing goods and food on credit. When the Native Americans got their shares of the proceeds for harvesting a whale, their income usually was inadequate to cover what they owed. Nonetheless, an increasing number of Indians took to whaling because it was still more lucrative and offered more status than the menial jobs available ashore.

The whaling contracts with the Native Americans began to disappear from the town records after 1680. This is probably the result of the Indians being so successful at their trade that the North Atlantic right whale was virtually extinct near the coast by the mid-eighteenth century.

Whaling from shore peaked in 1707, with four thousand barrels of oil processed from 111 right whales taken on Long Island. The number of whales taken could vary widely from year to year, as evidenced by the following year, when only six hundred barrels were filled.[20]

With fewer and fewer whales swimming near Long Island's coast, the industry shifted to larger vessels that would sail farther offshore in pursuit of humpback and other species. The Shinnecock and Montaukett harpooners and seamen, whose skills were still much in demand, went with them.[21]

THE HUNT GOES GLOBAL

The whaling industry's expansion beyond coastal waters required large, specially designed sailing vessels manned by sizeable crews who would be at sea for six months in the early days and later up to four years. The whaling ships would not return until their holds were full of kegs of oil. But the method of chasing and harpooning the whales remained the same. Once telltale spouts were spotted by lookouts in the rigging, the whaleboats, often equipped with sails, would be lowered and the crew would pursue the whales as they would have from shore. If the wind cooperated, the whaleship would sail to a whaleboat that had killed a prey. If the mothership was becalmed, the whaleboat crew might have to row back for miles, towing the whale sometimes as long as twenty-four hours. In either case, once the whale was at the whaleship, it would be dismantled and processed in a malodorous and smoky tryworks.[22]

One reason why the voyages lasted for years was that a very small percentage—probably between 10 and 20 percent—of the whales sighted were actually killed. For example, the crew of *Nathaniel P. Tallmadge* of Cold Spring Harbor spotted eighty-four whales between April and July of 1849. But they only succeeded in processing a handful. Some of the leviathans were lost after they had been harpooned. Some harpooned whales could tow a whaleboat for more than a dozen hours, during which time the harpoon lines might become tangled, forcing the mate in charge of the boat to cut the line. Sometimes the harpoons pulled free before the animal could be killed. In addition, many baleen whale species would sink before they could be towed back to the ship.[23]

Right whales remained the prey of choice, but increasingly the targets became bowhead and sperm whales. The latter got their name from spermaceti, the milky liquid found in their heads. It dried into a wax that made the best candles, with a clear almost smokeless light that burned steadily without an odor.[24]

The War of 1812 crimped the growth of the whaling industry on Long Island and the rest of the nation as the British captured many American vessels. Whaling greatly expanded after the war. By the mid-1840s, it was New York's and New England's second-largest industry. The expansion continued through the 1850s, when hunting whales became the fifth-largest industry in the country. Nationwide, it employed more than ten thousand seamen. At the industry's peak in the mid-nineteenth century, there were seventy-two American whaling ports serving as the base for 2,000 vessels. Three of those ports were on Long Island. Sag Harbor ranked sixth nationally, Greenport was seventeenth and Cold Spring Harbor twenty-seventh. The three harbors were the homeports for more than 143 whaling vessels that were responsible for more than one thousand voyages—almost six hundred from Sag Harbor alone. New Suffolk and Jamesport were smaller whaling ports.[25]

A BOON FOR AUXILIARY BUSINESSES

Besides employing those involved in hunting the whales, the industry provided jobs in a host of ancillary trades and businesses ashore: shipyards to build and maintain the vessels, sail lofts to cut and sew the canvas that propelled the ships, blacksmith shops to fashion harpoons and fittings, cooperages to make barrels and ropewalks to make the miles of cordage necessary for rigging and sailing a whaleship.

One of the ancillary businesses that thrived was the boatbuilding company of William Cooper of Sag Harbor. He became very wealthy by specializing in construction of the highly maneuverable whaleboats carried by every whaling ship.

The son of a boatbuilder, Cooper and his brother Huntting were building whaleboats in Middletown, Connecticut, in 1811. He was probably constructing whaleboats in Sag Harbor by the next year. Cooper's papers are in the collection of the Long Island Museum in Stony Brook, and the earliest whaleboat-related bills date to 1819. By 1830, Cooper had become a shareholder in the Long Island Whaling Company. The records indicate that Cooper built more than 920 small craft, including 747 whaleboats. In addition to his main Sag Harbor facility, Cooper maintained a shop in Greenport from 1838 to 1842. His whaleboat production spanned the most productive period in Sag

Harbor's whaling history from 1820 to 1867. Virtually every ship that sailed from Sag Harbor and other Long Island and Connecticut ports was outfitted with Cooper whaleboats.

To build them, he purchased large quantities of cedar planks along with some oak, white oak, pine, yellow pine, spruce, chestnut, ash, black oak and birch. It appears Cooper used steam to bend the ribs and planking. In 1843, the work was done by Cooper, two journeymen and two apprentices.

On the extended whaling voyages, the whaleboats got such a hard workout that they were usually worn out by the time the ships got home. Because of their hard use and occasional destruction by whales, vessels usually carried up to five spare whaleboats, which might include old ones from a previous voyage that were still serviceable. The limited lifespan of the boats guaranteed that Cooper had repeat customers.

Between 1830 and his death in 1857, Cooper owned shares in at least sixty-six whale ships. He also owned stock in two railroads. Thanks to his investments and revenue from boatbuilding, five years before he died, Cooper calculated his net worth at $51,642, a figure that when adjusted for inflation translated into $1,614,125 in 2016 dollars.[26] Cooper's whaleboat shop, including some of his original tools, has been re-created behind the Annie Cooper Boyd House, headquarters of the Sag Harbor Historical Society.

SAG HARBOR

In the eighteenth and nineteenth centuries, Sag Harbor was not only Long Island's biggest whaling port but also the most significant industrial and shipping center in Suffolk County. Over seven decades, more than one hundred whaling ships were fitted out in Sag Harbor, and many men from prominent local families with surnames such as Havens, Bennett, Lester and King served aboard them.[27]

A wharf with a tryworks was constructed in the village in 1761, and Long Wharf was added in 1770. The primary commodities shipped were whale oil and salt cod. Whaling activity greatly expanded after Captain Daniel Havens took the brig *America* to the South Atlantic in 1785 and returned a year later with a staggering three hundred barrels of oil. Driven by the whaling industry, economic development in Sag Harbor boomed and made many rich. The village became a federal port of entry in 1789, handling more vessels than New York City, and became the state's first customs port the following year.

At the high point, 1846–47, sixty-three vessels sailed from Sag Harbor employing about one thousand men. Thirty-two whaling ships arrived in the port that year with a total of 64,000 barrels of right whale oil, 4,000 barrels of sperm whale oil and 600,000 barrels of baleen.[28]

CAPTAIN MERCATOR COOPER

Mercator Cooper was not only the most famous early Sag Harbor whaling captain but also one of the most famous captains in the world. While many could boast of great adventures, it would be hard to top Cooper.

The Southampton mariner took the *Manhattan* from Sag Harbor to the South Pacific in 1845. He was not looking for a reason to visit Japan, a closed society that did not tolerate most foreigners. Eight years earlier, the last American ship to attempt to visit the feudal nation was driven away by cannonballs. Some shipwrecked foreign sailors who washed up on Japanese beaches were killed. But when Cooper glimpsed an opportunity to visit Japan, he didn't hesitate.

The *Manhattan* sailed from Sag Harbor on November 9, 1843. More than two years later, Cooper stopped at St. Peter's Island off the coast of Japan to look for water and firewood. His logbook entry for March 15, 1845, details that he came across something else. "We found 11 Japanese men that have been cast away," or shipwrecked. "We took them on board." The following day, "we fell in with a Japanese junk with her stern stove [or smashed] in and 11 men on board." Cooper rescued them as well.

Upon reaching the coast, he put three or four of the Japanese sailors aboard local craft to tell the shogun of Jeddo, the name of Tokyo at the time, that he planned to sail into the bay to hand over the rest of the rescued sailors. On April 18, a barge carrying an emissary from the emperor arrived to inform the captain that he could enter the bay. Cooper's log noted that "about three hundred Japanese boats with about 15 men in each took the ship in tow." Once the *Manhattan* was anchored in the bay, "they formed their boats around the ship with a guard of about three thousand men. They took all of our arms out to keep till we left. There were several of the nobility came on board to see the ship. They appeared very friendly." But there were limits to the hospitality. An interpreter made it clear that any American

Captain Mercator Cooper of Southampton, who visited Japan when it was off-limits to most foreigners and later became the first American to set foot on Antarctica. *Courtesy of the Southampton Historical Museum.*

leaving the ship would be killed, emphasizing the point by drawing his sword across his throat.

The Japanese visitors were fascinated by every aspect of the *Manhattan*, especially Pyrrhus Concer, a Southampton sailor who was the only black person on board, and a Shinnecock Indian named Eleazar. Having never seen dark-skinned people before, the Japanese wanted to touch the men's skin.

Cooper's April 20 logbook entry details provisions provided by the Japanese, who would accept no payment, including water, twenty sacks of rice, two sacks of wheat, a box of flour, eleven sacks of sweet potatoes, fifty fowl, two cords of wood, radishes and ten pounds of tea. Cooper added that the emperor's emissaries "thanked us for fetching them here. The Emperor sends his complements to me and thanks me for picking up their men and sends me word that I must not come again."

Cooper departed the next day. "We hove up our anchor and about 300 boats took us in tow," he wrote. They only released the *Manhattan* when it was twenty miles offshore. The captain retained a large nautical chart showing the waters around Japan; he would later give it to the U.S. Navy.

The *Manhattan* resumed whaling along the eastern coast of Russia, and the following year, Cooper sold the cargo in Amsterdam. The ship docked in Sag Harbor on October 14, 1846, after a voyage of two years, eleven months and five days.

Cooper wasn't done with his adventures. In August 1851, he left Sag Harbor as captain of the *Levant*, heading south in the Atlantic on a voyage in search of both whales and seals. On January 26, 1853, he sighted land in eastern Antarctica. The next morning, he sailed the ship closer to an ice shelf and ordered a small boat lowered. Cooper and his crew landed on the ice and saw penguins but no seals to kill. Cooper is credited with being the first American to set foot on the continent.[29]

Today, Mercator Cooper's imposing white house at 81 Windmill Lane is owned by the Rogers Memorial Library. A monument to the accomplishments of Cooper and the *Manhattan* was erected in Southampton Cemetery across the street from the captain's house.

Cooper's black crewman, Concer, was born an indentured servant in Southampton in 1814 and sold into slavery at age five. Named after a Greek king, he had been owned by the Pelletreau family and worked as a farmhand until he began shipping out on whalers at age eighteen. He was freed when he turned twenty-one. He worked his way up to the key position of boatsteerer. With the whaling industry petering out, Concer joined the 1849 gold rush in California before returning to Southampton a year later to be married. After Southampton became a summer colony following the Civil War, he ran a sailboat ferry across Lake Agawam, collecting a nickel from each passenger. He died on August 23, 1897, at age eighty-four. A monument was erected on Pine Lane across the street from his house, and an obelisk was placed over the grave he shares with his wife, Rachel, at the old North End Cemetery in the village. Its inscription reads: "Though born a slave he possessed those virtues, without which, kings are but slaves."[30]

Concer's house did not fare as well as Cooper's.

A Brooklyn couple bought the house, which had been altered, for $2.75 million in 2013. Historians and African American leaders fought to preserve the structure, but it was demolished the next year and the owners put the property on the market for $5 million. In 2015, the Town of Southampton bought the site for $4.3 million.

The Southampton African American Museum and Pyrrhus Concer Action Committee are hoping to build a replica of the ferryman's home using materials salvaged before the demolition. It would be used as an education center devoted to Concer and Long Island's overlooked African American history.[31]

GREENPORT

Between 1795 and 1859, the North Fork Harbor was the homeport at varying times for twenty-four whaling vessels that made 103 voyages around the world. In 1845 alone, Greenport was the base for a dozen whaleships.[32]

Before 1840, most of those ships sailed to the South Atlantic. They would depart in July or August and spend a year south of Brazil or near the Falkland Islands. But as the whales there became scarce, the ships increasingly headed for the Pacific and Indian Oceans. That meant voyages of two years or more that could cover thirty-seven thousand nautical miles. A typical crew would be twenty-five to thirty men.[33]

When several ships returned at the same time, Greenport would have been a bustling place. In 1843, for example, between the first week of May and the first week in June, the *Bayard*, *Delta* and *Triad* returned to the port carrying a combined total of 7,760 barrels of whale oil. Unloading, storing and shipping all of that cargo must have been a complicated enterprise. The vessels would remain in port only a few months for repairs and re-provisioning before heading out again.[34]

The Greenport fleet had its share of difficulties. The square-rigger *Potosi* was lost in the Falklands in 1831, and the *Delta* was damaged in a collision in 1841 but returned and was repaired before going on four more voyages. The barque *Noble* was badly damaged in a gale in 1843 and condemned in New Zealand. The second mate on the barque *Prudent* was killed by natives on Easter Island.[35]

Cold Spring Harbor

The hamlet's whaling activity began in 1836 when local businessmen John H. Jones persuaded his brother, insurance magnate Walter Restored Jones, and thirty-two other relatives and friends to revive the business of his great-grandfather Major Thomas Jones. They purchased the barque *Monmouth* in Boston and brought it back to Long Island to be reconfigured for whaling. Lacking experience in the trade, they decided to take *Monmouth* to Sag Harbor and have it sail under Captain Richard S. Topping. After only two weeks of preparation, Topping and crew departed on July 18, 1836, for the southern Atlantic Ocean. They returned to Cold Spring, as the community was then known, on April 10, 1837, with a meager cargo of oil valued at about $20,000. Topping returned to the same areas in 1837 and 1838 and grossed only about $25,000. Another voyage to the South Atlantic ended on May 24, 1839, with only about $13,000 worth of oil in the hold. To make matters worse, customs officials said the vessel's documentation papers were faulty and ruled the owners would have to pay the same high tariffs as foreign vessels. Their enthusiasm unquenched, the Jones brothers and other investors then bought the *Tuscarora* from its owners in New London, Connecticut, in 1837. It left on its first cruise from Cold Spring that year under Captain William Denison and returned twenty months later with 1,400 barrels of oil. The owners made a small profit. They decided they would do better with more capitalization, and the best way to acquire it was to incorporate. New York State passed an act of incorporation on March 24, 1838, to form the Cold Spring Whaling Company.

It took two years for the company to sell enough stock to buy *Monmouth* from the individual owners and another year after that to acquire *Tuscarora*. The company never was particularly profitable and offered its vessels for sale starting in 1848. John H. Jones and his associates purchased *Tuscarora* from the corporation that year to keep it from being broken up. Two years later, the company sold *Monmouth* to John Jones's son Townsend. In 1851, the directors filed an application with the state supreme court to dissolve the corporation.[36]

The seven other whaling ships that would sail from Cold Spring were owned by groups of individual investors. One of the vessels, the square-rigger *Sheffield*, was the largest whaler ever to sail from Long Island and the third-largest in the entire American whaling fleet. None of the vessels purchased was new, and only one, *Nathaniel P. Tallmadge*, had been built as a whaler. Because of the sand spit that blocked the entrance to the upper harbor, much of the outfitting of the whaleships was done in the outer harbor, with the equipment brought out on smaller vessels. John H. Jones built a sail loft and a large cooper shop to construct the barrels that would hold the whale oil on the west side of the harbor in an area that became known as Bungtown for the plugs that fill the openings in the barrels. The Cold Spring Harbor Laboratory now occupies the site, where some of the old whaling era buildings have been preserved. These include a circa 1825 warehouse, rescued from demolition and now known as the Wawepex Building, the headquarters for a children's nature study program, and the early nineteenth-century Yellow House, now a staff dwelling.[37]

Between 1836 and 1862, the nine vessels based in Cold Spring Harbor made forty-four voyages and returned with more than $1.5 million worth of oil and bone. The ships typically had a crew of from twenty-five to thirty-five men, depending on the size and whether the vessel carried three or four whaleboats. The average age was about twenty-three, with the officers generally in their late twenties or early thirties. The sailors had to be at least seventeen, but those as young as thirteen could sign on as cabin boys.[38]

Not surprisingly, considering how dangerous the industry was for vessels and sailors, most of the vessels sailing from Cold Spring suffered serious damage or worse. *Tuscarora* lost several men, its mainmast and rigging along with its whaleboats in an Indian Ocean storm in 1841. The third mate on the *Huntsville*, a man named Weeks, was killed by a whale on December 9, 1845. *Richmond* and *Edgar* were wrecked in Arctic waters in the summers of 1847 and 1855, respectively. *Edgar* was lost during its first voyage when it ran up on an island in dense fog. The loss of the two vessels was a financial calamity from which the owners never recovered.[39]

The fortunes of the Cold Spring whaling fleet began to ebb more quickly after 1855, when *Edgar* was lost and Walter R. Jones died. His brother John died four years later. Without the involvement of the brothers, their whaling ventures and other businesses, including a steamboat company, crumbled. The whaleships were sold off beginning in 1855.[40]

Captain Thomas Roys

Captain Thomas Welcome Roys, who sailed from Sag Harbor and Cold Spring Harbor, achieved several important firsts in the whaling industry.

Born upstate near Lake Ontario about 1816, he began his whaling career in 1833 aboard the *Hudson* of Sag Harbor. On his third voyage aboard, he was promoted to boatsteerer. Then he joined the *Gem*, also out of Sag Harbor, in that same position before moving up the ranks and then being hired as captain of the *Crescent*, another Sag Harbor ship. In 1843, he married Ann Eliza Green, daughter of the captain of the *Hudson*. She would die in 1847 soon after giving birth to their son Philander. That same year, he was signed on as captain of the Sag Harbor whaler *Josephine*. It was on this voyage that he learned from other whaling ship captains and a Russian naval officer of a large untapped population of a likely new species of whales in the northern Pacific and in the Arctic Ocean. The latter was north of the treacherous Bering Strait—a physical and psychological hurdle no whaling captain had ever dared traverse.[41]

Roys was undaunted. He got his opportunity to look for the "new fangled monsters" after he was named captain of the Sag Harbor whaler *Superior* in 1847. Failing to convince other captains to join him, disobeying the instructions of the vessel's owners and overruling the objections of his mates and crew, Roys ordered the *Superior* through the strait on July 23 of the next year. There he quickly found and personally harpooned one of the surprisingly docile "polar whales." Because of the whales' thick blubber, the still-fearful crew of the *Superior* filled all of the 1,800 barrels in the hold of the relatively small vessel in thirty-five days. That was a feat that would usually take at least two years.

The huge population of slow-moving bowhead whales—named by whalers because of their large bow-like mouths—discovered by Roys made whaling profitable for two more decades. One subspecies was named in his honor. Fifty whaleships, forty-six of them American, sailed through the Bering Strait the following year. The large number of American whalers in the Arctic Ocean spurred the purchase of Alaska by the United States in 1867.[42]

Roys was impatient to revisit the Arctic and do it on a larger vessel. His chance arrived in 1849, when he was recruited by Walter Restored Jones and his partners to take command of the huge Cold Spring Harbor whaleship *Sheffield*, which had previously served as a record-breaking transatlantic packet. He returned to the Arctic, assisted the search for the missing British explorer Sir John Franklin and again quickly filled the barrels onboard. It was the Cold Spring Harbor fleet's most successful voyage. *Sheffield* returned—five years later—having brought aboard a spectacular total of 8,600 barrels of oil and 115,000 pounds of bone.[43]

During the voyage, Roys wrote a natural history, "Description of Whales." The twenty-nine-page manuscript has been described as

Thomas Welcome Roys, the first captain to hunt whales in the Arctic Ocean, spent years developing a rocket harpoon gun. One experiment resulted in an explosion that led to the amputation of his left hand. *The National Air and Space Museum.*

the first written description of whale species. It included drawings of about eighteen species and detailed descriptions, natural history data, distribution patterns and feeding habits for sixteen of them. Roys generated scientific interest in the orca, or killer whale, which was little known then by Americans and had only been written about in some European scholarly journals. (The manuscript was stolen from the Mariners Museum in Virginia by an archivist working there sometime between 2000 and 2006. It turned up in a 2018 auction, was purchased by the Whaling Museum & Education Center in Cold Spring Harbor and then, after it was recognized, was to return to Virginia after remaining on loan in Cold Spring Harbor for a year.)[44]

Roys's next command, in 1855, was *Hannibal*, based in New London, Connecticut. About that time, he began working on an invention for which he would become even more widely known. Roys—at great personal cost—would spend years developing a shoulder-fired rocket harpoon, similar to a modern bazooka, that would make the hunt much more deadly for the whales and lead to the development of factory ships and a huge increase in the harvesting of whales.

On a *Hannibal* voyage to Hudson Bay in Canada, Roys killed a blue whale, the largest of all the leviathans. That gave him the idea that a larger harpoon gun might be used to hunt rorquals, a grouping of the largest whale species, which had previously not been hunted because of their size. But the conservative owners of *Hannibal* concluded that Roys was insane when he informed them of his purchase of "two rifles in pairs for killing [rorqual] whales" while in France. One of the owners boarded the next packet for that country and upon arriving in Lorient fired Roys on the spot.

But Lorient would also provide something in way of compensation. It was there that Roys met Marie Salliord, a woman half his age he would marry in 1860 before bringing her back to the hamlet of Peconic in Southold Town to set up housekeeping among other whaling families on "Blubber Row." She became a piano teacher and later ran off with their three children sometime after 1870, supposedly with one of his former shipmates, during one of his long voyages.[45]

Unfazed, Roys, with the help of several friends, bought the relatively small eighty-seven-foot Sag Harbor brig *William F. Safford* in 1856. The captain outfitted it with special harpoon guns of his own design and then traveled to both the Arctic Ocean and Antarctica in search of rorqual whales. He was testing his whaling guns on the *Safford* in the Bay of Biscay off the western coast of France later that year when he paid a terrible price for his experimentation. He wrote that

> *I took up one of my guns to try the explosion underwater....I fired the fuse, ignited the powder in the shell and it exploded, blowing up the gun and sent me backward about eight feet....I then saw lying upon the deck a finger with a ring upon it which I knew, and looking I saw my left hand was gone to the wrist, but for the moment it had given no pain, only a sensation of numbness. Walking into the cabin, I sat down and had it amputated* [by the first mate] *as well as we could with razors.*[46]

Roys sailed to Oporto, Portugal, where the rest of his lower arm had to be amputated. That did not stop him from continuing to work on his rocket harpoon concept in the following years. In 1857, the innovative captain received his first patent, in Great Britain, for explosive shells. His first American patent followed in 1861 for improvements in harpoon guns. That same year, he entered into a partnership with Gustavus A. Lilliedahl, a wealthy New York City pyrotechnics manufacturer. They worked together for six years trying to perfect rocket harpooning of whales.[47]

In 1865, Roys established the first shore-based whaling station, in Iceland, where he developed a method to process whales with bone grinders, presses and steam kettles, which was more efficient than the old method of cutting the blubber and boiling it in great kettles aboard ships. Nothing was wasted, not even the entrails. His method is still followed today by nations that hunt whales.[48]

In the following years, Roys continued his experiments on several ships. And then in 1871, he took command of the whaling brig *Byzantium* out of Victoria, British Columbia. His bad luck continued. In May, *Byzantium* struck rocks in British Columbia, and the crew had to abandon ship and spend a freezing night huddled on the beach. It was a financial disaster that marked Roys's last whaling venture as an entrepreneur.

The next year, he turned up in San Francisco, where he worked on manufacturing and improving his harpoons. Although they were sophisticated for their time, Roys never perfected his design.

In the winter of 1876–77, he surfaced in San Diego, where he joined a ship a few months later. He contracted yellow fever and was put ashore in Mazatlán, Mexico, where he died—broke and delirious—on January 29 of a stroke. The local United States consul and resident Americans contributed sixty dollars for a proper funeral.[49]

From 1857 until even two years after his death, Roys was granted sixteen patents in five countries. Most were for improved rocket harpoons. But one was for a "whale-raiser," a device to retrieve sunken whale carcasses from the seafloor.[50]

While he was known to every whale ship captain in the 1850s and 1860s, today Roys is only remembered by whaling historians, even though he was one of the first to apply methods of the machine age to the whaling industry.[51]

THE WHALING LIFE

The business was chronicled extensively in owners' ledgers, captains' logbooks and sailors' diaries. The captains detailed the whales they harpooned, those that eluded them, the number of oil barrels filled and the pounds of whalebone they were bringing home. Many of the captains illustrated their logs with drawings of whales, making the volumes not only invaluable historical documents but also works of art.

The Southampton Historical Museum has many fine examples. One belonged to James R. Foster of Southampton, second mate on the barque *Washington* out of Sag Harbor under Captain Henry Babcock on a voyage in the Atlantic Ocean that began on May 2, 1859, and concluded on May 7, 1862. The logbook includes this typical notation:

Sunday, Nov, the 24th. This day commences with clear and pleasant weather and a strong breeze from the N and E. steering a course N and W with all sails set at 4 pm raised a right Whale, lowered 2 boats, struck and killed him and took him alongside after…very strong breeze and a heavy sea.

Many of the logbooks chronicle heartbreak and disaster. J.B. Worth, a member of a Southold farm family who was captain of the *Konohassett*, left Sag Harbor in December 1845 with a crew of white farm boys, Indians and three black men—Reese Smith, Philip Smith and Solomon Ward. Five months later, he wrote matter-of-factly in his log: "May 24, 1 o'clock in the morning, ship K, under full sail before the wind, going at a rate of five knots, struck upon a coral reef which is not drawn on any chart. We were obliged to leave the ship in our boats with a little bread and water." The crew salvaged supplies and materials from the wreckage to build another ship—in only eighteen days. The twenty-two-foot-long *Konohassett Junior* carried Worth and six crewmen to the Sandwich Islands, now known as Hawaii, in forty-two days. The captain then sailed a larger vessel back to what became known as Hells Reef and rescued the remaining crew without the loss of a single life.[52]

Konohassett was one of twenty-seven whaleships that embarked from Sag Harbor in 1845. It was not the only one to sail into trouble. The captain and three crew members of the *American* were killed by a whale. The rest of the crew mutinied in the Sandwich Islands, where the ship was condemned as unfit for service. Other Long Island vessels struck uncharted reefs, lost crew to drowning or were crushed by ice sheets in the Arctic.[53]

A Hard Way to Make a Living

Whaleship owners tried to attract crew members by posting advertisements in harbor towns that promised "Chance of a Lifetime" or "Come See the World." Those who signed on might see a great deal of the world, but the

Help-wanted broadside for Cold Spring Harbor whalers. *Courtesy of the Whaling Museum & Education Center of Cold Spring Harbor.*

work was lowly paid, arduous and unpleasant. So anyone willing to do it would be hired.

"Whaling was the most dangerous job on the sea that ever existed," former Sag Harbor Whaling and Historical Museum curator George Finckenor remarked. "There was no romance associated with it at all—it was brutal. Few men wanted to do it." As a result, the ships often left port shorthanded, increasing the burden on those aboard until they could try to fill out their rosters closer to the whaling grounds in places like the Cape Verde Islands.[54]

Discipline aboard was harsh. Men who shirked their duty or committed other infractions could be clapped in irons or flogged, receiving sometimes more than twenty lashes. Captains, including Thomas Roys, also had to put down attempted mutinies or deal with sabotage of their vessels by disgruntled crew.[55]

As with whaling from shore, the share of the profits was based on skill. That meant the harpooners, no matter their race, were better compensated than others on the crew. But the officers made much more. And the owners, who might include the captain, did best of all. They could become wealthy and build gorgeous homes in whaling centers such as Sag Harbor and Cold Spring Harbor. Any profit from a voyage would be divided into thirds. One third was retained for maintenance of the vessel, another third was split by the owners and agents, while the last third was divided among the captain and crew. Their "lay" or share was determined by their place in the vessel's hierarchy. The captain got 1/10 or 1/16 of that third, while a seaman might get 1/200 or 1/225 of the profit.[56]

AN INTEGRATED INDUSTRY

As seen with the experience of Pyrrhus Concer, crews were diversified. The reason was that life on a whaling ship was so unappealing that anyone willing to sign on would be hired, regardless of race.

"Whaling was a cross between working in an oil refinery and a slaughterhouse, with the chance of drowning thrown in," said Richard Doctorow, collections director of the Sag Harbor Whaling and Historical Museum. "It was not a job the upper class would want to get involved in, and socially, sailors and whalers were at the bottom of the heap. Which meant that, of course, this was a job available for African Americans."[57]

The rosters were filled with the poor former slaves and Indians who could find no better work ashore. Native Americans worked alongside whites, African Americans, Polynesians and others under the command of—at least for the Long Island vessels—a white captain.

"It was the first integrated industry in the country," noted Nomi Dayan, executive director of the Whaling Museum & Education Center in Cold Spring Harbor and author of *Whaling on Long Island*. "It's not to say that racism was totally absent. On the whale ships, crews were often segregated."[58]

And whatever integration there was didn't reach all the way to the top in the Long Island industry. While blacks and other minorities served as mates, the positions just under the captains, there is no record of a captain who wasn't Caucasian. "There were no non-white whaling captains in the Sag Harbor whaling fleet," Doctorow told the author. "There were a number of non-white mates. On the national level, there were a number of non-white whaling captains out of New Bedford and other New England ports."

Historians estimate that between one-quarter and one-third of whalers were people of color. Queens College archaeologist Allison McGovern identified fifty-four men of color who sailed for just one of the approximately half-dozen major Sag Harbor whaling companies between 1828 and 1859. Many of the black and mixed-race men who sailed out of Long Island ports were from prominent families.[59]

As with the Native Americans in the early days of coastal whaling, shipping out for extended voyages provided for higher wages and socioeconomic upward mobility unavailable on land. But working in the industry meant sharing the risk and the potential for tremendous personal loss. This can be seen from the experience of the prominent Plato family of East Hampton. Around 1845, Isaac Plato, third mate on the Sag Harbor whaler *Hudson*, drowned in the Pacific Ocean. Eighteen years later, Silas B. Plato, believed to be his brother, became another whaling fatality. After Plato sailed out of New Bedford, Massachusetts, on the *Eagle* as second mate, probate records show that he died "fast to a whale" or drowned while tangled in the line attached to a harpoon, just like Herman Melville's fictional Captain Ahab in *Moby-Dick*.[60]

The fact that the Plato family members served as mates is evidence that "life at sea was a meritocracy," Doctorow said. "You don't get promoted if you don't know what you're doing. A whaling ship was one of those rare places in 19th century America where an African American could be the boss."[61]

Women at Sea

Not all of those aboard whaling and trading ships were men, and some of the best accounts of voyages were written by captains' wives.

Because whaling voyages could stretch out for years and even trading trips could last months, some captains would bring their wives along. At least forty-eight Long Island women are known to have sailed with their husbands on whaling or trading vessels.

One of them was Martha Smith Brewer Brown of Orient, a young mother who sailed with her husband, Edwin Peter Brown, on the whaleship *Lucy Ann*. When he headed for the Pacific on August 21, 1847, she was onboard. It turned out to be a voyage of two years filled with love, loneliness, happiness and hardship. She was not a mere spectator; she contributed in her own way to the success of the voyage.

Left: Captain Edwin Peter Brown. *Courtesy of the Oysterponds Historical Society.*

Right: Martha Smith Brewer Brown. *Courtesy of the Oysterponds Historical Society.*

In the beginning, Martha Brown was smitten by the romance of life at sea. If "moon light nights are incentives to make love, surely moon light nights on ship board are doubly so," she wrote as the *Lucy Ann* cruised the Pacific. Five months later, however, the romance had worn thin. "I have been sick most of this week and by dint of hard labor have only made one shirt with short sleeves," she wrote in her journal on March 25 "I have catched as many colds as there is days in the week, and nights to, for all what I know, and have come to the conclusion that if I go on deck and open my mouth I am sure to get a new addition."[62]

Brown was only twenty-six when she left home, and sailing with her husband meant leaving behind her two-year-old daughter, Ella. She might have regretted the decision to sail on March 8, 1848, when she wrote: "You can have no Idea how warm, or how hot rather, it is. There is heardly a bit of comfort to be taken but on deck, and that we have not had the privalage of enjoying untill today for it has rained every half hour for a week."[63]

Part of Brown's misery must have stemmed from the fact that she was pregnant. Finding herself in "circumstances," she and her husband decided that she would be put ashore in Honolulu to have the baby, which was not due for five months. She ended up being stranded there for seven months as one of six hundred non-Hawaiians on the island. Her husband left her with what she felt was so little cash that she could not afford to live in town with the other foreigners, so she rarely got to see the wives of other captains—her "whaling sisters." Her first entry ashore on April 30 noted that "I do not know of one here that I can call friend." The journal entries show how she longed for her husband. She lamented on November 5 that "I am not permitted to clasp the object of my fondest affection."[64]

A week later, the *Lucy Ann* returned to retrieve the captain's wife. Reuniting with her husband did nothing to rekindle Martha's original infatuation with life at sea. While sailing home, she wrote a message for him in the ship's logbook: "Adieu to Whale grounds and now for home and right glad am I. And now my Dear, alow me to inform you that this is the last time you are to leave, or visit these waters."

Captain Brown was not about to be dictated to by his wife, however. He made at least two more voyages before settling down ashore as a farmer in Orient when he was thirty-nine.[65]

Some other "whaling sisters" and women voyaging on other types of ships would have considered Martha Brown's life at sea enviable. As the trading ship *Frank N. Thayer* was sailing in the South China Sea in 1885, the Malay crew members mutinied. When they attempted to murder the captain, Robert Clarke of Quogue, his wife, whose name was not recorded, sprang to his rescue. She tackled a seaman who had sliced open her husband's chest and pushed his lung back inside his body. Then she held off the rebellious seamen with a pistol long enough to give her time to bandage the wound and organize an escape. They sailed in a small boat two hundred miles to the island of Saint Helena, and Captain Clarke survived the episode.[66]

Some of the women who sailed with their husbands died with them at sea. When the coastal schooner *Nahum Chapin* was wrecked within sight of its homeport of Quogue in the winter of 1897, Captain Ernest L. Arey, his wife—again her name not known—and their child all drowned.

Conditions aboard a ship for the women varied greatly from vessel to vessel and by the type of commerce it was engaged in. It was the worst on the whalers, with cramped quarters, horrendous smells and crew members of dubious character on voyages that lasted years. The opposite extreme was on international trading vessels on which the captains' wives presided over luxurious cabins.

One aspect of the sailing life that made it tolerable for the women was chance encounters with the spouses of other captains at sea—called "gamming"—or meeting women in foreign cities with American enclaves.

The sailors onboard ships carrying a woman who did not want to be separated from her husband had mixed feelings about serving on "hen frigates." The women could be a diversion and temper the often harsh discipline at sea, but they could also make the men more lonely because they could not bring their wives.[67]

The End of an Industry

A combination of factors killed the whaling industry. Even with the expansion into the Arctic Ocean, finding whales to process became increasingly difficult and the voyages longer and less profitable. While whale oil fueled the Industrial Revolution, it also lubricated its own demise as more manufacturing jobs were created ashore without the danger and miserable conditions afloat.

As Sag Harbor's industry reached its peak around 1845, the village was struck by a catastrophic fire. As it tried to rebuild, gold was discovered in California in January 1848. Whaling vessels cashed in on the gold rush by carrying would-be prospectors to the West Coast, only to have crew members jump ship to join the search for riches. That resulted in many vessels being sold or abandoned. One of the Sag Harbor whalers, the *Niantic*, was left to rot in San Francisco in 1849, and a fire two years later burned it to the waterline. A section of the hull was excavated in 1978.

The discovery of petroleum in Titusville, Pennsylvania, in 1859 heralded the replacement of whale oil by crude from underground. Confederate commerce raiders during the Civil War decimated the Union whaling fleet at sea and kept many other vessels idle in port. Early onset of ice in the Arctic trapped and destroyed many whalers in 1871 and 1876. Changing fashion tastes in 1908 made baleen for corset stays unnecessary.[68]

Greenport's last whaler was the *Kanowha*, a barque that sailed in 1855 to the Atlantic and Indian Oceans and returned in 1860 with 890 barrels of whale oil and 900 pounds of whale bones. The village then shifted its focus to shipping and fishing.[69]

The last Cold Spring Harbor whaler, *Alice*, sailed in 1858 on a voyage to the Pacific and was sold four years later on its return to its homeport. The demise of the community's last whaling company set the stage for the hamlet to become a summer resort destination.[70]

After a brief shipbuilding boom in the 1850s, the Sag Harbor industry slid into a final decline. The last voyage was made by the *Myra* in 1871.

The last whale killed from shore in East Hampton, on February 22, 1907. *Collection of the East Hampton Historical Society.*

Deemed unseaworthy and condemned in Barbados three years later, it was burned to recover the metal in its hull. The *Myra*'s Long Island crewmen found their way home six months later and never received any pay. The voyage marked the end of Long Island's whaling industry. Ten years after the last departure of *Myra*, the customshouse in Sag Harbor closed for lack of activity. (It is now a museum owned by Preservation Long Island.) Where the current Long Wharf stands, a fleet of stranded and derelict whaling ships accumulated, giving the area the nickname Rotten Row.[71]

One of the last whales successfully hunted off Long Island was a right whale taken off East Hampton by a crew led by Captain Joshua Edwards and his son Sam on February 22, 1907. The skeleton was shipped to the American Museum of Natural History in New York, where it was suspended from the ceiling as part of a display on the endangered creatures. The last recorded whaling activity around Long Island occurred in August 1918. A whale was spotted and killed off the Napeague Coast Guard Station by a crew that included members of the Edwards and Dominy families. They towed the carcass for fifteen hours around Montauk Point to a fish processing factory in Promised Land on Gardiners Bay. The whale yielded thirty barrels of oil, but there was no market for it.[72]

The legacy of the industry on Long Island industry is preserved at whaling museums in Sag Harbor and Cold Spring Harbor. It is also commemorated by the Broken Mast Monument in Sag Harbor's Oakland Cemetery. Underneath the depiction of a snapped ship's mast is an inscription that says that it demonstrates "lasting respect to those bold and enterprising ship masters…who periled their lives in a daring profession and perished in actual encounter with the Monsters of the deep."[73]

4

THE FISHERMEN

I n 1614, Dutch captain Adriaen Block discovered that the waters along the northern shoreline of Long Island were teeming with fish. But even though the fisheries of New England were a major factor in the American colonies' survival, nothing was done immediately to take advantage of the bounty.

Then in 1633, John Winthrop, the governor of Connecticut, dispatched the barque *Blessing of the Bay* across Long Island Sound. The voyage confirmed Block's reports, but there was no follow-up because, Winthrop wrote, the local Indians were "very treacherous." The Algonquian Indians on the East End at the time were dominated by the Pequot tribe in Connecticut. That ended in 1634 when the English in Connecticut wiped out the dominant tribe in the Pequot Wars, opening Long Island for settlement.[74]

After colonists from New England began to arrive on Long Island in the 1640s, they raised cattle for meat as well as hides and tallow that could be traded. But marine life also was essential for feeding the population and trade. The local waters were filled with cod, bass, tuna, bluefish, mackerel, flounder and other species into the early nineteenth century. The fishermen would drag a large net around a school of fish near the shore and then haul the net with the catch up on the beach. In the early years, up to thirty thousand fish might fill the net.

Favored fish such as striped bass, cod and salmon were kept for consumption, with some salted or smoked for winter. Less-prized fish were used for animal feed or fertilizer. After their final harvest in the fall, farmers often fished during the winter using trawl lines of baited hooks strung between buoys anchored to the seafloor to catch cod.[75]

MENHADEN

Native Americans in Massachusetts taught the European settlers there how to use a small bony silver fish for fertilizer. When some of those settlers relocated to Long Island, they began to spend some of their time in the spring and fall catching menhaden, a member of the herring family whose name in the Algonquin language means "that which enriches the soil." The fish—also called mossbunkers or bunkers by Long Islanders—was not considered fit to eat by most people. But the Massachusetts farmers and Indians—and possibly the Native Americans on Long Island—increased their crop yields by burying menhaden among their plants.[76]

Bunkers were used for only a short time as fertilizer because the farmers found that the oil in the fish eventually would harden the soil to a cement-like consistency. The practice was resumed in the early nineteenth century after it was rediscovered by Long Island agricultural innovator Ezra L'Hommedieu while he was experimenting with fertilizers to improve dwindling crop yields. Eventually, the new generation of farmers discovered why their predecessors had abandoned the use of menhaden and followed suit.[77]

There was renewed interest in menhaden in the mid-nineteenth century when the local whale population was just about fished out. This stemmed from discovery of a method to cook the bunker to extract the oil on an industrial scale and then grind up the remains for fertilizer. The first factory to do it was established in 1841 in Rhode Island. Nine years later, Daniel D. Wells and his son Henry E. built Long Island's first factory on Chequit Point on Shelter Island. It processed two to three million fish annually. Three years later, Wells and son responded to complaints about the odor by closing the plant and opening a new one at White Hill on the island that was the first steam-operated menhaden plant in the state. Later, they relocated the operation to East Hampton. When the steaming process was patented by William D. Hall of Wallingford, Connecticut, about 1853, Wells contested it but failed to overturn it. The Wells operation was soon followed by at least twenty-five factories on Peconic Bay alone, with at least one in every hamlet in Southold. Others were constructed along the beaches of the South Shore.[78]

As bunker oil began to eclipse whale oil as fuel for lamps and for use in other products as well, individual fishermen were replaced by companies formed to not only process the menhaden but catch the fish as well.

Farmers had initially caught menhaden by rowing out to a school of fish with a huge seine net that could be as long as three-quarters of a mile. The ends of the net would be brought ashore, where horses would pull the haul up onto the beach. Inside the net would be schools of menhaden ranging in size from 25,000 to 500,000 fish.

But by the mid-nineteenth century, the fishermen had to travel farther offshore to find schools of menhaden. That led to development of the purse seine. This was a cotton mesh net between 1,000 and 1,500 feet long, 50 to 60 feet deep and suspended from cork floats. A purse seine operation consisted of a main vessel with two smaller seine dories, similar to whaleboats, to handle each end of the net. Once the fish were encircled, the next step was "pursing" the seine, or closing the bottom ring to prevent the fish from escaping out the bottom. Then the men on the seine boats pulled the net out of the water and collected the fish.[79]

With dozens of bunker processing factories from Barren Island in Jamaica Bay to the East End, Long Island became a major part of an industry that supported factories all along the East Coast.[80]

Nineteenth-century promotional image of menhaden fish processing plant on the North Fork. *Courtesy of Oysterponds Historical Society.*

Two factors—complaints about the offensive odor and possible health hazards emanating from the factories and the use of larger steam-powered vessels in the late nineteenth century—drove many of the smaller companies out of business after the Civil War. By the 1870s, the factories in Southold and on Shelter Island had started to close, with the loss of hundreds of jobs. That set the stage for the area to blossom into a summer resort.[81]

Mossbunker processing continued mostly on the South Fork; in 1883, there were 90 factories operating around Peconic Bay that were supplied with menhaden by 212 sailing vessels and 83 steam-powered boats. The industry employed 2,313 men, many of them blacks from southern states. Many were clustered on an unpopulated narrow isthmus between Amagansett and Montauk named Promised Land, where no one would complain about the odor. By the end of the nineteenth century, the remaining factories clustered there were bought out and consolidated by the Smith Meal Company.[82]

According to a U.S. Bureau of Fisheries report in 1898, the Long Island menhaden fishery employed 9,348 men working on 601 vessels. Another agency report four years later stated that the demand for menhaden oil grew rapidly during the late 1800s. Eastern Long Island produced the most oil in the country and in 1902 generated 1.4 million gallons. The report said the principal uses were for curing leather, illumination, paint manufacturing and manufacturing of rope and wire.[83]

By the late 1960s, even with the use of aircraft for spotting the schools of fish, the menhaden had become increasingly scarce. Between 1960 and 1967, the Long Island catch dropped from eighty-five million pounds to five million pounds. The industry's decline had a dramatic effect on the economy of the East End, particularly in Greenport, which provided most of the supplies for the local industry.[84]

The last of the Montauk factories closed in the late 1960s for several reasons: the bunker had been fished almost to extinction, petroleum products had become cheaper than fish oil and other fertilizers had become available. Another factor was an acrimonious tug-of-war between commercial and recreational fishermen over the scarce resource. Mossbunkers became something caught just as bait for larger fish.[85]

FISHING FOR OTHER SPECIES

While catching menhaden was a huge business, fishing for cod, bluefish, striped bass, sturgeon and other species also employed thousands of Long Island men.

In Port Washington in the early 1800s, Portuguese net fishermen lived as squatters at Sheet's Creek. Immigrants from Nova Scotia who served as boating guides lived with their families on houseboats on Manhasset Bay. Freeport was another major fishing hub in Nassau County. In 1901, the village shipped almost one million pounds of fish to market, much of it to New York City.[86]

After the Long Island Rail Road reached Greenport in 1844, the North Fork village became the primary fishing, packing and shipping port on the East End. The steamboat *Shinnecock* sailed from nearby Orient with cargoes of salt cod and smoked eels destined for New York City markets.[87]

In the 1880s, Greenport was the base for twenty boats that hunted for bluefish in the summer and cod in the winter. Each vessel usually had a crew of three, and on a good day, a boat might return to port with five to six thousand fish.[88]

When the Long Island Rail Road (LIRR) extended its tracks on the South Fork from Bridgehampton to Montauk in 1895, Greenport was no longer the primary fish-shipping center for the East End. The rails ran right onto a fish dock at Fort Pond Bay, enabling a dedicated cargo train filled with sturgeon, caviar and black sea bass to run into the city every evening.[89]

Overfishing would eventually hobble the Long Island industry, but in the nineteenth century the quantity of the catch wasn't yet an issue. In East Hampton, Captain Jim Winters caught 144 porgies in one afternoon in 1890 while Jared Wood brought home more than 500 bonito in one afternoon after the turn of the century. And the small hamlet of Springs north of the village of East Hampton shipped more than 2,000 barrels of flounder between February and April 1887. Long Island also became a destination for recreational fishermen. By the time of the Civil War, East Hampton had begun to be known as a resort community that was a good place to catch bluefish.[90]

Long Island boatyards built specialized craft for the local fishermen and the conditions they faced. Skiffs were built along the South Shore suitable for the shallow waters and sandbars. Thomas Clapham built similar vessels in Roslyn on the North Shore.[91]

In the early twentieth century, the primary species caught on the South Fork was cod. The industry supported not only full-time fishermen but also idle construction workers and farmers during the winter. Usually, the fishermen would work in pairs, although sometimes they were joined by a third man who would gut and clean the fish and prepare clams as bait. It was hard work with long hours starting at four o'clock in the morning and often lasting late into the night. Early in the spring, the fishermen would set gill nets for sturgeon. Eventually, overfishing left no cod anywhere near Long Island, and other species were greatly diminished. Bluefish became scarce, and by 1908 they had all but vanished, only to come back stronger the next year through 1921 before declining. Sturgeon got smaller and then virtually disappeared.[92]

One of the most iconic Long Island maritime traditions is haul-seining: fishermen launch a dory from the beach through the surf to deploy a net and then pull the net with fish ashore. The preferred catch is striped bass. Early in the twentieth century, that highly prized species disappeared. Then the population rebounded in the late 1930s, only to become scarcer and sporadic in later years. In New York State, 820,250 pounds of striped bass

Haul seining in Amagansett in a photograph taken by Ray Prohaska about 1950. *East Hampton Historical Society Marine Museum Archive.*

were landed in 1981, and the total fell to 469,100 pounds the next year. Because the striped bass is highly treasured by sport fishermen, the scarcity precipitated decades of legal conflict. In 1983, New York State, spurred by recreational fishermen organizations and federal agencies, approved legislation that dramatically cut the striped bass catch limits for commercial fishermen. The commercial fishermen have received support for maintaining their way of life from advocates such as singer-songwriter Billy Joel, who owns properties on the East End.[93]

Status of the Industry

With fish populations dropping and government quotas tightening, in the past eight years the number of commercial fishing licenses issued on Long Island has dropped by 11 percent, from 1,030 in 2010 to 916 by mid-2018. The level of commercial fishing is one-sixth of what it was in the 1980s, according to the Montauk-based Long Island Commercial Fishing Association. Many commercial fisheries such as whelk and striped bass are closed to newcomers, although there are occasional lotteries for new whelk licenses. Some fishermen who want to remain out on the water are shifting to mariculture projects such as creating oyster farms.[94]

But even with overfishing that has depleted many species, the fishing industry remains a major Long Island economic generator. The New York State Department of Environmental Conservation reported that in 2015, the last year for which statistics were available, 24.7 million pounds of finfish were landed—most of it from Long Island—with a value of $49.5 million. The most productive commercial fishing center in the state was Shinnecock Inlet in Hampton Bays, which ranked 94th in the list of highest-grossing fishing ports in the nation with a catch of 4.1 million pounds worth $4.9 million. Greenport was number two on Long Island, ranked 126th nationally, with landings totaling 200,000 pounds with a value of $300,000.

Recreational fishing also is a major economic force on Long Island, with anglers supporting boats heading out daily in the warmer months from Freeport, Captree State Park, Montauk and other harbors.

Those seeking finfish are not the only ones on Long Island waters trying to harvest seafood. Shallower water is where baymen search for oysters, clams and other shellfish. Their story is told in the next chapter.

5

SHELLFISHING

Early European settlers learned from the Native American inhabitants about the variety and value of shellfish in Long Island waters. Individually and later through companies, they began harvesting oysters, clams and other species from the local bays.

The fishermen who pursued the shellfish—known as baymen—initially used open rowboats and long iron rakes or tongs to dig the bivalves out of the bottom. As the industry developed, rowboats were supplemented before the Civil War by wide-hulled sloops or schooners with huge mainsails for fishing in deeper water by towing metal cage-like dredges.[95]

Baymen were so prevalent around the Long Island shoreline that they constituted a large percentage of the volunteers in the 127th New York Infantry Regiment, which recruited along the North Shore of Suffolk County and the East End during the Civil War. Soldiers from other regiments tried to insult the Long Islanders by calling them clamdiggers. But the men of the 127th liked the sobriquet so much that they adopted the nickname for themselves.[96]

Initially, Long Island shellfish was carried to New York City by boat, but by the late 1860s much of the transportation was handled by the LIRR.[97]

THE SOUTH SHORE

In the early nineteenth century, oysters from the Great South Bay—especially those from off Blue Point—became an international delicacy that fostered a huge industry with revenues in the millions of dollars. By 1890 there were twenty-five packinghouses along the South Shore, with much of the product shipped from Bay Shore, Oakdale, Sayville and Patchogue. These hamlets shipped sixty to seventy thousand barrels of oysters annually. Shells from the oysters were so plentiful that the streets of Sayville were covered with them to prevent ruts.[98]

The Great South Bay oysters made the entrepreneurs who bought and sold them rich and provided jobs for thousands of others who dredged the bay for the bivalves or processed them ashore. The shellfish would be brought to factories where they would be shucked—or opened—with special knives and the meat inside placed in wooden kegs and later cans.[99]

The Great South Bay was not uniformly suited for the growth of shellfish. The western end near Fire Island Inlet was saltier. Oysters and clams would set, or reproduce, better in the brackish water in the eastern part of the bay but grow fatter faster in the saltier water to the west. In addition, the fresher water curbed the growth of the oysters' natural enemies such as starfish. So

Illustrations of oystering in the Great South Bay in *Harper's Weekly* in 1886. *Author's collection.*

about 1847, the baymen began to collect small bivalves known as seed oysters in the eastern part of the bay and transplant them to the west to enhance their growth. About this time, officials in the town of Brookhaven decided to cash in on and regulate the industry by leasing two-acre underwater parcels for two dollars a year. As part of the regulatory effort and to prevent poaching and taking undersized shellfish, the town began issuing licenses and hired inspectors it called "toleration officers."[100]

The Great South Bay oyster fishery received a boost in the 1870s when Connecticut entrepreneurs figured out a way to grow seed oysters in hatcheries. The seed oysters were then shipped to Long Island and sowed across the bay.

Most of the South Shore oystermen were Dutch immigrants. Jacob Ockers of Blue Point was the first dealer to export large quantities to Europe. He shipped thirty thousand oysters there every year during the 1890s, earning himself the title of the "Oyster King." Ockers, who was born in Holland in 1847 and came to America three years later, began crewing on his father's oyster schooner at age eight. He owned his own boat before he turned seventeen. When he set up an oyster processing plant in Oakdale in 1876, it made him the largest dealer of the acclaimed Blue Point oysters. He got rich buying shellfish from other baymen and shipping it to New York City by water. As Ockers's empire grew, he controlled oyster beds from New Jersey to Massachusetts and owned ten schooners in part or outright.[101]

The two decades beginning in the 1890s were the high point for the industry, with more than 150,000 barrels of oysters a year shipped from the South Shore. The Blue Point oysters were so prized that in 1908 the state legislature passed a law stating that only oysters that had spent at least three months growing in the Great South Bay could be described as Blue Points.[102]

By the beginning of the twentieth century, the fishermen were working from boats propelled by engines, further boosting yields. But this also led to overfishing and depletion of the natural population of oysters. Exacerbating the problem was contaminated runoff from farms and increasing residential development.[103]

Acts of nature also helped curtail oystering. A storm in March 1931 created a new inlet south of Moriches. Over the next few years, the influx of water from the Atlantic increased the salinity of the eastern part of the bay, allowing predators to wipe out the best oyster beds. The South Shore baymen began switching to dredging clams, while those on the East End began harvesting scallops.[104]

Baymen work the Great South Bay around 1900. *Courtesy of Nassau County Photo Archives Center.*

The Great Hurricane of 1938, also known as the Long Island Express, had an even bigger impact on the industry. The huge waves ripped about one-third of the bay's oysters and clams from their beds and killed them by burying them in deep water. That killed some of the shellfishing companies as well. But there also was a long-term impact from the storm. The waves and tidal surge carved a new inlet across Fire Island at Moriches. As with the 1931 storm, the inflow of ocean water increased the salinity of the Great South Bay, resulting in a die-off of oysters. The saltier water, however, was a boon for the clam population. Those bivalves replaced oysters as the primary shellfishing catch. But the clams were not in as much demand as oysters, so the baymen made less bringing them to market. Many of the clams raked or dredged from the bay bottoms made their way to New York, where they were cut up for chowder or eaten steamed, fried or raw "on the half shell." As Long Island became more of a vacation destination, visitors would rake their own clams at low tide and then feast at clambakes on the beach.[105]

By 1969, the baymen in the Great South Bay were harvesting half of the clams consumed in the United States. But overfishing and pollution continued to take their toll. The first algae blooms began to appear, smothering the bivalves. The number of commercial shellfishing permits issued for the bay almost doubled to 9,500 between 1970 and 1977. After 1976, when a record of more than eight million pounds of shellfish came out of the bay, the Long Island harvest began to decline.[106]

THE DOXSEE FAMILY

Besides Ockers, the other big name in South Shore shellfishing was Doxsee. In 1865, James Harvey Doxsee was running his family's Islip farm, which included a cannery on the Great South Bay that processed corn, tomatoes and other vegetables. According to undocumented family lore, two men whose names have not been recorded rented the cannery and attempted to process seafood. But their cans did not properly preserve the product. So Doxsee and brother-in-law Selah Whitman took over the operation after a year and eventually solved the spoilage problem. J.H. Doxsee & Sons became the first Long Island company to can hard-shelled clams and bottle clam juice. In 1872, it also began to can "American Lunch Fish," which was menhaden or bunker fish processed to compete with sardines after Doxsee figured out how to dissolve the bones.

The Islip cannery closed in 1905. (Two historical markers near the Islip town dock commemorate the company.) But five years earlier, with the Great South Bay harvests dwindling, Doxsee's eldest son, Henry, set up a branch operation in Ocracoke, North Carolina. A decade later, his son James Harvey II moved it to Marco Island, Florida, where canning continued until 1948. That branch of the family business was sold several times and is now part of the Bumble Bee line, which sometimes includes Doxsee clam juice produced in Cape May, New Jersey.

When Henry went south, another of Doxsee's sons, John C., under the name of Deep Sea Fish Company, began setting traps in the Atlantic Ocean from a fishing camp located where the Fire Island Coast Guard station is now situated. Deep Sea Fish published brochures that claimed clam juice would cure indigestion, dyspepsia, disordered stomach, constipation and hangovers, and it provided recipes for its use. In 1919, John moved the operation to Meadow Island in the bay near Jones Inlet. John's sons, Robert L. and Spencer, moved the business to Point Lookout on Reynolds Channel in 1933 and renamed it Bright Eye Fish Company because bright eyes are the hallmark of fresh fish. There was no community of Point Lookout at the time. The company set up a tent and then a little cottage and a dock. They staked "pound traps," a maze of nets to catch migrating fish, to the bay bottom and caught albacore, bonito, mackerel, butterfish, porgies, bluefish, fluke and squid. A processing plant came later.

The Doxsees encountered setbacks over the years, not surprising for a business dependent on an uncertain Mother Nature. The Great Hurricane of 1938 and another in 1944 destroyed the family's nets. A month before the second storm, the company had begun a transition to dredging for surf clams—primarily used for fried clam strips—while also netting finfish. But after the second hurricane, the Doxsees focused entirely on offshore clams.

Initially, the clams were raked out of the bottom by steel "dry" dredges. Later, the company utilized hydraulic dredges to dislodge the clams. At its peak, during World War II, the company owned five boats and bought seafood from seventeen independent baymen. It employed about one hundred workers, half on the boats and the rest shucking and packaging clams. In the beginning, the clams shucked in Point Lookout were shipped to a cannery in Maine. But about 1960—around the time Robert L. Doxsee, who had been mayor of Freeport in the late 1940s, turned the business over to his son, Robert Doxsee Jr.—the company now named Long Island Sea Clam Company began shipping frozen chopped clams packed in half-gallon milk cartons all around the country.

Robert Jr. had to endure the family's worst setback. In 1975 one of its boats, *Doxsee Girls*, with its crew of four was lost in a line squall off the Virginia coast.

With catches diminishing, in 2008 Doxsee made a dramatic change. He ended the wholesale processing operation and demolished the processing plant. "It was time," Doxsee said. "I was old. The plant was old. The business was no longer viable." Declining catches and increased regulations to protect the marine life that was left were part of the equation, he added.

With the main plant razed, Doxsee continued selling frozen products retail out of a shed next door. More of the company was chipped away in 2010 when Doxsee sold the remaining two boats and shifted to buying shucked clams from other processors. That downsized version of Doxsee Sea Clam Company continued until superstorm Sandy arrived in October 2012. The storm surge wrecked the dock and last processing shed, ending the family's long and fabled fishing history.[107]

THE NORTH SHORE

Before World War II, there were about 150 oyster companies working Long Island Sound and its harbors, including 4 in aptly named Oyster Bay. That harbor became the primary center for harvesting oysters as well as clams. Around the turn of the twentieth century, a fleet of about forty large oyster-dredging sloops operated in Oyster Bay. When a sloop had a full load of shellfish, it sailed to New York City and docked at a market for several days until the crew sold their entire catch. Despite some degradation of water quality from runoff, Oyster Bay today remains the leading source of shellfish in the state.[108]

On the North Shore, Oyster Bay had competition from Manhasset Bay, Hempstead Harbor and the waters of Huntington and Smithtown. In 1880, the harvest of hard shell clams along the North Shore is believed to have been more than 300,000 bushels. Manhasset Bay, fifteen miles from New York City and with abundant clam and oyster beds, was known in the early nineteenth century as "the shellfish garden" of the metropolis. Hundreds of local families supported themselves harvesting oysters, clams and eels or working for the businesses that supplied them. The fishing shacks owned by the baymen, who formed an important local political power base, were given names like "City Hall" and "Tammany Hall."[109]

While Ockers was the most famous name in oysters on the South Shore, Frank M. Flower & Sons became the best-known shellfishing enterprise on the North Shore. That company is still going strong on the waters of Oyster Bay. The firm, with facilities in Oyster Bay and Bayville, traces its history back to 1876 when William A. Flower built a house on the shore of Mill Neck and staked out three acres of oyster beds in Mill Neck Creek, an arm of Oyster Bay. His three sons helped rake up the oysters from rowboats. Frank was the only son to stick with the business. He began dredging with sailboats and then gasoline-powered vessels around the turn of the century, and he also began harvesting clams. In 1934, with the help of his sons, Allen, Butler and Roswell, he moved the business across the creek to Bayville. After the natural "set" of oysters and clams began to decline in the 1950s because of overharvesting and bad weather, the three brothers created a hatchery at the Bayville complex in 1963 to grow seed shellfish. When they have grown to sufficient size, the oysters and clams are placed in cages in Mill Neck Creek and then spread on the more than 1,800 acres of bay bottom leased from the Town of Oyster Bay through 2024. Those leases have been controversial, with an association of independent baymen involved in long-term litigation with the company and town. The baymen also contend the firm's hydraulic dredging damages marine life by stirring up the bottom, a charge not validated by state or federal agencies to date.

While other small startup oyster and clam fishing companies—some with their own hatchery operations—have emerged in recent years, Flower, now owned by three longtime employees, remains by far Long Island's largest operation. The Bayville hatchery produces 100 million seed oysters and 100 million clams annually.[110]

Out on the North Fork, when the natural population of oysters began to decline, James M. Monsell developed an oyster farming industry in the area in the late 1880s. After Suffolk County passed the Oyster Grounds Act in 1879 to open shellfish areas for leasing, Monsell acquired access to oyster beds in Peconic and Gardiners Bays that eventually totaled hundreds of thousands of acres. Millions of seed oysters that Monsell could later harvest were spread over the beds. Other individuals and companies joined the business. By the early 1930s, there were twenty-eight oyster companies situated in the Greenport area employing more than five hundred people. In 1936, more than 2.5 million bushels of oysters were shipped out of Greenport.[111]

SCALLOPS

On the East End, the bay scallop fishery also was once a major industry. But pollution and resulting algae blooms caused the scallop population to plummet in some years. Peconic Bay scallops, which are generally smaller than sea scallops, are considered a delicacy and fetch high prices when they are available.

The amount of scallops available can vary wildly from year to year. In 1946, the bay scallop harvest in New York waters totaled only 12,881 bushels, according to the state Department of Environmental Conservation. By 1960, the total soared to 140,495 bushels. In 2010, 40,396 pounds of bay scallops were brought ashore. There was a large bounce to 100,066 pounds in 2014. In 2015, it was 65,378, and then in 2016 it dropped to just 30,575 pounds.

The Peconic Bay scallop fishery rebounded strongly in 2017 to a total of 108,800 pounds, the best results since 1974 and a significant boost for the East End shellfishing industry already benefiting from improved oyster yields. Fish dealers bought hundreds of pounds a day and would have bought more but they could not hire enough shuckers. The bay scallops harvested also were larger in 2017 than they had been in several years. This was believed to be the result of baymen throwing smaller scallops back the previous year to give them additional growing time.[112]

Lobstering

The lobster fishery along the North Shore of Long Island has followed the same pattern as other fisheries: plenty followed by a drastic drop-off. Whether the cause is overfishing, warmer water temperatures or pesticide pollution, as the lobstermen suspect, the result is a scarcity of lobsters.

During lobstering's glory years in the 1980s and '90s, the industry generated $100 million a year on Long Island. There were once as many as seven hundred members in the local lobstermen's association, but now only about a dozen remain. During the good years, Long Island compared favorably against other top lobstering areas such as Maine and Massachusetts, according to Bob Bayer, head of the Lobster Institute at the University of Maine.

Lobster landings, or reported catches, in the state, most of them in Nassau and Suffolk Counties, totaled more than 9 million pounds in 1996 and then dropped precipitously to under 1 million pounds in 2011, the most recent statistics available from the Department of Environmental Conservation. The 2011 landings were slightly lower than the total in 1981, when the trend began to rise steeply toward the 1996 record level. By 2016, the total was only 218,000 pounds, according to the Atlantic States Marine Fisheries Commission.

After the successful 1996 season, there was an influx of fishermen getting into the business. But then came what the lobstermen call "the die-off," the death of millions of lobsters in 1999 that they attribute to a concentration of mosquito insecticide that made its way into the sea. Most of those who once set traps for lobsters now fish for conch or other species, have moved to Maine to continue lobstering or have taken jobs ashore.[113]

BAY HOUSES

One unusual vestige of the baymen's lifestyle can still be seen on the marsh islands dotting the waters along the South Shore in the towns of Hempstead and Islip. Bay houses are structures of varying architectural styles built by baymen to provide shelter so they could harvest shellfish and small bait fish without having to return to shore every night.

The structures, some appearing ramshackle and others fashioned with obvious care, are called by various names such as gunnin' shacks, bungalows or bay shacks, as well as bay houses. Some of them are more than a century old. Most are two or three rooms with a porch and deck. The buildings are supported by telephone poles driven into the ground and resting on mud sills, which are long planks resting on the marshland. They have been handed down from generation to generation. Used initially by commercial fishermen, baymen and professional duck hunters, most now are used for recreational fishing and hunting.

Between 1870 and 1918, many of the baymen made a living by duck hunting as "market gunners." Some lived in the bay houses year-round. The feathers were purchased to make women's hats, and local restaurants bought the duck meat. Market gunning was outlawed in 1918 as a conservation measure. After that, the baymen used their houses for personal hunting or as a base for guiding recreational hunters. Others were built after World War II as getaways by people who didn't make their living on the water.[114]

At one time, bay houses could be found in most of the towns on Long Island, on both the northern and southern coasts. But after Congress passed the Clean Water Act in 1972, the federal government pressured the state and towns to remove the structures and their accompanying outhouses to protect water quality. While Islip and Hempstead allowed the houses to remain, each must now have a composting toilet.

In the 1950s, Hempstead responded to the demand by recreational fishermen, hunters and others by granting an unprecedented number of leases, and the number of houses increased exponentially. But many in the two towns have disappeared, victims of government regulation and actions, erosion from boat wakes and the force of storms. In 1933, the Meadowbrook and Wantagh Parkways were built on marshlands where many of the houses had been built, resulting several dozen being demolished or moved. In the 1950s, there were more than two hundred bay houses in Hempstead. The numbers dropped precipitously in subsequent years in part because the town at the time prohibited owners who leased their land from the town from transferring the lease to anyone, including family members. The town had also stated that it would terminate all leases in 1993 and then remove all the structures. But in 1983, Hempstead officials relented and imposed a new policy allowing the owners, who pay a fee in lieu of taxes, to transfer the lease to a family member or someone with a long-standing relationship with the family.[115]

Before Hurricane Sandy in 2012, about forty structures remained in Hempstead waters. After the storm, there were only fourteen. A half-dozen were rebuilt. The storm destroyed four of the forty houses in Islip.[116]

Kevin Braunlich owns a Hempstead bay house on the site of a shack built by his grandfather and father in 1957. After the structure was destroyed in a 1997 fire, the retired town parks worker rebuilt it. "I fish for flounder, weakfish, clams, and hang out," Braunlich said. "People drive hundreds of miles to go upstate to rough it. I've got a half-hour boat ride."[117]

STATUS OF THE SHELLFISHING INDUSTRY

While the harvest of shellfish in recent years is well below historical record levels, it's still a sizable industry. And a growing number of small mariculture companies and government-assisted projects are making it bigger. In New York State, in 2016, the most recent year for which statistics are available from the state Department of Environmental Conservation, the hard clams brought ashore—all from Nassau and Suffolk Counties—totaled 181,853 bushels worth $12 million. Almost 49,000 bushels of oysters were harvested with a value of almost $4 million.

Although it's unlikely that the shellfish population will ever approach its historic numbers, town governments including Hempstead, Oyster Bay and Brookhaven backed by state grants have been spending hundreds of thousands of dollars to expand hatcheries and buy seed clams to spread over the bays. Their goal is to boost local shellfishing companies and improve water quality because clams and oysters are effective filtering devices that remove pollution. There also is a growing number of small commercial shellfish farming operations around the island such as Blue Island Oyster Farm, which operates on five acres of bay bottom leased from the Town of Islip, and Thatch Island Oyster Farms, which leases two and a half acres from Islip; they grow more than half a million oysters a year combined.[118]

Much of the shellfish harvested from Long Island waters was carried to market by water, especially in the early years. The story of that maritime trade is related in the next chapter.

MARITIME TRADE

Most of Long Island's early settlements were clustered along the shorelines to enable easy access, trade and gathering of seafood. Colonial Long Island ports were shipping corn and wheat, wood, fish, livestock and whale oil to other cities in America, the Caribbean islands and even to Europe by 1675.[119]

Some of the grain shipped to New York City and beyond came from tidal mills. Most mills on Long Island were built adjacent to streams and rivers flowing into bays or Long Island Sound. But some were built adjacent to these bodies of water to take advantage of the rise and fall of the tides twice a day. One of these tidal mills was the Lefferts Mill in Lloyd Harbor, built in 1795 and still standing on the western shore of Huntington Harbor. The tides, as high as nine feet, would flow into the pond behind the mill and then drain out over the mill's waterwheel to create grinding power. Another surviving example is the circa 1702 Saddle Rock Tidal Grist Mill on the Great Neck Peninsula. It is owned by Nassau County and, like Lefferts, is a museum.[120]

THE RISE OF FEVERSHAM

In the late 1600s, much of Long Island's shipping was done through a port few people today know existed. Feversham was located at Conscience Point on Peconic Bay in the town of Southampton, in the area of today's North Sea. It was not only the most active port on Long Island but also the third-busiest in all of the colonies behind Boston and Philadelphia.

Southampton Town was founded in 1640 by colonists from Massachusetts who landed at Conscience Point but settled farther south in what is now the village of Southampton. Feversham was established ten years later and named for a small port town in England. It was created by entrepreneur John Ogden, who was given a land grant by Southampton officials in return for a promise to settle twenty-three families along the town's northern shoreline. Tom Edmonds, executive director of the Southampton Historical Museum and Research Center, who has been researching Feversham, has gleaned that the community had several farmhouses clustered plantation-style, two taverns, a warehouse, a brick kiln and a customs house. The harbor enabled the South Fork to thrive. (Suffolk County's population surpassed the towns in present-day Nassau until the twentieth century, and from the colonial era through the early nineteenth century, much of Suffolk's population was concentrated on the East End.)

"Long Island in the seventeenth century was full of virgin forests [for timber] and people were raising cattle and other goods on the rich fertile

A regularly scheduled packet boat schooner in Roslyn in 1890. *Courtesy of Nassau County Photo Archives Center.*

soil," Edmonds said. "The pioneers were able to grow really great crops, and they would ship flour and timber to England and take in rum and sugar from Barbados." By the 1680s, Feversham was exporting whale oil to Boston and London and cordwood to North Carolina. Edmonds found one entry in town records showing one thousand pounds of dried pork sent to Virginia. Passengers traveled from Feversham to Connecticut, Boston, London and Barbados. The harbor was too shallow to dock large ships, so smaller boats ferried cargo to and from shore.

Feversham was the only major port on Long Island until after 1700. It would be supplanted by Sag Harbor, which was settled in 1730 but didn't see major development until the end of the century, about the time Feversham disappeared from maps. Sag Harbor had the advantages of a deep-water harbor, increasing trade, particularly with the West Indies, and the growing whaling industry. Feversham became a sleepy farming community that specialized in growing apples. All that is left from Ogden's time is a 1661 farmhouse and the foundation of a brick kiln from the 1600s.[121]

Sag Harbor grew to the point that in 1789 it was named one of America's earliest official ports of entry by the first Congress. (Its first customshouse is now a museum owned by Preservation Long Island.)[122]

OYSTER BAY BECOMES A TRADING CENTER

A century after Feversham was founded, Oyster Bay became a regional trading center.

The waterfront community became the base for entrepreneur Samuel Townsend, whose businesses dominated activity in the surrounding agricultural enclaves in the mid-eighteenth century. The farmers in this period were already more oriented toward growing for the market than only for local consumption. Many Long Island communities, including Oyster Bay, had close economic ties with New York City, Connecticut and other nearby population centers. At the same time, the local farmers and artisans, no matter how poor or apparently self-sufficient they were, were regular consumers of imported merchandise.

Samuel Townsend was born into a prominent Long Island family. The prior three generations had dominated the politics and business activities in the town. Samuel, educated in accounting and navigation, relocated the family's store from Jericho to the shoreline in Oyster Bay. The well-protected harbor and gently sloping waterfront favored trading and shipbuilding—and Townsend would be active in both. Partnering with his younger brother Jacob and Captains Joseph Milliken and John Aspinwall, Townsend began construction of a coastal trading sloop and a warehouse in the spring of 1747.

Through his store, Townsend quickly became a major regional buyer of agricultural products, from cattle and hogs to barrels of flour. The merchant acquired these items for export. Townsend owned a wharf at the end of Ships Point Lane and ships that docked there. His fleet began with the aptly named *Prosperity*, which was eventually joined by *Sarah*, *Solomon*, *Audrey*, *Polly*, *Sally* and *Elizabeth*. With all of the ships coming and going in Oyster Bay, it was natural that there would also be shipyards. There were at least two (see chapter 8).[123]

The quantities of food and goods dispatched by Townsend were significant. In one 1746 shipment to New York, he included 226 hams, 10 double casks of biscuits, 3 hogsheads of lard, 49 pounds of old pewter, 90 double casks of pickled tongues, 8 barrels of tallow, 9 containers of butter and 100 pounds of beeswax. To transport all of these items, he steadily purchased barrels and the components to make them locally. In 1748, he purchased 100 barrels from David Weekes and 1,000 barrel hoops from Thomas Seaman.

A cargo schooner docked in Baldwin in undated photo. *Courtesy of Nassau County Photo Archives Center.*

Vessels leaving Oyster Bay for other ports, including those in Canada and the Caribbean, usually would first sail to New York to report in the customshouse and confer with merchants before continuing on. Townsend's ships typically went to the Caribbean, especially Jamaica, Barbados and the Virgin Islands. On one 1754 trip, a Townsend ship supplied sixteen merchants in Jamaica. The captains would return to Long Island with sugar, molasses, rum, wine, indigo, lumber and other products to exchange for European imports. Once they arrived in Oyster Bay, the cargoes would go into Townsend's warehouse and then eventually to the store to be sold to the farmers, completing the commercial chain that began with the sale of their products to Townsend. The store was a busy place. In the middle of the century, with all of the goods Townsend was importing, it was open six days a week and served up to twenty customers daily.

The trading vessels were augmented by weekly packet boats serving Oyster Bay that carried passengers, cargo, letters, newspapers and even winning lottery tickets.[124]

Other Long Island ports in the eighteenth century also engaged in maritime trade, although on a smaller scale than Oyster Bay. Shelter Island, for example, also was a busy port, as the Sylvester family regularly shipped what it grew on its plantation there to the island of Barbados, where the Sylvesters had extensive holdings.[125]

The Nineteenth Century

As the population of Long Island grew in the nineteenth century, the need for vessels to provide transportation for people and goods grew accordingly. There were many coastal sloops and schooners moving between Long Island ports and New York City and New England. In the 1800s, regularly scheduled packet vessels traveled up and down the sound and along the South Shore carrying lumber, farm produce and passengers to New York City and returned with merchandise along with manure and ashes to fertilize farms. By 1824, there were one hundred vessels of various types regularly traveling between the town of Brookhaven and New York City. Even the small community of Stony Brook boasted of being the homeport of 24 trading vessels that by the 1830s transported more than four thousand cords of wood annually to New York City and New England. The larger vessels serving Long Island ports carried lumber, bricks, sand, clay and gravel to Central America and even Africa. The growing trade resulted in Port Jefferson becoming an official U.S. port of entry in 1852. In 1875, 239 ships unloaded thirty thousand tons of goods at the port. The trading activity supported many ancillary businesses in the harbor towns.[126]

Eventually, beginning in the twentieth century, most products coming to or leaving Long Island would travel by truck, although the Long Island Rail Road has carried some of the freight since the last half of the nineteenth century. But certain heavy commodities, particularly fuel oil as well as sand and gravel, are still transported on Long Island Sound by barge.

It's a far cry from the early days of sail when almost every commodity moved by water. Most of it was legal. But some goods were stolen and smuggled by pirates.

7

PIRATES

L ong Island was a good hiding place for pirates in the seventeenth
century. It was near New York City but so sparsely populated that the
chances of being spotted or apprehended by the colonial authorities
were slim.

Smuggling of pirated goods was a big business, with powerful government
officials complicit in the enterprise and sharing the profits. The pirates used
the harbors around Long Island to repair their ships and offload their illegal
goods, which included slaves, sugar, textiles, jewels and spices.

The best known of these outlaws was Captain William Kidd, one of
the most infamous pirates in history, who buried some of his treasure on
Gardiners Island.

Kidd, a native of Scotland, went to sea as a young man on a merchant
vessel that traveled between New York and London. He went to London
in 1695 seeking a commission as a privateer, a private citizen authorized
by the government to capture French and Spanish shipping. There he met
the Earl of Bellomont, a member of Parliament who became governor of
the Massachusetts Bay Colony and later governor of New York. Bellomont
supported Kidd's initiative and became his business partner. Kidd outfitted a
ship named *Adventure Galley* and sailed to the Indian Ocean. In May 1698, the
vessel reached Madagascar, where 90 of the 150 men of his crew deserted
and Kidd abandoned the deteriorated ship.

The privateer seized a Moorish trading vessel, *Quedah Merchant*, and
by the following spring was in the West Indies. In the interim, the British

Kidd at Gardiner's Island, by Howard Pyle. *Art and Picture Collection, the New York Public Library. New York Public Library Digital Collections.*

government had declared Kidd to be a pirate. And Bellomont, now governor in Massachusetts, declared war on pirates, especially his former business partner. The governor wrote in May 1699 that the inhabitants of Long Island were "a lawless and unruly people" who protected pirates who were "settled among them."

When Kidd learned what the British government had done, he transferred some of his treasure to a sloop named *St. Anthony* and sailed for New England to resolve his legal issues with the British authorities. His first stop was Oyster Bay, where he contacted attorney James Emmot and arranged for him to approach the governor. While the lawyer headed for Boston, Kidd took precautions. He sent some jewels to the governor's wife. Then the captain traveled on one of his captured vessels, the *San Antonio*, to Gardiners Island, where he buried a lot of his loot a half mile inland from the western shore with the consent of the island's owner, Jonathan Gardiner. Kidd marked the spot with a cairn, or large pile of rocks, which still stands on the island near a granite marker erected in the nineteenth century by the family. For his trouble, Kidd gave Gardiner an expensive silk fabric, a piece of which hangs on the wall of the island's manor house.

Kidd then sailed to Boston, carrying proof that the ships he had seized were French. But Bellomont had him arrested on July 6 and sent a messenger to Gardiners Island to seize the booty. It was estimated to be worth more than $1 million in today's money. Gardiner gave a statement to the governor that the day he buried treasure, Kidd convinced him to "take three negroes, two boys and a girl, ashore, to keep till he, the said Kidd, should call for them." Gardiner also said the captain had given him cloth and "four pieces of Arabian Gold" and had buried "a chest and a box of Gold, a bundle of quilts, and four bales of goods." Gardiner also said two members of the captain's crew gave him "two bags of Silver...Which weighed 30 pounds...A small bundle of gold, gold dust of about a pound weight...a sash and a pair of worsted stockings."

Kidd was sent to London for trial and in February 1700 was charged with murdering one of his crewmen, William Moore. Two deserters from his crew testified against the captain. He was convicted and sentenced to hang. If that wasn't bad enough, he was then tried for piracy and convicted on that charge as well. On May 23, 1701, Kidd went to the gallows. When the trapdoor opened, the rope broke and he survived. Kidd was carried back up to the platform. The second time, the rope held.[127]

8

SHIPBUILDERS AND BOATYARDS

A s Long Island's population expanded, so did the demand for ships. Construction of ships is believed to have begun in Oyster Bay shortly after the town was founded in the 1650s. The first record of a ship being constructed on the Island is found in Brookhaven Town records in 1662. Between 1694 and 1707, six vessels—five sloops and a barque (the preferred spelling today)—were built at Gardiners Island, Southold and Cow Neck (now Port Washington), none of which evolved into major shipbuilding centers.[128]

America's major centers for shipbuilding in the age of wooden vessels were the cities of New York, Brooklyn, Boston and Philadelphia. The rest of Long Island was able to play an important part in the industry because of its deep protected harbors and proximity to major trade routes and New York City. To meet the need for transporting increasing numbers of passengers and cargo, shipyards were created in most coastal communities by 1840.

Shipbuilding had become a major local industry by 1855, a peak year for shipbuilding locally and nationally. Suffolk County had at least twenty-five shipyards, an increase of five over 1840, and they were much larger in scale, employing 419 workers. Fourteen of the companies were located in the Port Jefferson–Setauket area, five in Greenport or elsewhere in Southold, four in Northport or elsewhere in Huntington and one each in the towns of Islip and Smithtown. The Suffolk boatyards built at least 15 percent of the ships in the state.[129]

Larger vessels were constructed in only a few major ports, almost entirely in Suffolk, the state's largest shipbuilding center outside of New York City and Brooklyn. Major ship construction also was a North Shore endeavor. The South Shore lacked the deep harbors necessary. Patchogue did become an active boatbuilding center in the second half of the nineteenth century, but the craft built there were primarily small and used for fishing on the Great South Bay. Surprisingly, even though they were centers of the whaling industry with protected harbors, Sag Harbor and Cold Spring Harbor never became significant shipbuilding sites, while Greenport did.[130]

Building wooden vessels required a range of trades. Rather than working from blueprints, a shipwright, or ship designer, would carve a one-sided wood "half model" whose dimensions would be "lofted" or transferred full-size onto the wooden floor of a shop as a guide for cutting the frame timbers. After lumbermen cut down trees, they were shaped at the shipyards by sawyers. The shipwrights then fashioned the vessels from the keel up, attaching frames and planking using an assortment of hand tools from an auger to drill holes to an adze to shape the edges of the timber. Shipsmiths forged iron rings and other fittings, while blockmakers made the wooden blocks, or pulleys, for the rigging. Caulkers used oakum, a fiber similar to unraveled rope, to fill the seams between planks and covered them with hot tar-like pitch to make the deck and hull watertight. Workers in long and narrow "rope walk" buildings twisted fibers into rope for the rigging. Finally, riggers and sailmakers assembled the system of rope and sails to power the ship.

The shipyard owners enjoyed considerable economic success and became leaders in their communities. Life was less pleasurable for their employees. They worked long hours six days a week, had no job security and rarely received pay increases, especially after the Civil War.[131]

The demand for construction of wooden ships nationally ebbed after 1855, in part because of overproduction in previous years, when many vessels were built to carry prospectors to California after the discovery of gold there in 1848. Another factor was the Civil War, which decimated the shipping and shipbuilding industries. After the war ended in 1865, neither rebounded to its previous prosperity. The decline of the whaling industry also reduced the need for wooden sailing vessels. But the most important reason was that iron- and steel-hulled steamships fabricated elsewhere were capturing an increasing share of trade. The decline in the industry can be seen from census figures. In 1870, there were 251 Suffolk men listed as working in shipbuilding trades. The number dropped to 200 in 1880. At the close of the nineteenth century, some of the larger Long Island shipyards segued into building steel vessels and steamships. But most of the large yards and small boat shops shifted their operations to handling repairs or building and maintaining pleasure craft.[132]

OYSTER BAY

Oyster Bay was the earliest Long Island shipbuilding center. It was a natural location with its gently sloping waterfront, protected harbor and proximity to New York City. Construction of vessels probably began shortly after the town was settled in the early 1650s. In 1681, a town meeting granted John Newman a home lot and yard for "the building of vessels." Several other shipwrights, including Samuel Andrews, William Frost and Samuel Powell, were also operating in the same time period.[133]

Although Oyster Bay was still a small hamlet in the mid-eighteenth century, it was the home for many ship owners. And most of their vessels appear to have been built locally. A three-decade boom in shipbuilding began around 1745 after Jericho merchant Samuel Townsend relocated his busy store to the harbor. During the next five years he commissioned three trading vessels—*Prosperity*, *Solomon* and *Sarah*.[134]

The craftsmen in Oyster Bay built everything from small open fishing boats to sailing vessels called snows, which were large enough for transatlantic voyages. The most common type of construction was sloops, single-masted craft forty-five to fifty feet in length and used for coastal trading. It would take six months to a year to build a trading ship. The ship carpenters in Oyster Bay included one Native American, John Rumpas, and at least one enslaved African American. Most of the merchant vessels were equipped with cannons to ward off marauders.

The American Revolution hobbled the industry, as the British occupied Long Island and the volume of trade in and out of Oyster Bay was drastically reduced. There was little improvement after the end of the war, when a deep depression and the loss of traditional trading partners who had been allied with the British crippled northern port towns.[135]

As shipbuilding was revived in later years, the work was generally done elsewhere. The exception was Jakobson Shipyard Inc., established in Brooklyn as Jakobson & Petersen in 1895. Founder Daniel Jakobson was succeeded in 1925 by his son Irving, who moved the company to Oyster Bay in 1938. The company's primary business was building tugboats for railroads and other customers, but it also built fireboats for the City of Baltimore. During World War II, Jakobson built submarine-chasers, minesweepers and tugboats for the military (see chapter 25). The shipyard was acquired by Moran Towing after the war. Shipbuilding ended in 1984, and the company shut down in 1993 because of environmental problems. It was removed from the state's hazardous waste site list two years later after a voluntary cleanup by Moran. The State of New York and Town of Oyster Bay bought the 5.2-acre property in 1997 for parkland. One building was left standing and houses the offices of the nonprofit WaterFront Center. A new building erected on an old foundation is being used to build a replica of the oyster dredge *Ida May* (see chapter 29).[136]

PORT JEFFERSON

Almost a century after ship construction began in Oyster Bay, the area around Port Jefferson—then called Drowned Meadow—began its rise to becoming Long Island's second most prolific shipbuilding hub after Brooklyn.

The first report in Brookhaven Town records of a ship being constructed is in 1662. Richard Bullick, "a traveller," was allowed to buy timber and planks from John Ketcham and given four months to complete a vessel and then leave town. His goods would be forfeited if he misbehaved during his stay.[137] Benjamin Floyd constructed a large vessel named the *Boyne* in Setauket prior to 1787. Believed to be the first oceangoing vessel built in the area, it carried as many as seventy-two passengers from Amsterdam and London to New York.[138]

The impetus for creation of a significant shipbuilding industry in Drowned Meadow was the decision in 1779 by John Willse, a fourteen-year-old New Jersey farmhand, to take a job at a farm on George's Neck, now Poquott, northwest of Port Jefferson. By 1797, he was building vessels as a sideline to his farm chores. The following year, he purchased land on the southeast corner of the harbor and built a sloop designed to carry lumber. He built at least five more ships on the site before his death in 1815. Willse had hired Richard Mather sometime before 1809 as an apprentice, and five years after that Mather married Willse's daughter Irena. He became the community's largest shipbuilder after the death of his father-in-law. Mather died in 1816 from injuries sustained when he fell off the deck of a sloop under construction. Mather's demise brought a three-year lull to shipbuilding in the village. But in 1819, work resumed at the Willse yard under the direction of William L. Jones, who had been an apprentice with Mather's brother Titus and married Mather's widow. Jones built two vessels during the 1820s, and his stepson John R. Mather helped foster the shipbuilding boom in Port Jefferson in the 1840s.[139]

In the nineteenth century, the village's population was only about three hundred, but most of the adult males worked in the shipyards. From the late 1700s until 1884, they built 327 wooden vessels, about 40 percent of the ships constructed in Suffolk County. Among the noteworthy vessels was the schooner *Edward L. Frost*. Built in 1847 by C.L. and J.M. Bayles, it was the first American ship to bring cargo from Japan in 1856 after trade had been established by Commodore Matthew Perry. The schooner *Henry James*, built in 1854, was converted into a Union navy mortar ship during the Civil War and took part in the bombardment and capture of New Orleans in 1862.[140]

The war crimped shipbuilding other than for military vessels. And after the war, the business continued to shrink. In 1870, there were eleven shipbuilders in Port Jefferson, and by 1891 there were only three. The surviving shipyards focused increasingly on small commercial vessels and pleasure craft. Forty of the forty-three vessels built between 1891 and 1917 were steam launches, recreational yachts and small working vessels. Some of the exceptions were noteworthy. In 1906–7, the *Lake*, a torpedo boat prototype, was built at the Hawkins yard for the U.S. Navy. But the vessel flunked its sea trials in the harbor and was never accepted by the service. One major exception for John Titus Mather was the large steam ferry *Park City* built for the Bridgeport & Port Jefferson Steamboat Company at his Mather & Wood yard in 1898. Mather & Wood also launched the four-masted schooner *Martha E. Wallace*, the last large sailing ship built in the village, in 1902. With a length of 218 feet, it was the largest sailing vessel ever built on Long Island. Mather closed the business in 1908. James E. Bayles constructed thirty-seven vessels, mostly pleasure craft, between 1884 and 1917. One standout was *Zoroya*, a 184-foot luxury steam yacht constructed in 1901. When Bayles closed his yard in 1917, it marked the end of Long Island's wooden shipbuilding era.[141]

After the United States entered World War I in 1917, the federal government paid to upgrade the moribund yards so it could construct steel-hulled vessels. Between 1917 and 1919, the number of workers more than quadrupled from 250 to over 1,100. They built dozens of ships, including

Launching of the *Martha E. Wallace*, the largest vessel ever built in Port Jefferson. *Courtesy of the Incorporated Village of Port Jefferson, portjeff.com/village-history.*

in 1919 two oceangoing tugboats as well as two freighters, which were the largest ever built in Suffolk County. When the war ended, so did shipbuilding in Port Jefferson. The cancellation of government contracts was not offset by spending for new pleasure craft. The wartime modifications to the shipyards left them unsuitable for that kind of work.[142]

Northport

In the early years of the wooden shipbuilding industry, Northport was Port Jefferson's closest competitor. Construction there commenced slightly later, about 1812, when shipwright C. Beebe began work. By about 1820, Isaac Scudder Ketcham was building ships, and in 1828 a firm named Bunce and Bayles was in operation. Another decade would pass before the village's major shipbuilders—Jesse Jarvis, Moses Hartt and Jesse Carll—established their yards.[143]

The Carll facility is believed to have been the largest on Long Island. At the age of seventeen, Jesse Carll began to learn the trade from James

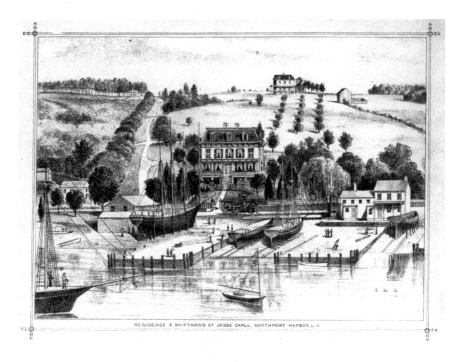

Residence & Shipyards of Jesse Carll, Northport Harbor, L.I., by Edward Lange, published in an 1882 book. *Courtesy of the Northport Historical Society.*

and C. Lloyd Bayles, noted Port Jefferson shipbuilders. Carll and his older brother David opened their yard with an investment of $400. By the time they built their third vessel, a barque named *Storm Bird* completed in eighty-seven days, the shipyard had developed a reputation for skill and efficiency. Carll employed between seventy-five and one hundred "mechanics" at the yard. Jesse Jr. took over the business after his father died in 1902. The Carll shipyard was a driving force in the local economy for four decades.[144]

More than 180 ships had been launched in Northport by 1884. But the business declined as it did in other harbor towns. While there were seven builders in 1870, by 1891 there were only three. By the early twentieth century, only the Carll yard remained, and it was doing primarily repair work. During World War I, the property was leased to a company that constructed scows for the navy. During the 1920s, shipbuilding ceased and the property was given to the village to become a park.[145]

Greenport

The first vessel built in the North Fork community is believed to have been a sloop named *Van Buren* constructed by Caleb Horton in 1834. By the end of the nineteenth century and through World War II, Greenport was a major shipbuilding center. The twenty-five shipbuilders located there over the years built more than 550 sizable vessels.[146]

Most of the early vessels were schooners for coastal trade. There is no record of any ships being built between 1858 and 1863, which coincides with the lead-up to the Civil War and the first two years of the conflict, so owners might have been reluctant to invest in shipping during that turbulent time. Ship construction resumed in 1864, a year before the war ended, with three vessels built. Only one ship was built in 1865, but it was a large one: the 370-foot steamship *Nebraska*.[147]

The largest sailing ship built in Greenport was the barkentine *Wandering Jew*, launched in 1880 with more than three thousand people witnessing the ceremonies. The ship did not have an auspicious debut. The wind picked up so strongly after the ship was launched that it was blown up onto the beach and had to be rescued by fishing boats and towed back to the pier at the Smith & Terry shipyard. The bad luck continued: the *Wandering Jew* was driven ashore and wrecked in South Carolina during a 1898 hurricane.[148]

Construction of wooden vessels tapered off almost completely not long after the launch of the *Wandering Jew* in 1880. Census records show only a dozen shipwrights working that year.[149]

The oldest Greenport facility and the only one to survive, with changes in ownership and name, is Greenport Basin and Construction Company. Founded about 1830 on the site of a menhaden fish processing factory, it constructed numerous commercial vessels. The shipyard also built hundreds of landing craft for amphibious assaults and thirty-nine wooden minesweepers for the navy during World War II (see chapter 25). After the conflict, the facility became Brigham Shipyard and in 1966 Greenport Yacht & Ship Building Co. The firm, which retains its historic marine railway to raise vessels out of the harbor, no longer builds ships—it just maintains them.[150]

Hanff's Boatyard is located on property on Stirling Creek where boats have been built since John Wesley Ketcham began operating there around 1907. He sold the business in 1934 to Charles L. Hanff, whose two sons, Bill and Walter, continued to build fishing boats, ferries, barges, recreational boats and other watercraft using traditional wood framing methods along with modern steel technology. When they became too old to continue the business, they sold it in 1994 to John Costello and his brother George. After George's death, John continued to build barges and rents the old Hanff woodshop to Donn Costanzo, owner of Wooden Boat Works, which repairs old wooden craft and builds replicas of them. The boatbuilding sheds date to the Hanff era, while the marine railway for launching boats was originally built by Ketcham.

GIL SMITH

Anyone who wanted to sail faster than everyone else on the Great South Bay around the turn of the twentieth century would make their way to the Patchogue boatbuilding shop of Gilbert Monroe Smith. The Manorville native created about four hundred sailboats—Smith never kept track. They were renowned for their beauty, handling and shallow draft for navigating over the sandbars in the bay as well as their speed. His yachts featured long overhanging sterns, wide beams and roomy cockpits that allowed them to accommodate many passengers and carry large sails.

As a boy, Smith carved model boats to sail in ponds and puddles but never had any training in boat design. He worked as a crewman on schooners traveling to Spain and Cuba, as well as on ships supplying the Union army during the Civil War. When the fighting ceased, Smith built a house in Canoe Place and worked as a bayman, duck hunter and hunting guide, fashioning his own decoys and gunning boats. Then he began building sailboats for customers.

In 1876, Smith moved his family to Patchogue, then a center for yachting on the Great South Bay. He rented a shop on the Patchogue River and began creating catboats that were twelve to sixteen feet long for local baymen. (Catboats have one large mainsail hanging from a gaff or spar connected to a single mast mounted just inches behind the bow.) Many of his customers served as crew on the large yachts owned by local estate owners. That helped spread Smith's reputation for building fast boats, and he began to get commissions. One came from Frederick G. Bourne of Oakdale, president of the Singer Sewing Machine Company, whose estate became La Salle Military Academy, and another from Bayard Cutting of Great River, whose property is now a state park. In 1906, Smith was hired

Boat builder Gil Smith at the helm. *Courtesy of the Long Island Maritime Museum.*

by a syndicate looking for a boat to sail against a German team for the President Taft Cup. Smith's boat won.

The boat builder usually worked with only one or two employees and his wife, Marion, who sewed sails on the only machine in the shop. Smith made everything except the rigging and hardware with hand tools. He continued building boats until he suffered a stroke at age ninety-three. He died four years later in 1940. Smith's son, Asa, continued the business for another decade until his death.

Some of the boats Smith built over six decades are preserved at the Long Island Maritime Museum in West Sayville, the East Hampton Historical Society and the Bellport Historical Society. One of Smith's designs, *Elvira*, a thirty-eight-foot sloop constructed in 1906, was relaunched in July 2018 after a thirteen-year restoration by the nonprofit Carmans River Maritime Center (see chapter 29).[151]

Purdy Boat Company

In the 1920s and 1930s, many rich and famous men who wanted a quality wooden boat gravitated to the Purdy Boat Company on the shores of Manhasset Bay in Port Washington. Its customers included Walter P. Chrysler, C. Douglas Dillon and Harold Vanderbilt.

In the 1890s, James Gilbert Purdy and some of his sons, including Gil and Ned, went to work at the Seabury boatbuilding company on the Hudson River in Nyack. After Ned and Gil moved to Consolidated Shipbuilding on the Harlem River in Manhattan, they got their big break from Carl Fisher, the auto industry pioneer and real estate entrepreneur who developed land in Montauk. While he was creating the resort community of Miami Beach, Fisher visited Consolidated and was so impressed by the skills of the brothers working in the design department that he hired them to set up their own shop.

The Purdy Boat Company built its first two craft for Fisher in 1916 in garages on the infield of the Indianapolis Speedway. Fisher relocated the company several times before establishing its final location in Port Washington

The Purdy Boat Company shop on Manhasset Bay around 1926. *Courtesy of Alan Dinn and the Port Washington Public Library.*

in 1925. With his financial empire crumbling, Fisher gave the Purdy Boat Company to the Purdy family in 1927, probably to protect it from creditors. The following spring, an employee left a battery charger running in Harold Vanderbilt's seaplane hangar adjacent to the Purdy building, starting a fire that destroyed the shop. It was replaced by a fire-resistant structure.

The company built yachts, hydroplane racers, dinghies, fishing boats and launches. The total was about 322 vessels, from *Shadow III* in 1915 to *Amp III* in 1954. Purdy's most famous design was *Aphrodite*, a sleek seventy-four-foot "commuter yacht" built at a cost of $90,000 in 1936 for financier John Hay "Jock" Whitney of Manhasset to commute to Manhattan. The contract required the boat to reach a speed of thirty-eight miles per hour.

During World War II, the Purdys built eighty-eight boats for the U.S. Navy, including thirty-six-footers designed to rescue downed pilots and forty-five-foot "picket," or patrol, boats. Some of the Purdy-built luxury yachts, including *Aphrodite*, served during the war as patrol craft.

Ultimately, the family could not compete with mass-produced runabouts and cabin cruisers from manufacturers who often pirated ideas from the company. So after 1954, Purdy hung on by doing maintenance and storing boats until the family sold off the property between the early 1950s and 1977 for residential development.[152]

SMALL SURVIVING BOATYARDS

Long Island harbors were once lined by small boatbuilding and repair shops. As suburban development that began after World War II continues to sprawl, property values and tax rates have soared and tight economic times have reduced the number of Long Islanders who can afford a pleasure craft. This has led to many of the small shops being replaced by housing developments or other commercial uses. Some disappear because there is no one to take over from an aging craftsman. But about two dozen historic boatyards remain, some still building small craft, while others now only repair them.

Here are a few of the companies:

FRANK M. WEEKS YACHT YARD on the Patchogue River in Patchogue is one of the oldest family-run boatyards in the country. The Weeks family has lived or worked along the river since before 1807. As a boy, Frank M. Weeks worked as an apprentice for Martinus Smith, who owned and operated a shipyard that is now part of the Weeks' property. In 1898, when he was about fifteen, Weeks built and sold his first boat—a small catboat he called *Onion* because he paid for the materials by selling homegrown onions. After Smith's death, he purchased part of the property in 1917 and the remainder in 1928. He built and designed many types of boats, including different lines of sailboats, such as South Bay Scooters. The business is still housed in historic buildings: a wooden shop built after the Civil War by Smith and corrugated sheet metal buildings with dirt floors built before 1920 that are illuminated only by skylights. The company, now run by Kevin Weeks, Frank's grandson, occasionally makes Force 5 fourteen-foot fiberglass sailing dinghies, DN mahogany iceboats and other one-off projects. But most of the work now involves repairs.[153]

KNUTSON YACHT HAVEN MARINA in Halesite is the current name of one of the oldest operating yards on Long Island, dating to the mid-nineteenth century. Some of the buildings from that era survive with their original equipment. After it was operated by several previous owners, Thomas Knutson purchased the facility in 1937. The Thomas Knutson Shipbuilding Corporation built wooden boats and ships for local industries until World War II, when it began to construct submarine-chasers, boats to rescue downed pilots, patrol boats and landing craft for the military, leading to a major expansion. The yard milled its own lumber.

Unlike some shipyards elsewhere on Long Island, the Knutsons were able to remain in operation after the war. With the growth of suburbia, the boatyard switched to building mostly leisure craft. One of its most popular boats was the K-37, a sailboat that commanded the impressive sum of $16,000 in the 1960s. In the mid-1950s, as fiberglass began to replace wooden boats, the yard shifted to maintaining and repairing the newer craft. The operation is managed by Dan Knutson, the third generation of his family to work there.[154]

COECLES HARBOR MARINA & BOATYARD, a historic facility on Shelter Island, has been owned since 1973 by the Needham family. The boatbuilding arm of the business, CH Marine, is best known for building four boats for singer-songwriter Billy Joel, including the downeaster *Alexa*, made famous by the song of the same name. The yard continues to build one or two boats a year from its production models, the thirty-eight-foot Shelter Island Runabout and thirty-foot Shelter Island Nomad. It also handles refit work on older boats.

Hampton Shipyards in East Quogue is the workplace of the Scopinich family. Its boatbuilding story began in Freeport, where three generations created fishermen's garveys, flat-bottomed workboats. They focused on military boats during the two world wars, and the yard built both rumrunners and the U.S. Coast Guard patrol craft that chased them during Prohibition. When their father and uncle decided to sell the property in 1956, Fred and Mario Scopinich bought the abandoned Hampton Shipyard, which dates to the late 1800s. They began building twenty-eight-foot wooden Columbia recreational fishing boats and then expanded the line. Today, Fred's son, Fred III, and grandson Kevin are running the company, but he is still involved. In 2018, the yard fabricated its last Columbia cruiser. "I just couldn't get the help anymore, and the kids weren't interested" in boatbuilding, Fred Scopinich explained. The company built almost seven hundred Columbia boats ranging from twenty-five to forty-five feet since 1956. The Scopinich family still handles repairs and runs a marina.[155]

Steiger Craft in Bellport is one of the last production fiberglass boatbuilders on Long Island and the most prolific—the only one turning out one hundred boats a year. The company was founded by commercial fisherman Alan Steiger as a clamming supply store in 1972. "When I had some time I would build wooden workboats," said Steiger, the son of a marine carpenter. Although he did not enjoy commercial fishing, he said, "I always knew I wanted to do something with the water." So, in 1974 Steiger began building fiberglass boats.

Although Steiger Craft boats were originally designed with relatively flat bottoms for the shallow waters of the bay, in the mid-1990s he developed deep-V-bottom models for open-water recreational fishing. Steiger, like other manufacturers, has seen the market for recreational boats cool in recent years. "At one point we were building 300 or 400 bare-boned sixteen-footers a year," Steiger recalled.[156]

Although Steiger never built for the military, vessels constructed on Long Island would play a role in America's wars, starting with the War for Independence.

THE AMERICAN REVOLUTION

The first naval battle in Long Island history was fought over cattle and sheep. And it would become a historical footnote as America's first amphibious landing of troops.

When the American Revolution erupted in the spring of 1775, the British began to use Gardiners Bay between the north and south forks as a rendezvous point. From that base, they organized what some labeled "predatory excursions" to requisition provisions from East End farmers. In early August, the British began removing livestock and supplies from the islands off the North Fork. They helped themselves to 1,100 sheep and cattle from Fishers Island alone.

To stop the deprivations and protect Patriot families, and because he needed sustenance for his own troops, American commander in chief George Washington ordered General David Wooster to transport soldiers from the North Fork across the Plum Gut channel to the west side of Plum Island near the current lighthouse to thwart livestock raids by the British. Wooster wrote after his August 14 foray that

> a large [British] *sloop-of-war and twelve transports sailed round Plum-Island. After they had gone through the gut, I sent one hundred twenty men in three boats, which are all the boats we then had, to said island, if possible to get off the stock, with orders to return immediately upon the first appearance* [of the enemy back in Plum Gut] *lest their retreat might be cut off....Before the last boat got over, the sloop-of-war was observed to*

be returning, and the wind and tide favoring her, our boats were obliged, to put back again, the hindmost of which had several cannon fired at her, but at so great a distance they did no damage. A cutter came within fifteen or twenty rods [about three hundred feet] *of our last but discovering that there were armed men in the boat, stopped their pursuit. Our soldiers in the boat, and some others on the beach, then fired at them, but I fancy to little effect, as our boat was obliged to make all sail possible to keep out of the reach of the cannon from the sloop-of-war, which was close behind them.*

After the British ship anchored and took away nine head of cattle, Wooster went to Plum Island and removed the remaining cattle and sheep that had eluded the enemy.

By the time the Continental Congress recommended later that month that all livestock be removed from Plum and Gardiners Islands, British general Thomas Gage had taken at least eighty-six head of cattle and between two and three thousand sheep from those islands.[157]

After the Battle of Long Island—also known as the Battle of Brooklyn—on August 27, 1776, the British were in control of all the land from New York Harbor to Montauk Point as well as Long Island Sound and Gardiners Bay. Many Patriots and their families fled to New England to escape what became a seven-year occupation. In Sag Harbor, for example, on September 15, 1776, the wharves were crowded with refugees awaiting passage across the sound. Captain Zebulon Cooper made several trips to Connecticut to transport some of them. On one voyage, he carried sixty-three people, ten cows, two horses, thirty sheep, seventeen hogs and thirty-three loads of household goods.[158]

Some of the Patriots who had left for Connecticut joined with New England troops in making raids across Long Island Sound to harass the redcoat occupiers. They used wooden whaleboats, about thirty feet long with pointed ends so they could be rowed quickly in either direction and handle rough surf. Designed to chase and kill whales from a mother whaleship, they proved equally functional for carrying armed men quickly and unobtrusively across the sound. Whaleboats were light enough to be carried on the soldiers' shoulders and could be fitted with a sail to augment the six or eight oars. They were often armed with a small swivel cannon in the bow.

Whaleboat warfare worked both ways. The British used the tactic first in 1777. On April 25, General William Tryon, who had been the colonial governor of New York, led two thousand men north across the sound and destroyed a section of Danbury, Connecticut. That prompted the Americans to retaliate with a raid on Sag Harbor, the largest community in Suffolk County. Other British raids from Long Island targeted the Connecticut towns of Greenwich, New Haven, Fairfield, Norwalk and New London.[159]

The Patriots made forays from Connecticut to North Hempstead, Oyster Bay, Huntington, Setauket, Port Jefferson and, most famously, Sag Harbor. The aim of the Patriot raiders was to kill enemy soldiers or capture them to gain intelligence or exchange them for Americans in British hands, keep the British preoccupied and off-balance and gain provisions for the Americans while depriving the British of them. Most of the American targets were in Suffolk County, where the anti-British sentiment was the strongest. Fort Franklin (named after Benjamin Franklin's son William, the former royal governor of New Jersey) in Lloyd Neck, Fort St. George in Mastic, Fort Slongo in what is now Fort Salonga and other sites were attacked successfully.[160]

The Meigs Raid, or the Battle of Sag Harbor, occurred on May 23, 1777. After the British occupied Long Island in 1776, they built a fort with walls about fifty feet long atop Burying Yard Hill at Union and Madison Streets. It was a breastwork strengthened by a palisades and garrisoned by about sixty troops.

The American raid was commanded by Lieutenant Colonel Return Jonathan Meigs, a veteran of the Battle of Bunker Hill and the attack on Quebec under General Benedict Arnold. The force of 170 men in thirteen whaleboats escorted by two armed sloops left Guilford, Connecticut, on the afternoon of May 23. Avoiding British vessels, they landed at about 6:00 p.m. on Hashamomuck Beach in Southold, one of the narrowest stretches of the North Fork. They carried their boats across three hundred yards of sand and rowed across Southold Bay and Shelter Island Sound before landing at midnight on a beach four miles west of Sag Harbor. At 2:00 a.m., Meigs launched the attack. A pair of guards was captured at an outpost and forced to lead the Americans to the British headquarters at the Howell Tavern on Main Street, where they captured the commanding officer, Captain James Raymond. Then they assaulted the fort, killing 6 defenders and capturing 53. When the Patriots arrived at the Long Wharf, a twelve-gun schooner began shelling them. But they were still able to set afire twelve brigs and sloops. The Americans took 90 British sailors prisoner and captured hay, rum, grain and military supplies. The raiders, with their prisoners and captured provisions, returned to Connecticut twenty-five hours after their departure—without the loss of a single American.

Congress voted to recognize Meigs for his heroic "prudence, activity, enterprise, and valor," by awarding him a presentation sword that is now

Lieutenant Colonel Return Jonathan Meigs, who led an American whaleboat raid from Connecticut to Sag Harbor during the American Revolution. *Collection of the East Hampton Historical Society.*

in the collection of the Smithsonian Institution. In 1902, Sag Harbor erected monuments at the sites of the fort and the British outpost on Brick Kiln Road.[161]

Fort Setauket differed from other forts constructed by the British. Rather than constructing a redoubt—an enclosed defensive emplacement constructed from earthen berms—and a vertical log palisade, in this case they decided to fortify the existing Presbyterian church. Its congregation was considered disloyal to the Crown. The ground level was possibly used as a stable but more likely as a guardhouse, and swivel guns were mounted in the upper windows. A six-foot wall of earth was constructed thirty feet out from the church with six-foot-high pickets embedded atop it.

The Americans attacked the garrison that numbered between 50 and 260 soldiers, depending on the account, in the summer of 1777. On August 25, between 150 and 500 men, again depending on the account, under General Samuel Holden Parsons landed at Mount Misery with several artillery pieces. After the Americans' demand that the defenders surrender, firing by cannon and muskets ensued for more than two hours. The skirmishing ended when the Americans learned British reinforcements had been sighted on Long Island Sound. The raiders returned to their boats and Connecticut.

Fort Setauket remained unchallenged for the duration of the war. Then residents restored the church and removed the earthworks. (Years later, the church was struck by lightning and burned to the ground. It was replaced by the existing structure in 1812.)[162]

There were at least two raids on Fort Franklin, situated on a high bluff on the west side of Lloyd Neck and commanding the entrance to Oyster Bay and Cold Spring Harbor. It was not only the largest British fortification on Long Island during the war but also saw the most combat. It began as a woodcutters' camp in 1777 to supply troops, primarily in Brooklyn and Manhattan, with fuel. It also became a refugee camp for Loyalists forced to flee New England. The British built the fortification to protect the woodcutters and refugees from whaleboat raids across Long Island Sound by the Patriots.

Lieutenant Colonel John Graves Simcoe of the Queen's Rangers, based in Oyster Bay, assumed command of the Lloyd Neck site after 1778. He ordered the original small square redoubt strengthened with eight-foot-tall wooden pickets. He also had abatis—felled trees with sharpened branches facing out—dug into the ground outside of the earthworks. Simcoe had two cannons placed overlooking the harbor and two guns mounted on the opposite side facing east. A small blockhouse was erected by 1780 with a

parade ground later added on the east side of the fort. Eventually, a unit of militia called the Associated Loyalists was formed and based at the fort at the time it was named Fort Franklin.

Despite Simcoe's efforts to make the fort more formidable, it still proved to be an irresistible target for the Patriots. On September 15, 1779, Major Benjamin Tallmadge of Setauket, General Washington's spy chief, attacked the woodcutters' camp outside the fort with only 130 dismounted light dragoons and captured most of the 500 Tories there before returning to Connecticut. Tallmadge apparently chose not to overreach by attacking the fort at that time.

But he would return two years later with a larger rebel force of about 450, including a battalion of allied French soldiers. They landed on the northern shore of Lloyd Neck on July 12, 1781, and climbed up through the woods for a mile to attack the east side of the fort, where Tallmadge believed no cannons had been placed. Between 600 and 700 Loyalists awaited them. Both sides advanced across the parade ground and then began firing when 150 yards apart. The American commander quickly realized the larger defending force would not give ground and shifted his attention to the undefended huts south of the fort. The enemy responded by opening fire with the cannons on the east side of the fort, which had been unknown to the Americans. Tallmadge, lacking his own artillery, realized he had no alternative but retreat. Fort Franklin remained a Loyalist outpost and refugee camp until the end of the war. It was described as the largest Loyalist refugee camp of the revolution in 1781 with 800 inhabitants.

(The Fort Franklin site remained undisturbed until 1879, when Anne Alden purchased the property. She had a Shingle-style house designed by famous architect Charles McKim for the western portion of the fort site. Workers constructing the foundation found an array of relics from the fort: musket balls, cannonballs and even the gravestone of a Loyalist soldier. These were incorporated into the garden wall at what was named the Fort Hill estate. Remnants of the earthworks remain visible on the property.)[163]

Tallmadge led a more dazzling whaleboat raid on November 23, 1780, to attack Fort St. George at the Manor of St. George, located on Bellport Bay on Smith Point in Mastic, now present-day Shirley. General Henry Clinton, the region's British commander, had ordered Captain Thomas Hazard to establish the fort. Fifty Loyalist troops from Rhode Island had constructed a triangular stockade with walls 200 to 250 feet long of sharpened logs anchored by the manor house, another plantation structure and a blockhouse earlier that year. The enclosure encompassed several acres with a redoubt in the center. It was further protected by a deep ditch. Two cannons were placed to defend the supply base. The Rhode Island men had remained to garrison the fort, which also became the home of Loyalist refugees in September 1780 after the British evacuated Newport, Rhode Island. The garrison troops became known as Thomas Hazard's Corps of Refugees.

Washington ordered Tallmadge to attack a site in Coram where forage for horses and livestock had been collected and then Fort St. George if possible. The twenty-six-year-old major of the Second Light Dragoons, who had earlier crossed the sound to reconnoiter the British fortifications, set out with two companies of dismounted horsemen on November 21. The crossing took five hours. After hiding the whaleboats in the woods, the soldiers marched five miles until they were engulfed by a storm and retreated to the beach to spend the rest of the night under their boats. When the weather cleared the following afternoon, they set out again. They halted at 4:00 a.m., two miles from the fort. Tallmadge ordered the attack to be launched simultaneously on all three sides when the officers heard the signal: a cry of "Washington and glory!" The assault was to be made with unloaded muskets, relying on bayonets and surprise. But as the Americans closed on the fort, a Loyalist guard fired an alarm shot. The sentry was bayoneted, and Tallmadge ordered his "pioneer," or engineering, troops to use their axes to cut down the main gate. Once inside the palisade, the Americans captured most of the fort within ten minutes. But many of the Loyalists remained in the two houses. Tallmadge wrote in a memoir that

> *while we were standing, elated with victory, in the center of the fort, a volley of musketry was discharged from the windows of one of the large houses, which induced me to order my whole detachment to load and return the fire. I soon found it necessary to lead the column directly to the house, which, being strongly barricaded, required the aid of the pioneers with their axes. As soon as the troops could enter, the confusion and conflict were great. A considerable portion of those who had fired after the fort was taken, and the colors had been struck, were thrown headlong from the windows of the second story to the ground. Having forfeited their lives by the usages of war, all would have been killed had I not ordered the slaughter to cease.*

When all of the resistance was extinguished, seven Loyalists had been killed or wounded and fifty-three officers and men captured in the Battle of Fort St. George. Only one of Tallmadge's men was wounded. "All things were now secured and quiet," Tallmadge wrote, "and I have never seen the sun rise more pleasantly."

Observing that ships at the dock were preparing to escape with their cargo, Tallmadge had his men fire on them with the fort's cannons, burning and sinking them. Then the Americans turned their attention to destroying the fort, which was accomplished by 8:00 a.m. The prisoners were led out of the fort and made to carry captured supplies back across the width of the island to the whaleboats waiting at the Long Island Sound beach.

Tallmadge, meanwhile, told that the British had stockpiled three hundred tons of hay in Coram, led a dozen men on horses liberated from the Loyalists to destroy it. His party reached Coram in an hour and a half, overwhelmed the guards and set fire to the hay before reuniting with his force at the shore at 4:00 p.m. By midnight, they were back in Fairfield, Connecticut.

Washington and Congress, which passed a resolution praising Tallmadge, were thrilled at the success of the raid. Not surprisingly, it outraged the British and their Loyalist allies. On December 2, 1780, *Rivington's Royal Gazette*, a New York City Tory newspaper, wrote:

> *Mr. Isaac Hart of Newport in Rhode Island, formerly an eminent merchant and ever a loyal subject, was inhumanly fired upon and bayoneted, wounded in fifteen different parts of his body, and beat with their muskets in the most shocking manner in the very act of imploring quarter, and died of his wounds in a few hours after....A poor woman was also fired on at another house and barbarously wounded through both breasts, of which wound she now lingers a specimen of rebel savages and degeneracy.*

(The site of Fort St. George was acquired by the Town of Brookhaven in 1974 and is preserved as a park. The manor house on the property, built after the war, is now a museum.)[164]

One of the last engagements of the war on Long Island was the Battle of Fort Slongo, fought on October 3, 1781. The British outpost on Long Island Sound just east of the Huntington-Smithtown border was likely named for George Slongo, the Philadelphia contractor who built it, probably between 1778 and 1779. It was a hollow square about fifty feet on each side with a wooden palisade about seven feet tall erected on a berm. A blockhouse was constructed in the center. The size of the garrison ranged between fifty and ninety troops.

Tallmadge, now promoted to colonel, sent a reconnaissance party led by Sergeant Elijah Churchill of the Second Continental Light Dragoons across the sound to scout the fort. It was followed by the main attack force of one hundred men dispatched from Norwalk. In his journal, Tallmadge writes "on the evening of October 2, '81, 9 o'clock, I embarked from Saugatuck River part of my detachment, and placed Major [Lemuel] Truscott as the head of it....The troops landed on L.I. by 4 o'clock, and at dawn of day the attack was made and the fortress subdued."

After the Americans ascended the bluff, a sentry posted outside the redoubt fired his musket to sound the alarm and then rushed inside. The panicked soldier failed to close the gate behind him, and Truscott's men gained entry. The Americans profited from most of the British officers having imbibed heavily at a party at the Milford Inn at nearby Middleville—now considered part of Fort Salonga—the night before and the commander, a Major Valentine, having reported to New York City to discuss military matters. The Americans killed four of the enemy and wounded two. Twenty-one officers and men were captured. Only one of the raiders—Churchill—was seriously wounded.

Tallmadge wrote that "the Blockhouse and other combustible materials were burned, and the troops and prisoners returned in safety, bringing off one piece of handsome brass field artillery....The colors [flag] of the Fort, a brass 3 pounder [cannon], a number of small arms, ammunition, &c., were the trophies of the victory." Two four-pound cannons were spiked—spikes were hammered into their touchholes, where the powder was ignited, to make them unusable.

The berms on which the palisade had been placed remain, about two feet high and visible in the backyard of a private home overlooking the sound near a historical marker commemorating the battle. They represent the best-preserved remnants of the British wartime presence on Long Island.

Sergeant Churchill, twenty-seven, became the first American soldier to be honored with the forerunner of the Purple Heart medal. The Badge of Military Merit, created by Washington, was presented to the Connecticut soldier on May 3, 1783, in Newburgh, New York. Churchill was cited for bravery in the 1780 raid on Fort St. George and the 1781 raid on Fort Slongo. Washington devised the badge on August 7, 1782, and said it was for "any singularly meritorious action." His wife, Martha, sewed the first one using purple cloth provided by the Marquis de Lafayette. (Churchill's badge is on display at the New Windsor Cantonment State Historic Site near Newburgh. The Badge of Military Merit fell out of use after the war, but it was revived and redesigned as the Purple Heart for Americans killed or wounded in combat in 1932.)[165]

HMS *Culloden* ran aground on the north side of Montauk in a 1771 winter storm and was burned by the crew to keep the vessel out of American hands. The remains of the wreck lie off what is now called Culloden Point. *Courtesy of the Dan Berg Wreck Valley Collection.*

Not all of the military action around Long Island during the rebellion occurred on land. The British navy controlled the waters around Long Island, but not without cost. On January 24, 1781, the seventy-four-gun HMS *Culloden* was in Block Island Sound on blockade duty when a nor'easter blew in. The 170-foot-long frigate built in 1776 and two other men-of-war tried to clear Montauk Point to ride out the storm in the Atlantic. But *Culloden* never made it. Captain George Balfour was following the lights of HMS *Bedford* when around 12:30 a.m. that ship reversed course. Balfour, however, continued on but took the precaution of ordering depth soundings be taken every half hour. Nonetheless, at 4:00 a.m. the northern shore of Montauk loomed off the bow, and before any action could be taken, *Culloden* went aground. All 650 crew members survived. When the weather cleared, Balfour tried to refloat his vessel without success. The captain then ordered that everything of value be transferred ashore. Later, two vessels salvaged most of Culloden's cannons, gun carriages and anchors. The only guns left behind were obsolete thirty-two-pound iron cannons. They were spiked so they could not be put to use by the Americans or their French allies. Then

Culloden was set afire and burned to the waterline. Despite British efforts to keep any *Culloden* armament out of enemy hands, Joseph Woodbridge of Groton, Connecticut, salvaged sixteen of the remaining cannons the following July and offered them to General Washington.

The remnants of the wreck remained undisturbed until several decades ago when a group of divers illegally salvaged a cannon and other artifacts. They were later recovered and turned over to the East Hampton Town Maritime Museum in Amagansett, where they can still be seen. Today, the wreckage—listed in the National Register of Historic Places and protected by New York State law—lies mostly covered by sand in twenty feet of water just off Culloden Point in Montauk. Four cannons and wooden planks are still visible occasionally. The town of East Hampton and Suffolk County jointly own 14.3 acres of adjacent parkland.[166]

During the Revolutionary War, the captains of British warships patrolling farther west in Long Island Sound took note of a large glacial erratic boulder protruding from the sandy bluff on the west side of Huntington Bay. They decided it was a perfect target for their gun crews to practice their marksmanship. Their name for the New England boulder dragged to Long Island by a glacier, Target Rock, has been handed down through the subsequent centuries. The glacial erratic was located near a British fortification known as East Fort on the east side of Lloyd Neck. (Target Rock has remained a point of interest. Someone painted a bull's-eye on it in the early twentieth century. Over the years, the bluff has eroded, leaving the boulder standing out in the bay.)[167]

At the end of the war, when America had won its freedom, the waters around Long Island still had a role to play in the independence story. The Loyalists or Tories who had supported the Crown during the war realized they were no longer welcome and their property was likely to be confiscated if they had not transferred ownership to Patriot relatives. So they prepared for life in exile as passengers on several fleets of transport vessels headed for the British Isles, the British West Indies and Canada in 1783. Most went to Canada, where the British government had promised them free land.

Estimates are as high as 100,000 Loyalists had to flee from the former thirteen colonies at the end of the war. Among them were about 35,000 residents of the new state of New York.

The first fleet carrying Loyalists from the New York region sailed for Canada in late spring of 1783. After two days of loading families and their possessions, on May 27, 1783, *Two Sisters* left Oyster Bay near where Fort Franklin had been built on Lloyd Neck during the war. A second ship that came to Oyster Bay to carry away Loyalists was set afire by angry Patriots.

Two Sisters sailed to New York Harbor, where it waited two weeks for a dozen other ships carrying Loyalists from other areas to congregate. Then on June 11, the fleet sailed for Canada.

Among the 250 passengers aboard *Two Sisters* was Sarah Frost, who traveled with her husband, William, and their two children. They arrived in Nova Scotia on June 28 to find an encampment that included a few tents and small log shacks spread over a rocky wooded landscape. Frost described it as "the roughest land I ever saw." She had reason to be depressed; her family had already been displaced once by the war. They originally lived in Stamford, Connecticut, where they had been driven from their home by the Patriots because of their support for the British, even though her parents were Patriots. So the Frosts had settled on Lloyd Neck under the protection of the British garrison.

Another passenger on *Two Sisters* was Peter Walters, owner of a two-hundred-acre Woodbury farm, who had been a lieutenant commanding a Loyalist unit. Walters and some of the other Oyster Bay refugees settled in Digby in Nova Scotia. He remained for a year before returning to Woodbury to retrieve his farm, which had been held for him by his brother-in-law, Obadiah Valentine. Despite the lingering bitterness over the war, Walters resumed his life as a successful farmer and held several important public positions. He became captain in Samuel Youngs's militia regiment in 1791 and was promoted to first major in 1798, resigning in 1804 when he reached the age of fifty. He was elected to several positions in the town of Oyster Bay, starting in 1788 when he became "pounder" and was reelected each year through 1795. (In colonial times, public impoundments were established to contain cattle, swine and sheep, and the manager of these facilities was given the title pounder.) He was then elected highway overseer in 1796 and was reelected annually through 1802. He was elected "fence viewer" in 1798 and was reelected each year through his death in 1817.

The second large fleet sailed for Nova Scotia in the fall. The dozen ships carrying 2,500 Americans loyal to King George III was commanded by Colonel Richard Hewlett, owner of a large tract in present-day East Rockaway who had commanded a battalion of Loyalist troops on Long Island. Hewlett settled along the Saint John River and called the community he founded Hampstead after the one he had been forced to leave, Hempstead.[168]

Long Island played a prominent role in the Revolution. Its most important contribution in helping to end the war was as the base for the famed Culper Spy Ring. The story of its efforts to gather intelligence for Washington is told in the next chapter.

THE CULPER SPY RING

T he intelligence network that helped George Washington defeat the British during the American Revolution depended on a critical Long Island nautical link.

The American commander in chief knew that gaining information about British military activity through a spy system was critical if the underdog Americans were to have a chance to successfully fight for their independence. So with the British in control of New York City and Long Island, Washington moved slowly and cautiously to create his ring of agents in those areas.

The first spy to operate successfully on Long Island was Major John Clark, who gathered intelligence from a network of contacts during much of 1777. He sent his messages through Major Benjamin Tallmadge, a Setauket native and a dragoon officer in Connecticut who became Washington's spy chief. The messages were probably passed to Tallmadge by whaleboat captain Caleb Brewster, a friend and early classmate of Tallmadge.

When Clark left the island, Tallmadge needed another spy there or preferably a network of spies. He was fortunate in that he already had in place much of the infrastructure of what would become the Culper Spy Ring thanks to the cross-sound connection through Brewster.[169]

The Culper organization began in 1778 with Setauket farmer Abraham Woodhull, using the alias Samuel Culper, traveling to Manhattan and reporting what he could observe. But when his absences in Setauket began to attract attention, Woodhull recruited Robert Townsend of Oyster Bay to take over the snooping in Manhattan. Townsend, the purchasing agent

Ink drawing of Culper Spy Ring member Robert Townsend, done in 1813 by his nephew Peter. *Courtesy of Raynham Hall Museum.*

in the city for his merchant father, Samuel, accepted with one condition: no one—not even Washington—could ever know his identity. To protect himself, he adopted the alias of Culper Jr., since Woodhull was already Culper Sr. (The identity of Culper Jr. was only revealed in the 1930s when Long Island historian Morton Pennypacker employed a handwriting expert to match Culper Jr.'s handwriting with Townsend's.) Tallmadge adopted the code name of John Bolton.

Townsend was aided by the fact that besides serving as a merchant he also worked part-time as a volunteer journalist for *Rivington's Gazette*. Writing for the pro-British New York City newspaper provided perfect cover for spying on the redcoats. Townsend also became a silent partner in a nearby Wall Street coffeehouse run by the paper's proprietor, James Rivington, where British officers keen on being mentioned in print were eager to talk to the reporter/spy.

To ensure that the intelligence would not be intercepted, it was sent via a circuitous route from Manhattan to Washington's headquarters in New

Jersey. Townsend passed his information on to Setauket tavern owner Austin Roe when he traveled into the city, ostensibly to purchase supplies for his business. Roe would make the fifty-five-mile trip into New York about once a week, based on the available records, and then leave the information from Townsend in a secret location in one of Woodhull's farm fields. Brewster would transfer the information across Long Island Sound by whaleboat, avoiding British vessels by traveling at night.

Legend has it that Woodhull's neighbor, Anna Smith Strong, would hang out laundry to dry in a pattern that would indicate where Woodhull should meet Brewster, although the story has been questioned by historians in recent years. Strong—whose husband, Judge Selah Strong, had been imprisoned by the British in New York for "surreptitious correspondence with the enemy"—supposedly would hang out a black petticoat when she knew that Brewster, known as Agent 725, had arrived from Connecticut. She would add one to six white handkerchiefs to inform Woodhull at which of six coves Brewster would be waiting.

Whether aided by Strong's laundry or not, Brewster initially would turn over the information to Tallmadge, waiting at Fairfield. But eventually, Washington told his spy chief that his time was too valuable for him to wait in Fairfield so he should select a few of his dragoons to carry the messages to Tallmadge. He would relay Townsend's information to Washington's headquarters in New Jersey. If Washington was seeking specific information about the British, his request would work its way to Townsend by reversing the route.

Later in the war, Washington decided it was taking too long for the intelligence to reach him; at the same time, the British began to become suspicious about the activity in Setauket. The American commander wrote in a June 27, 1779 letter to Tallmadge that Culper Jr. "should endeavor to hit upon some certain mode of conveying his information quickly, for it is of little avail to be told of things after they had become... known to every body."

So a shorter route was planned to cross the sound near Cow Neck, present-day Port Washington. It proved impractical so the intelligence continued to move through Setauket.

Washington knew it was vital to his strategic planning to know expeditiously the number of British troops and navy vessels in the city and details of the forts protecting it. But he also knew that the key to successful spying was extreme discretion. "There can be scarcely any need," Washington wrote to Tallmadge on July 10, 1779, from New

Jersey, "of recommending the greatest...secrecy in the business so critical and dangerous."[170]

The Culper intelligence proved highly valuable to George Washington and the American cause. Perhaps the best example occurred in 1780. When the British were threatening Rhode Island as a French fleet of nine vessels carrying five thousand troops was preparing to sail into Newport, Washington feared his allies could be heading for disaster. "As we may every moment expect the arrival of the French fleet a revival of the correspondence with the Culpers will be of very great importance," the commander in chief wrote from New Jersey on July 11 to Tallmadge. Washington did not know that the French had actually arrived a day earlier. Nonetheless, Tallmadge got a message to Caleb Brewster in Fairfield, Connecticut, and he and his crew rowed his whaleboat across the sound to Setauket. A courier raced to Manhattan and contacted Townsend. Culper Jr. learned that the British under the command of General Henry Clinton had eight thousand troops planning to embark from Whitestone in Queens to Newport to attack the French before they could prepare. He wrote a message in invisible ink on July 20 that was in Washington's hands by 4:00 p.m. the next day, the fastest delivery of a dispatch ever made by the spy ring. The American commander knew the British feared an attack on New York City since they had taken control in September 1776. Washington didn't have the men to make such an attack, so he resorted to subterfuge. He and his staff invented a plan for a twelve-thousand-man attack on the city, put it in an official dispatch pouch and gave it to a man who agreed to pose as a Tory farmer. He gave it to the British, saying he had found it on a roadside. The ruse worked, and Clinton used a series of signal fires along the North Shore to reach the fleet off Huntington and recall it.[171]

LIGHTHOUSES

The newly formed Congress of the United States deemed construction of lighthouses so important to the development of the fledgling country's economy that the ninth law it passed, in August 1789, provided that the government would build and maintain the critical aids to navigation.

Eventually, twenty-one lighthouses would be built—and in some cases rebuilt—around what is now Nassau and Suffolk Counties. Eighteen of them were built in Suffolk County, believed to be the most of any county in the United States. (Door County in Wisconsin, with ten lighthouses, is number two.) And eight of the eighteen are situated in the town of Southold, giving it more lighthouses than any other township in the country.[172]

They are described here—briefly, because several comprehensive books have been written on the subject—in the order of their construction.

MONTAUK POINT. The first lighthouse on Long Island was authorized by President George Washington in 1792. New York State provided the land. Lit in 1797, it is the fourth-oldest operating lighthouse in the United States. The eighty-foot octagonal tower was built by famous lighthouse architect John McComb Jr. In 1860, a major renovation raised the tower's height by fourteen feet and added a larger keepers' quarters, which is now a museum. Its familiar reddish-brown stripe was added in 1903.

In 1987, the lighthouse was automated and leased to the Montauk Historical Society, which opened it to the public as a museum and acquired ownership in 1997. More than two-thirds of the land between the lighthouse and the tip of Montauk Point has eroded since the 1790s, and terracing and placement of boulders have been employed in recent decades to slow the process.[173]

EATONS NECK. The octagonal sandstone tower located at the Eatons Neck Coast Guard Station was built in 1799 by John McComb Jr., the contractor for the Montauk Point Lighthouse. It was renovated in 1868. The 50-foot tower sits on a cliff that raises the light to 144 feet above Long Island Sound. It marks a rocky headland that had claimed more ships than any other location on the North Shore. The keeper's quarters was demolished in 1969 and replaced by eleven housing units for U.S. Coast Guard personnel. Because of severe erosion of the bluff in the early 1990s that caused cracks in the structures at the station, the Coast Guard in 1996 raised the issue of relocating the operation. Boaters, local officials and residents opposed the idea, and it was dropped several years later.[174]

LITTLE GULL ISLAND. A fifty-foot-tall beacon was constructed in 1805 on the two-acre rocky outcrop seven miles off Orient Point at the end of the North Fork. It was first lit the following year to help mariners navigate the Race, the sluiceway that connects Long Island Sound and Block Island Sound with currents that can exceed six miles per hour. During the War of 1812, the British, who controlled the waterways off the East End, landed on Little Gull Island on January 28, 1813, and insisted that keeper Giles Holt extinguish the light because it helped American vessels traverse the area. When he refused, the British removed the illuminating apparatus from the top of the tower. After the Civil War, the government decided to build a taller lighthouse. The eighty-one-foot tower was completed in 1869. It is one of the last masonry lighthouses built on the East Coast. A new stone keeper's dwelling was also built at that time.

The light station was severely damaged in the Great Hurricane of 1938. When a 1944 fire destroyed most of the keeper's house and damaged the tower, the dwelling was replaced by a one-story building that was removed by the Coast Guard in 2002. The light in the tower was automated in 1978. The Fresnel lens was removed in 1995 and replaced with a modern optical system. The original lens was placed on display at East End Seaport Maritime Museum in Greenport. In 2009, the federal government offered the lighthouse to other government agencies and nonprofit organizations, but there were no takers. It was then sold at auction in 2012 for $381,000 to Connecticut machine tool company owner Fred Plumb, who has said he wants to restore the beacon and make it accessible to the public. The Coast Guard continues to maintain the light and foghorn.[175]

SANDS POINT. Ship captain and Revolutionary War veteran Noah Mason built the 80-foot-tall octagonal brownstone tower in 1809 and served as its first keeper. A Colonial-style keeper's house was added in 1868. Long Island's third-oldest remaining light tower was deactivated in 1922. It was replaced by a small tower at the end of a reef 325 feet offshore, which, in turn, was replaced by another tower in 1968.

Alva Belmont, a prominent figure in the women's suffrage movement, bought the five-acre property in 1924. She combined it with the adjacent site of the former Sands Point Hotel, where she had already built a French Gothic–style mansion called Beacon Towers. In 1927, she sold the properties to newspaper publisher William Randolph Hearst. He and his wife lived in the keeper's quarters and used the mansion for guests until they left in 1937. The mansion was leveled in 1941 and houses built around the old lighthouse.[176]

OLD FIELD POINT. The original lighthouse, an octagonal stone tower thirty feet from the base to the lantern, was first lit in 1824. It was rebuilt in 1869 with granite blocks and a cast-iron tower of the same design as the lighthouse on Plum Island. The Coast Guard discontinued the light in 1933 and replaced it with an automated light on a skeleton tower. Two years later, Congress approved the transfer of the site to the village of Old Field, which uses the keeper's quarters as a village hall. The Coast Guard reactivated the light in the tower in 1991.[177]

FIRE ISLAND. The first lighthouse was built in 1826. It failed to prevent many shipwrecks because the light was only seventy-four feet above sea level and the lighting mechanism was primitive.

As New York became the nation's busiest port, Fire Island's lighthouse was replaced in 1858 by the current 166-foot brick tower 200 feet to the northeast. It became the state's tallest lighthouse, supplanting Shinnecock Bay, and received its distinctive black-and-white stripes in 1891. The lighthouse was augmented by a series of three lightships, or floating lighthouses, stationed six miles offshore from 1896 to 1942.

The second beacon was discontinued at the end of 1973, and the light shifted to the water tower at Robert Moses State Park. Boaters and preservationists, fearful that the lighthouse would be demolished, formed the Fire Island Lighthouse Preservation Society in 1978. Three years later, the Coast Guard declared the structure beyond repair and announced its intention to demolish the tower, generating a public outcry. The next year, the Fire Island Lighthouse Preservation Society was incorporated to raise funds to restore the light station. Also in 1982, the Coast Guard ceded control of the property and responsibility for maintenance to the National Park Service and, in 1983, transferred ownership to that agency. The lighthouse was relighted in 1986, and the keeper's quarters became a museum the next year after the preservation organization raised more than $1.5 million. The tower was restored and opened to visitors for the first time in 1989 after the society raised an additional $500,000. In 2007, the original first-order Fresnel lens, which had been on loan at the Franklin Institute in Philadelphia since 1933, returned to Long Island. A new display building for the lens opened in 2011.[178]

PLUM ISLAND. Built in 1827, it was reconstructed in 1870 in the same Victorian style as the Old Field Lighthouse. The beacon was discontinued in 1978 and replaced with a light on a steel tower. The site was turned over to the U.S. Department of Agriculture, which eventually sealed off the deteriorating structure. The lighthouse's 1897 Fresnel-style lens was removed and loaned to the East End Seaport Museum in Greenport in 1994. The structure was added to the National Register of Historic Places in 2001 after being nominated by the Long Island chapter of the U.S. Lighthouse Society. The organization also procured $500,000 worth of boulders to stabilize the eroding bluff below the lighthouse. The Department of Homeland Security acquired the site in 2003 and continued discussions about restoration with nonprofit organizations. But nothing has been done pending the planned sale of the island by the government when the Plum Island Animal Disease Center closes and its research is relocated to Iowa.[179]

CEDAR ISLAND. A thirty-five-foot-tall wooden lighthouse was built on the island north of Sag Harbor in 1839 to guide vessels in and out of Long Island's busiest port. It was rebuilt with granite in 1868. The lighthouse was discontinued in 1934 and sold to a New York City attorney for $2,000 in 1937, and it changed hands several times after that. The Great Hurricane of 1938 filled in the two-hundred-yard channel between the island and the South Fork, making the island a peninsula that is now part of Suffolk County's Cedar Point Park in East Hampton.

Suffolk acquired the lighthouse in 1967. After an arson fire in 1974 gutted the structure, the county installed a new roof and bricked up the doors and windows. Preservationists have been working with the county ever since to restore the interior, but several projects faltered before making major progress. In the summer of 2017, an architectural firm was hired to design a renovation plan after the Suffolk County legislature voted the previous November to appropriate $500,000 for the work. It was intended to be the first step toward converting the lighthouse into a self-sustaining bed-and-breakfast inn.[180]

NORTH DUMPLING. A lighthouse was built on North Dumpling Island north of Fishers Island in 1849. It was rebuilt in 1870 and again in 1980. The Great Hurricane of 1938 destroyed the bell tower, boathouse and storehouse. The sixty-foot-tall Second Empire–style lighthouse was automated in 1959, and the island was sold to a New York City businessman for $18,000. He resold it in 1980 for $95,000 to yachtsman David Leavitt of New York City. He refurbished the facilities and had the Coast Guard relocate the light back into the stone tower after it had been shifted to a skeletal steel structure. The island's fifth owner, since 1986, is inventor and entrepreneur Dean Kamen, best known for developing the Segway scooter.[181]

EXECUTION ROCKS. Built on a reef in Long Island Sound a mile north of Sands Point and illuminated in 1850, it was reconstructed in 1868. Legend has it that its name stems from the practice of the British, who occupied Long Island during the American Revolution, to chain prisoners to the rocks at low tide and let them drown as the water rose, but there's no evidence this ever happened. The name is more likely the result of the reef ripping out the bottoms of numerous ships before the lighthouse was constructed. When the lighthouse was automated in 1979, the keeper was removed and the Fresnel lens at the top of the tower was replaced by an automated rotating beacon. When the government declared the site surplus, a Philadelphia nonprofit organization, Historically Significant Structures, purchased it in 2009 and has been working on a restoration. Tours have been given intermittently, and the group allows overnight stays as a fundraising mechanism.[182]

GARDINERS ISLAND. In 1851, the federal government purchased a fourteen-acre sandspit known as Gardiner's Point that ran north off the tip of Gardiners Island between the North Fork and South Fork for $400 to build a lighthouse. A one-and-a-half-story stone structure was completed in 1854 at a cost of $7,000. The choice of the site would prove unwise. In the following decades, storms eroded the sandspit, leaving the lighthouse on its own small island, and undermined the lighthouse foundation. Rather than build a proposed breakwater to protect the lighthouse, in March 1894 the government discontinued it. That led to several vessels running aground on Gardiner's Point. The lighthouse eventually collapsed, and the government built Fort Tyler on the site in 1900. The ruins of the fort remain the property of the federal government.[183]

LLOYD HARBOR. The square brick tower, thirty-four feet from its base to the light apparatus, was built on a sandspit jutting out from Lloyd Neck at the entrance to Lloyd Harbor in 1857. It was attached to a two-story wood-frame keeper's quarters. The beacon was augmented by a new Lloyd Harbor Lighthouse—now named the Huntington Harbor Lighthouse—nearby at the entrances to Huntington and Lloyd Harbors in 1912. The original lighthouse was extinguished by the Coast Guard in 1925 and destroyed by a fire in 1947.[184]

The Lloyd Harbor Lighthouse was built at the entrance to Lloyd Harbor in 1857. It was extinguished by the Coast Guard in 1925 and destroyed by a fire in 1947. *Courtesy of Lighthouse Digest.*

HORTON POINT. The 58-foot-tall square brick and stone tower and two-story Federal-style keeper's dwelling were built on a 110-foot bluff overlooking Long Island Sound in Southold in 1857. The lighthouse was decommissioned by the Coast Guard in 1933 and replaced by a light on a steel tower. The 7.62-acre site was transferred to the Southold Park District in December 1937. During World War II, the Civilian Defense Corps and military units used the tower as a lookout post. After the war, the lighthouse was vacant for many years, and in the 1960s there was discussion about its demolition. But the Southold Historical Society and the Park District stepped in, and efforts to restore the building began in the 1970s. It opened as a maritime museum in 1977. After a restoration project, the light was moved back into the old tower on June 7, 1990.[185]

SHINNECOCK BAY. Initially named the Great West Bay Lighthouse, the beacon was built in Hampton Bays in 1858 to fill the sixty-seven-mile gap between the Montauk Point and Fire Island lighthouses. At 160 feet, the brick lighthouse was the tallest in the state when completed. It was renamed the Shinnecock Bay Lighthouse in 1893, although local residents have long called it the Ponquogue Light because it was built on Ponquogue Point. The aid to navigation was discontinued in 1931 and replaced by a metal skeleton tower. It was demolished in 1948 after Southampton officials declined the Coast Guard's offer to donate it to the town. The only original building left at the site, now a Coast Guard station, is a brick oil house from 1902.[186]

Demolition of the abandoned Shinnecock Bay Lighthouse in 1948. *Courtesy of* Lighthouse Digest.

LONG BEACH BAR. More popularly known as Bug Light because it initially sat on spindly metal legs, the beacon was built at the entrance to Peconic Bay off Orient in 1870 and was lit on December 1, 1871. The foundation of "screwpile" metal legs drilled into the seafloor was replaced with reinforced concrete in 1926 to allow for installation of a central heating system. It was discontinued in 1948 and sold at auction by the government to the Orient Marine Historical Association in 1956.

Destroyed by arsonists on July 4, 1963, the lighthouse was replaced by a replica created by the East End Seaport Foundation in 1990. The following year, the Coast Guard agreed to take over operation of the light mechanism that initially was operated as a private aid to navigation. The foundation allowed donors to spend the night at the lighthouse, the only Long Island beacon where this was permitted until the new owners of Execution Rocks followed suit in the past few years.[187]

LATIMER REEF. After years of building offshore stone lighthouses on stone foundations, the U.S. Lighthouse Board decided in the 1880s to shift to a less expensive technique. It began deploying prefabricated circular cast-iron caisson foundations that were bolted together on-site. These were topped with prefabricated iron towers, often containing Victorian architectural details. This lighthouse was built with that technique on the west end of a rocky shoal in eastern Fishers Island Sound to replace a lightship that had been stationed nearby. It was built of cast iron lined with bricks on a cement-filled cast-iron base thirty feet in diameter. The three-story lighthouse was equipped with a fifth-order Fresnel lens mounted fifty-five feet above the water. It was lit on July 1, 1884. A modern lens was installed in 1983. It's the oldest cast-iron lighthouse in the region.[188]

STEPPING STONES. The rocks that break the surface of Long Island Sound north of Great Neck were known as the Devil's Stepping Stones in colonial times. The westernmost Long Island Sound lighthouse was completed there in 1877 at a time when the government began building offshore beacons with no land access. To create a foundation for the forty-six-foot-high red brick tower, nine hundred tons of boulders were dropped into the sound. The Second Empire–style lighthouse was automated in 1966. Stepping Stones was given by the federal government to the Town of North Hempstead in 2008. After several years with no action by the town to restore the beacon, the National Park Service threatened to take it back. But after a change in the town administration, officials are working with the Stepping Stones Lighthouse Preservation Society, formed in 2012, Great Neck Historical Society and Great Neck Park District to undertake an estimated $4 million restoration program.[189]

Race Rock. This lighthouse has the most dramatic construction story of any Long Island beacon. It was built on a reef only three feet underwater half a mile west of Fishers Island. Many engineers thought the task was impossible because of the strong currents that run through the Race, a channel connecting Long Island Sound and Block Island Sound. The lighthouse would be built, but it would take nine years.

The government had ten thousand tons of stones for a foundation placed on the reef in 1870, only to have them swept away by the tidal current, which can run at more than six miles an hour. Next, the engineers tried building a wall around the reef with stones weighing three to five tons. This foundation was then filled with cement. It took two more years to erect the sixty-seven-foot Victorian-style granite tower. The project claimed the lives of several workmen and cost $278,716 instead of the original $8,000 allocated. On January 1, 1879, the fourth-order Fresnel lens, sixty feet above the water, was illuminated for the first time. The lighthouse was automated in 1978 and the original lens replaced by a modern rotating beacon. The federal government gave the lighthouse to the New London Maritime Society in 2013.[190]

Cold Spring Harbor. It was built in 1890 at the entrance to Cold Spring Harbor and Oyster Bay with the light forty and a half feet above mean high water. President Theodore Roosevelt would row out from his home at nearby Sagamore Hill with his children and visit keeper Arthur Jensen after he was appointed in 1908 following the drowning of his predecessor.

The light was automated in 1948. The small wooden structure was deactivated by the Coast Guard in 1965, removed from its caisson foundation and slated for demolition. Artist Mary Glenn, who lived across the water in Centre Island, saw the lighthouse floating next to its foundation. She and her husband, J. Wooderson Glenn, arranged to buy it for one dollar and had it towed to the shoreline of their property. Then a truck winch was used to pull it across marshland, where it was set on a new foundation next to a tidal creek to become Mary Glenn's studio. It's the only Long Island lighthouse to be relocated and repurposed. The foundation caisson remains out in the harbor entrance, topped by a skeletal light tower.[191]

ORIENT POINT. This is the second lighthouse in the region built with a prefabricated circular cast-iron caisson foundation bolted together on-site and topped with a prefabricated iron tower. It was erected in 1899 to mark the channel at Plum Gut between Orient Point and Plum Island. The beacon, nicknamed the Coffee Pot, rises sixty-four feet above sea level. It was automated in 1958. The Coast Guard plan to demolish the lighthouse in 1970 resulted in a huge outcry that saved the beacon.[192]

HUNTINGTON HARBOR. The last Long Island lighthouse to be built, the forty-eight-foot-high structure was erected at the entrance of Huntington and Lloyd Harbors in 1912. It was constructed with reinforced concrete, a material first used for lighthouses after a 1908 earthquake in California destroyed a lighthouse there. The only concrete lighthouse on the East Coast, it was designed in the Venetian Renaissance (Beaux-Arts) style. It replaced a wooden two-story structure erected in 1857 across the water on the shore of Lloyd Neck. The Huntington light originally carried the same name—Lloyd Harbor Lighthouse—until it was renamed for the busier of the two harbors.

After the Coast Guard automated the light in 1949, there was little maintenance. In 1984, the structure was crumbling, and the agency proposed demolishing the lighthouse and replacing it with a light on a steel tower. The outcry from boaters and other residents spurred concerned citizens led by Janis Harrington, with the help of her father-in-law, Dr. Douglas Harrington, to organize the Save Huntington's Lighthouse Inc. in 1985. The Coast Guard shelved the demolition plan and leased the structure to the nonprofit group in 1988, and the beacon was added to the National Register of Historic Places. The nonprofit organization, renamed Huntington Lighthouse Preservation Society in 2003, restored the structure and opened it for tours. The lighthouse is now owned by the preservation society and is an active aid to navigation maintained by the Coast Guard. In the summer of 2018, the group completed a two-year renovation of the unstable stone foundation at a cost of more than $1 million. Adding 350 tons of stone around the foundation, replacing the windows and doing masonry repairs are planned for the future as funding allows.[193]

Today, many of Long Island's lighthouses remain active aids to navigation maintained by the Coast Guard, even if the structures have been turned over to someone else. Some of the lighthouses, such as Montauk Point, Fire Island

and Horton Point, are museums open to the public. Whatever their status, Long Island is fortunate that only one of the beacons—Shinnecock—has been intentionally demolished, while the rest have been saved to help tell the story of the region's maritime heritage.

WAR OF 1812

T he United States declared war against Great Britain on June 18, 1812, in part because for more than a decade the Royal Navy had been "impressing" crew members of American ships. At least twenty Long Islanders were among those forcibly removed from merchant vessels on suspicion of being British deserters.

But it wasn't until March 20, 1813, that the Royal Navy took action to repeat its blockade strategy from the American Revolution. When eight British warships arrived off the East End to bottle up Long Island Sound, they faced little opposition from the tiny U.S. Navy because its few men-of-war were dry-docked in Brooklyn for repairs. It fell to other arms of the government and privateers—private vessels commissioned by the government to capture enemy vessels—to take on the British.

Britannia was not content just to rule the waves during the war. Its forces raided several harbors. They tried to copy the Revolution's American raid on Sag Harbor, still Long Island's most important trading and manufacturing center. The American generals were aware of this and had protected the town with a garrison of three thousand soldiers. Despite the lopsided odds, about one hundred British marines landed on the wharf on July 11, 1813, and began firing cannons. "Solid shot were screaming overhead, houses were being shattered and pandemonium reigned generally," wrote witness A.M. Cook of Bridgehampton. With American militiamen converging on the town, the British had time to set afire only one sloop before cannon balls from the fort drove them away. The American forces led by Captain David

Hand extinguished the fires and recovered abandoned British weapons. The attack caused extensive damage to the village, while the war devastated its commercial shipping industry. "We formerly had twenty to twenty-five coasting vessels employed in southern trade and in carrying wood to market," Congressman Ebenezer Sage wrote. "Three or four of them remained."[194]

Also in 1813, two British warships sailed into Port Jefferson Harbor after dark. They captured seven merchant ships before fleeing. The only threat came from Fort Nonsense in what is now Poquott. Its soldiers opened up on the ships with their single cannon. In trying to evade the fire, one of the British ships ran aground and was burned by its crew to keep the vessel out of American hands.

On May 30, 1814, British ships attacked Wading River, burning small American vessels and about three hundred cords of wood lying on the beach awaiting transport. The next day, HMS *Sylph* attempted to land marines to capture the sloop *Nancy* nearby at Northville and fired on the militia atop the bluff. Despite reinforcement by another ship, likely HMS *Maidstone*, the British were driven off by the Americans under Captain John Terry.[195]

Residents of Babylon feared they were encountering British spies when a whaleboat came ashore in 1814. But the man in charge turned out to be Captain David Porter of the American frigate *Essex*—with an amazing tale to relate.

Essex had been captured by a British squadron in the Pacific Ocean off the coast of Chile. Porter and his crew was set free in a small boat, *Essex Jr.*, after promising never again to bear arms against the British. Rather than sailing into a neutral port in Chile and face being detained, Porter made the incredible choice to head for New York. He and his men spent seventy-three days at sea, sailing around Cape Horn and then up the eastern coasts of South and North America. After completing the amazing journey, *Essex Jr.* was stopped by HMS *Saturn*, which was on blockade duty at the entrance to New York Harbor. After hearing Porter's account, the British captain allowed *Essex Jr.* to proceed. But then the Americans were halted by another British vessel and held. Taking advantage of fog, Porter and ten crew members managed to escape in a whaleboat. They rowed for sixty miles, survived the dangerous surf of Fire Island Inlet and crossed the Great South Bay to Babylon. Porter convinced the residents they were not British spies by producing his naval commission. Then the citizens placed the whaleboat on a wagon, and captain and crew climbed aboard for a trip to the Brooklyn Navy Yard, where they were greeted as heroes.[196]

The closest to a full-scale naval battle in Long Island waters came in late spring of 1814 when Commodore Stephen Decatur sailed with *United States*, *Hornet* and *Macedonian* from New York City down the sound eastward toward the British blockading fleet patrolling off the East End. But on June 1, Decatur, after receiving inflated reports of British strength, withdrew into the Thames River at New London. While the *Hornet* escaped the next year, the other two ships were bottled up for the rest of the war. That left only privateers to carry on the fight. The privateer sloop of war *Beaver*, fitted out on the East End, captured eleven British prizes. While the British blockaders could not cover all the waterways adequately, they did capture more than two dozen Long Island merchant ships before a peace treaty was signed.[197]

The strangest incident of naval warfare during the conflict occurred in June 1814. A partially submerged vessel steamed out of New York Harbor and into Long Island Sound on June 19. It was one of America's first submarines, a weapon designed to offset Great Britain's naval superiority. The craft, built by a man named Berrian, was named *Torpedo Boat* and likened to a turtle because of its curved, iron-clad deck. The twenty-three-foot semi-submersible was designed so that its hull was just about even with the surface of the water. It carried five torpedoes designed by steamboat inventor Robert Fulton. One would be attached to a spar sticking out from the bow, and it would be exploded under the hull of an enemy vessel.

Its maiden voyage turned out badly. *Torpedo Boat* was bound for New London, Connecticut, with a twelve-man crew. The plan was to use the novel weapon to sink British warships blockading Long Island Sound. But on June 23, *Torpedo Boat* was washed ashore at Horton Point in Southold. The crew and local farmers attempted over several days to refloat the craft. Then on June 26, the British warships *Maidstone* and *Sylph* appeared and launched small boats with the intent of burning the vessel on the beach. American militiamen, including sixty-seven-year-old Noah Terry, who climbed up on the submarine and defiantly waved his hat, could not keep the British from landing and burning *Torpedo Boat*.[198]

The defense of the revenue cutter *Eagle* against an attack by the British brig HMS *Dispatch* and an accompanying sloop was one of the more dramatic incidents of the war. Under the command of Captain Frederick Lee of Guilford, Connecticut, the New Haven–based vessel captured a number of valuable British ships. But the cutter's luck ran out on October 11, 1814, when it sailed out of New Haven and encountered the British man-of-war *Suzan* and the eighteen-gun *Dispatch*. Lee tried to escape by sailing south toward Long Island. Two of *Dispatch*'s longboats were manned by a boarding party ready to take the under-gunned cutter. *Eagle*'s crew managed to drive off the launches, but the British warship's heavy guns forced Lee to beach his vessel off Friar's Head, a 160-foot-high bluff fifteen miles east of Port Jefferson. The cuttermen and volunteers removed *Eagle*'s cannons and hauled them up the bluff and took the *Dispatch* under fire. Local militia, already entrenched on the bluff, also commenced fire. The fighting lasted from mid-morning until late afternoon. The October 18, 1814 edition of the *New York Evening Post* reported that

> *having expended all the wadding of the four pounders on the hill, during the warmest of the firing, several of the crew volunteered and went on board the cutter to obtain more. At this moment the masts were shot away, when the brave volunteers erected a flag upon her stern; this was soon shot away, but was immediately replaced by a heroic tar, amidst the cheers of his undaunted comrades, which was returned by a whole broadside from the enemy. When the crew of the Cutter had expended all their large shot and fixed ammunition, they tore up the log book to make cartridges and returned the enemy's small shot which lodged in the hull.*[199]

Unable to overcome the stubborn defense, the British ships left, and the next day the Americans began repairing *Eagle*. The following day, *Dispatch* returned with a larger British frigate, HMS *Narcissus*, mounting thirty-two guns. Though Lee and the militia again attempted to protect the ship, the British were able to tow *Eagle* away. In all of the fighting, only one combatant on each side was injured.[200]

HMS *Sylph*, one of the vessels that had destroyed the semisubmersible *Torpedo Boat*, came to its own unhappy end. On January 16, 1815, the ship, under the command of Captain Henry Dickens, was sailing from southern waters back to New London when it ran aground near Shinnecock Point in Southampton about 2:00 a.m. There were a dozen officers and a crew of 121 on the twenty-two-gun vessel. When the ship hit the offshore sandbar, the crew scrambled up the masts to escape the crashing surf. "A number of men assembled on the beach and attempted to rescue the people on the vessel, which was fast breaking up," the *Brooklyn Times* recounted. "The surf was running very high, a furious snowstorm was raging, and the weather was bitterly cold. After several efforts the villagers succeeded in launching a fishing boat and after desperate exertions the purser and five seamen were brought ashore. All others were lost" when the ship capsized and broke in half about 9:00 a.m. Other accounts say the purser, William B. Parsons, and

Illustration first published in London in 1818 of HMS *Sylph* off Little Gull Island Lighthouse. *Courtesy of the East Hampton Library, Long Island Collection.*

two seamen were saved by clinging to wreckage and that the three men were saved by the fishermen. One witness to the tragedy saw a spar come ashore through the breakers with twelve frozen bodies lashed to it, their legs sticking up into the air.

Another witness to the demise of the *Sylph* was Henry Thomas Dering. In a letter to his sister that is owned by the Southold Historical Society, he wrote that

> *when I arrived at the place what a scene there was 5 poor seamen holding onto the keel of a Ship which was bottom upwards and the sea breaking over them and they crying for help, but no one able to assist them.... There was five that was on the keel from 8 o'clock in the morning until 3 in the afternoon. In vain did active young men try to get them a rope one of the sailors throwing off his coat leaped in to the sea endeavoring to catch the rope but did not. He held his hand above water and cryed for help but no one could help him and another out of the five sliped down and expired on the spars that surrounded the wreck. The people at last succeeded in saving the other three. They were hardly able to help themselves being badly bruised.*

Those rescued were taken to New York as prisoners of war. British admiral William Hotham thanked the local inhabitants for their humane treatment of the survivors. The dead were buried in Patchogue, Fire Island, Southampton and Islip.

In cruel timing, *Sylph* was lost two weeks after the Treaty of Ghent ending the war was ratified, but word of it had not reached the combatants.[201]

A memorial plaque carved from red cedar salvaged from the remains of the *Sylph* is mounted in St. Andrew's Dune Church in Southampton. For many years, one of its cannons was located on the Bridgehampton commons, where it was fired to mark Independence Day. It was also moved around to celebrate weddings. C.H. Hildreth wrote in the *Bridgehampton News* in 1910 that "the wonder is, that nobody ever got killed or hurt....When Captain Charles A. Pierson was married...they got the gun so near the house that some 40 panes of glass were broken and other damage done."

In recent years, a group of divers tried to locate the wreck, an effort recounted in the 2011 documentary *Search for the HMS Sylph*.

Overall, the story of the War of 1812 on Long Island waters was one of blockades and minor skirmishes. Other than the deaths on the *Sylph* caused by an act of nature, all of the firing of cannons and muskets resulted in no recorded loss of life on either side.[202]

13

STEAMBOATS AND FERRIES

T he earliest travel from Long Island to Manhattan or Connecticut was generally done by canoe, rowboat or sailboat subject to the wind and tides. In the eighteenth century, travel by water became more predictable with the introduction of ferries powered by horses walking on treadmills to turn paddlewheels. While faster and more reliable, horse-propelled ferries were not immune from mishaps. In 1741, one of these ferries that had been operated successfully from what is today Lattingtown to Rye in Westchester for two years by Thomas Jones of Oyster Bay capsized in a storm. Jones, his African American helper, five passengers and six horses drowned.[203]

The introduction of steam power made travel even more reliable, although boilers introduced the risk of fire and explosions. Robert Fulton and his financial backer, Robert Livingston, initiated steam-powered ferry service between Manhattan and Brooklyn in 1814.

A ticket for the ferry *Nassau*, which traveled between Brooklyn and Manhattan. *From Harper's Weekly, 1872.*

The *Nassau* made its maiden voyage on May 10. The *Long Island Star* reported enthusiastically that "this noble boat surpassed the expectations of the public in the rapidity of her movements." The trips across the East River took between five and twelve minutes, depending on tide and weather. On the first day, the *Nassau* carried 549 passengers, some of whom purchased ten-dollar annual commutation tickets. But the vessel's inaugural trips were not without problems. The newspaper noted that the chief engineer of Fulton's manufacturing plant, "Mr. Lewis Roda accidentally got hurled into the machinery…which cut off his left arm a little below the elbow, and broke his neck. He expired in about three hours after."[204]

STEAMBOAT SERVICE TO NEW ENGLAND

The following year brought another major development. On March 21, 1815, Captain Elihu Bunker steered the first powered vessel through the treacherous rocks and whirlpools of Hell Gate on the East River between Queens and Randall's Island and into Long Island Sound. The 134-foot *Fulton*, which could travel no faster than eight miles per hour, took eleven hours to make the seventy-five-mile trip to New Haven, Connecticut.[205]

Bunker's success led to the next milestone in marine transportation on Long Island Sound—regularly scheduled steamboat service to take passengers part of the way to Boston. Before the Cape Cod Canal opened in 1914, travelers avoided going all the way to Boston by water because it meant an unpleasant ocean voyage to get around Cape Cod. As a result, steamboat lines began running to New England towns where they could connect with stagecoaches and later train lines in cities including New Haven, Stonington, Norwich and New London, Connecticut; Providence, Rhode Island; and Fall River and New Bedford, Massachusetts. The alternative was a four-day stagecoach ride with three short overnight sleeping stops.[206]

The first steamboat line ran between New York and New Haven. It was established by Robert Fulton's company in 1815, eight years after he introduced the first successful steamboat on the Hudson River. The service was initially provided by the *Fulton*, which had a large noisy engine in the center between two paddlewheels with a small crowded cabin toward the stern for the passengers. Nonetheless, the business was successful, and the line added additional steamboats with improvements. Service was extended to New London, and President James Monroe took advantage of it when after his inauguration in March 1817 he toured New England.[207]

New York subsequently gave the company the exclusive right to operate steamboats in state waters. Connecticut retaliated by refusing to permit the New York company to operate within its waters. That forced its competitors to operate on the Long Island side of the sound and then out to Narragansett Bay in Rhode Island and up to Providence, which turned out to be the most direct and fastest way to get to Boston. Going by steamboat meant an overnight trip of about twelve hours plus six hours on the stagecoach from Providence to Boston.[208]

The early steamboats devoured cords of wood so quickly that the captains would pick up schooners full of wood off Fishers Island and tow them to refuel without stopping. That procedure was eliminated with the successful trial of a coal-fired boiler in 1836. Unfortunately, the existing boilers had difficulty containing the sustained higher pressure from coal fires, leading to an increased number of explosions and deaths. The problem was compounded by boat captains racing one another to gain bragging rights and, hopefully, more passengers. In one widely publicized incident, the two boilers on the side-wheeler *New England* exploded in the Connecticut River after it successfully raced the *Providence* down the sound in 1833. Fifteen people died immediately or from their injuries. Some captains dealt with the anxiety over boiler explosions by placing their passengers on a sailing vessel and then towing it with the steamboat. Other companies moved the boiler from the hold to the upper deck so that if it exploded the force would go upward.[209]

An 1824 Supreme Court ruling that state-granted monopolies were unconstitutional led to a golden age of steamboat travel on what became known as the "American Mediterranean." By the end of the decade, competition became cutthroat, with companies offering low fares, luxury accommodations and higher speeds. The latter resulted in more boiler explosions.[210]

Cornelius Vanderbilt was one of the men who entered into the newly competitive steamboat business, and he would remain active for three decades. "The Commodore," as he called himself, started out as a boatman in New York Harbor and then began operating steamboats on the Hudson. In 1828, the young captain was part of a group of New York entrepreneurs who established a line from New York to Providence with the steamer *Chancellor Livingston*, named for Fulton's partner. A group of Providence businessmen countered by beginning their own line in 1832 with the steamer *Providence*.[211]

In 1835, Vanderbilt added a new steamer on the Providence route that would become infamous. The *Lexington* was 205 feet long and built with boilers designed to handle the highest pressure while traveling down the sound at top speed. On its maiden voyage in January, the vessel completed the 210-mile trip to Providence at an average record-setting speed of 17 miles per hour. The competing line responded by adding three large steamers, none as fast as *Lexington*. During the 1830s, steamboats also were running to several points in southern Connecticut: Norwich, New London, New Haven, Bridgeport and up the Connecticut River to Hartford. The Hartford route became the most popular.[212]

When the railroad from Boston was extended southwest to Stonington, Connecticut, in 1837, the steamboats began running there instead of Providence. The trip was faster, but passengers arrived at Stonington to transfer to the train at three o'clock in the morning. To keep Providence in the mix, local businessmen started their own line. The railroad responded by buying *Lexington* from Vanderbilt and running it to Providence.[213]

STEAMBOAT DISASTERS

The story of the *Lexington* ended—badly—in 1840. On the night of January 13, the five-year-old pride of the Navigation Company left Manhattan at 4:00 p.m. in a cold spell that had left sheets of ice floating on the sound. At 7:30 p.m., Stephen Manchester, the pilot steering the steamboat, heard a cry of "Fire!" above the routine clanking and chuffing. He spun around and was horrified to see smoke and flames pouring from around the smokestack. Manchester attempted to turn the vessel toward Eatons Neck, but it was four miles away and the tiller ropes had burned through so the ship continued out of control, heading northeast at thirteen miles per hour. The *Lexington* carried a cargo of 150 cotton bales, some stored around the smokestack. While these fueled the fire, they would later serve as life rafts.

When the fire broke out on the freight deck, Captain George Child raced there and directed crew members to start a fire pump and form a bucket brigade. Realizing the effort was hopeless, Child shouted to the passengers to head for the three lifeboats. Unfortunately, the flames kept the crew from extinguishing the boilers, so the *Lexington* continued to plow through the waves. The forward speed caused the lifeboats to capsize as soon as they were lowered, throwing the occupants into the freezing water.

Those who survived owed their lives to the quick thinking of Chester Hilliard, a twenty-four-year-old captain traveling as a passenger. Hilliard realized it would be futile to try to escape until the ship's speed diminished. When it slowed after about fifteen minutes, he organized the deckhands and passengers to throw cotton bales overboard. He and one of the ship's firemen, Benjamin Cox, shoved the last bale into the sound and climbed onto it about 8:00 p.m. A few minutes later, the center of the main deck collapsed, throwing those gathered there into the middle of the fire.

Hilliard survived and a week later told a coroner's inquest how he managed it: "We were sitting astride of the bale with our feet in the water....About 4 o'clock, the bale capsized." The two men were able to climb back aboard the makeshift raft, but eventually Cox was so cold he could no longer hold on or speak. "I rubbed him and beat his flesh," Hilliard said. Then a large wave shook the bale, and "Cox slipped off and I saw him no more." About seven hours later, a Captain Meeker of the sloop *Merchant* spotted Hilliard waving his hat and rescued him.

After Hilliard abandoned ship, about thirty others remained on the bow with pilot Manchester. After consuming the center of the ship, the fire had died down. But by midnight, Manchester was convinced the *Lexington* could not remain afloat much longer. So the pilot managed to climb aboard a cotton bale occupied by a man named McKinney. At 3:00 a.m., McKinney died and the hulk of the ship sank in 140 feet of water northwest of Port Jefferson, leaving all but 4 of the 143 passengers and crew dead in the first and worst steamboat fire on Long Island Sound.

Manchester told the inquest that "my hands were then so frozen that I could not use them at all." But when he saw the *Merchant* at noon, an hour after the vessel had rescued Hilliard, he was able to raise a handkerchief between his hands and capture the captain's attention. Meeker was not done saving survivors. Two hours after rescuing Manchester, the *Merchant*'s skipper noticed fireman Charles Smith on a bale and took him aboard.

The most amazing survival story was that of Second Mate David Crowley. When he went over the side with a flaming cotton bale, the water extinguished the bale's fire. The *Long Island Democrat* noted that Crowley "drifted ashore near Riverhead...having been 40 hours exposed to the severity of the weather, after which he made his way through large quantities of ice and snow, before gaining the beach, and then walked three-quarters of a mile to the house where he is now. His feet and hands are a little frozen." Having drifted nearly fifty miles to Baiting Hollow and knocked on the door of a house before collapsing, Crowley was expected to lose his toes and a finger. Yet he still had the presence of mind to retrieve the cotton bale as a souvenir after being revived. (He kept it until the outbreak of the Civil War, when he donated it to be used for Union uniforms. Cotton from some of the other bales was made into souvenir shirts.) In the days after the fire, bodies and baggage washed up along fifteen miles of Long Island shoreline. After some of the baggage was plundered, guards were stationed on the beaches.

The inquest jury excoriated the owners and crew of the *Lexington*. "Had the buckets been manned at the commencement of the fire, it would have been immediately extinguished," the jury's report stated. Had the crew been more disciplined, the lifeboats could have been successfully launched. It condemned "the odious practice of carrying cotton…on board of passenger boats, in a manner in which it shall be liable to take fire." But it was not until a dozen years later, when the steamboat *Henry Clay* burned on the Hudson, that new safety rules were instituted.

There are two interesting footnotes to the fiery disaster. Poet Henry Wadsworth Longfellow had booked passage but had to remain in New York for a lecture and avoided almost certain death. And young engraver Nathaniel Currier was asked by the *New York Sun* to produce an image of the burning steamboat. It was one of the first color engravings in a daily newspaper, and it made the artist famous.[214]

On Thanksgiving Day in 1846, fire led to another steamboat disaster on the *Atlantic*, the largest and finest passenger vessel on the sound. It had been launched in May by the Norwich & Worcester Railroad Company with luxurious features, including the then novel gas-burning light fixtures. The ship, under the command of a Captain Dustan, departed New London at 2:00 a.m. on a cold, windy night carrying more than one hundred passengers and crew. Nine miles outside the harbor, a steam pipe burst, and with the ship powerless, deckhands rushed to drop the anchors. As crew members reassured passengers while passing out lifejackets, the wind continued to

The steamboat *Atlantic* before it ran aground on Fishers Island in 1846. *Historical Collections of the Great Lakes, Bowling Green State University.*

increase. To prevent the ship from dragging its anchors, the captain ordered the crew to reduce the windage by chopping down the smokestack and pilothouse. Other crewmen lightened the ship by throwing cargo overboard.

At dawn, the ship's flag was lowered to half-mast as a distress signal. The steamer *Mohegan* and other passenger vessels approached to offer assistance but could do nothing in the terrible weather conditions. When the wind changed direction and increased in intensity in the afternoon, the anchors began to drag, and the ship began moving toward the coast of Fishers Island. At four o'clock the next morning, a huge wave hit the stern, and both anchor lines parted with loud cracks. The captain remained on deck despite the entreaties of his crew to take shelter. "The *Atlantic* goes, I go with her," he replied. The *Atlantic* struck the rocks at the base of North Hill and shattered. After a few minutes, only the engine and one mast with the ship's bell still ringing from it remained above the waves. Only fifty-six survived. The captain was among the dead.

The death toll could have included Daniel Webster, the statesman and orator, as well as his wife and friends, who had been booked on the *Atlantic* but had decided to remain overnight in New London.[215]

THE FALL RIVER LINE AND ITS COMPETITORS

After a decade as the leading steamboat port, Stonington was overtaken by Fall River, Massachusetts, when a railroad was built to that city from Boston. In 1847, a group of investors in the railroad began the most famous steamboat company, the Fall River Line, to connect that city with New York. From its first boat, the *Bay State*, to its final one, the *Commonwealth*, ninety years later, the company set the standard for luxury travel on the sound. In 1894, the Fall River Line launched *Priscilla*, the best known and most admired of all the sound steamers.[216]

Competition for faster and more luxurious boats continued among numerous companies. In 1867, a group of New York financiers took on the Fall River Line by starting Merchant's Steamship Company to offer new service to Bristol, Rhode Island, which was closer to Boston by rail than Providence or Fall River. They ordered two identical 373-foot-long vessels that would be larger and more luxurious than anything else afloat on the sound. The *Bristol* and the *Providence*, the first steamers in the region with two full passenger decks above the main deck, were designed and constructed by

The Fall River Line's *Priscilla. Library of Congress.*

William H. Webb, the famous New York shipbuilder who founded the naval architecture college in Glen Cove that bears his name. When the Bristol line folded after only two years, the two steamers ended up running on the competing Fall River Line.[217]

Some of the steamboats that ran down the sound, particularly those of the Fall River Line and its direct competitors, were among the largest and most luxurious on inland waters in the United States. They typically ran at night to connect with the trains in New England early in the morning. So the competing lines would leave late in the afternoon or early evening and race down the sound. The vessels had staterooms lining large saloons. Most of the accommodations were cramped with a double-deck bed, although some were larger "bridal rooms" with brass beds and velvet curtains. The main saloon featured patterned carpets and potted palms in keeping with Edwardian decoration tastes.[218]

The steamboat industry experienced two periods of consolidation. In the 1830s and 1840s, Vanderbilt, after engaging in price wars that brought other operators to the brink of bankruptcy, purchased all of his major competitors. Then about 1849, he sold all of the steamboat lines to focus on oceangoing steamships and then railroads. In the 1890s, J.P. Morgan, a board member who controlled the New Haven Railroad, created a monopoly of all transportation companies in southern New England, with the marine operations run by a subsidiary named the New England Steamship Company.[219]

Not long after, new small lines emerged in New England to compete. One was the Joy Line, which began in 1899. Although its boats were slow, its prices were low, attracting a new class of passengers who could not afford a trip on the luxury boats. The company was eventually bought out by the railroad and kept in business to avoid other low-fare competitors from emerging.[220]

In the twentieth century, there were several attempts to compete with the New Haven Railroad monopoly. After the Cape Cod Canal opened in 1914, bigger and faster boats ran directly to Boston via Buzzards Bay. In 1931, the Eastern Steamship Company built the *Acadia* and the *St. John*, which proved to be the last steamers built for the Sound trade. The Colonial Line, which operated between New York City and Providence, was the most successful of the railroad's competitors. Business remained strong for all of the lines through the 1920s, but by the beginning of the next decade, passenger and freight traffic dropped dramatically. Through the 1930s, one company after another gave up the business. Part of the reason was the Great Depression, which left people unable to afford traveling. Competition from motor vehicles was another factor. In 1937, the Fall River Line suspended its service after ninety years. Its famous steamers *Commonwealth*, *Priscilla*, *Providence* and *Plymouth* were towed to Baltimore and scrapped. After the New Haven ended its sound operations during labor unrest that same year, Colonial boats continued to operate for five years. The last of its steamers was requisitioned by the federal government for use in World War II in March 1942. Steamboat service on Long Island Sound never resumed.[221]

SERVICE TO AND FROM LONG ISLAND

The first steamboat to provide regularly scheduled service to and from the North Shore was the *Linneus*, which began operating to Glen Cove in 1829. That vessel along with the *Mayflower*, *George Law* and *Pilot Boy* later served Oyster Bay, docking at the end of Steamboat Landing Road. Other boats traveled to Bayville, Cold Spring Harbor, Lloyd Neck and Northport in the late 1860s and following decades. Often it was the extension of Long Island Rail Road tracks into a community that spelled the end of steamboat service.[222]

While the larger night boats ran from Manhattan to New England ports, some smaller vessels provided transportation from Long Island for passengers and freight, including agricultural products and seafood, to the city and harbors across Long Island Sound.

On the East End, the Long Island Rail Road reached Greenport in 1844 with the goal of serving passengers headed for Boston. Twenty steamboats began traveling from the North Fork to Connecticut and Rhode Island ports so travelers and freight could connect with trains to the principal New England city. On the South Fork, two lines combined in the late 1880s to form the Montauk Steamboat Company. Its boats, which included *Shelter Island* and *Montauk*, ran only in the summers with routes from New York to Greenport, Shelter Island and Sag Harbor. About 1896, the line was acquired by the Long Island Rail Road to eliminate competition with its trains. But the railroad kept the line going until around 1920.[223]

From the 1840s to the early twentieth century, some of the steamboats transporting passengers and freight to and from Manhattan were considered "commuter boats." Despite the name, they did not carry commuters in the modern sense. They were not used by people working in the city because Suffolk and the part of Queens that would become Nassau had not yet developed into suburbs. The vessels, which lacked staterooms and luxurious furnishings, were used instead by merchants needing to go to the city to order new stock or businessmen bringing back supplies. Farmers also used the service to bring produce and live poultry to the city on the open freight decks. The boats would leave early in the morning and make several stops on the way to docking in lower Manhattan in the late morning. They would leave the city in late afternoon to reverse their route to Long Island. One of the boats, the two-hundred-foot-long *Glen Cove*, was equipped with a calliope on the upper deck for serenading residents living along Hempstead Harbor.

The most luxurious of the commuter boats serving that harbor was the *Seawanhaka*. Introduced in 1866, it served Roslyn, Sea Cliff, Glen Cove and Great Neck for fourteen years. Then, on the afternoon of June 28, 1880, it was steaming up the East River on the return trip to Long Island when it caught fire. The captain had to navigate through Hell Gate before finding a place to beach the vessel. The boat was destroyed, and forty people died. *Seawanhaka* was replaced by other boats until the route was abandoned during World War I.[224]

The *Rye Cliff* was another ferry that came to a fiery end. It was one of five ferries that ran between Manhattan or Westchester to Sea Cliff, which started as Methodist camp meeting community in the 1880s and transformed into a resort community by the early 1900s. The 137.5-foot-

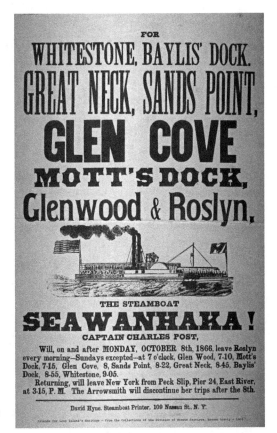

Right: An advertising poster for the ferry *Seawanhaka*. *Courtesy of Ian Zwerling.*

Below: Steamboat ferry *Seawanhaka* painted by Charles T. Vincent in 1880. *Courtesy of Nassau County Photo Archives Center.*

long side-wheel steamboat was launched in 1898. After going through several name changes and different uses, the vessel was operated by the Oakland Steamboat Company between Sea Cliff and Rye Beach in Westchester six times daily during the summer season. On September 28, 1918, the ferry was tied up at the village pier, having completed its last run for the year two days earlier. When a fire broke out, the engineer and firemen who shoveled coal into the boilers were almost trapped below decks but managed to escape without serious injury. The *Rye Cliff* burned to the waterline and destroyed the pier before drifting several hundred yards offshore and sinking in twenty-five feet of water in Hempstead Harbor. One of the boilers was recovered and used in a Roslyn elementary school. Because the ferry service was on its way out as a result of better rail and road transportation options, the pier was never rebuilt. (The wreck was explored by a team of divers between 1992 and 2010, with artifacts donated to the Glen Cove Public Library and for a permanent exhibit at the Sea Cliff Village Museum.)[225]

Sailing packets, or vessels operating on a schedule, began to make the seventeen-mile trip between Port Jefferson and Bridgeport a few times each week in the 1830s. The Bridgeport & Port Jefferson Steamboat Company

The Sea Cliff ferry landing. *Courtesy of the Sea Cliff Village Museum.*

was established in 1883 to offer more regular and reliable service. One of those responsible was the promoter and showman Phineas Taylor Barnum, then in his seventies. P.T. Barnum was a resident of Bridgeport, and the idea of establishing a ferry company is believed to have been the idea of his friend Captain Charles E. Tooker, a sailor who lived directly across Long Island Sound in Port Jefferson. The twenty-seven stockholders who signed the Articles of Association elected Barnum as the first president. Tooker and his brother-in-law, Edward Davis, owned the controlling interest. The main reason for establishing the ferry service was to link the agriculture of Long Island with industrial New England.

The company's first vessel was a 120.6-foot utilitarian steamboat christened the *Nonowantuc*. It was built by the renowned shipbuilding firm of Mather & Wood in Port Jefferson and could carry 350 passengers. The passengers were primarily Long Island farmers taking their crops to more urban Bridgeport and then coming back with supplies and for Bridgeport merchants and salesmen visiting Long Island to take orders for meat, groceries and hardware. In the 1890s, the company tried to boost its revenue by promoting tourist traffic in both directions, and it successfully marketed Port Jefferson as a recreational destination. Besides landing in town, the steamboat also stopped at California Grove, later called Valley Grove, on the west side of the harbor, where Barnum owned a large tract of land and built a pavilion, restaurant and picnic area and provided music.

With business booming, the company added another steamboat from Mather & Wood in 1898. Compared to the *Nonowantuc*, the *Park City*—the nickname for Bridgeport—was luxurious, and it could carry six hundred passengers. A succession of other boats followed. While the advent of the automobile killed many steamboat companies in the 1920s and 1930s, carrying cars across the sound stabilized the revenue stream for the Bridgeport & Port Jefferson Steamboat Company.

The Great Hurricane of 1938 gave the company a scare. The *Park City* left Port Jefferson at 2:00 p.m. on September 21 and then was not heard from until the following morning. Shortly after sailing, the vessel was hit by ninety-mile-per-hour winds. So much water entered the hull that the boiler had to be extinguished to prevent an explosion, forcing the captain to anchor in the sound. With no steam to power the main pumps, the crew of nine and two male passengers had to use hand pumps to keep the ship afloat. When the *Park City* failed to arrive in Bridgeport, the company organized a frantic search. The ferry was located by another vessel at 7:00

The ferry pier in Port Jefferson sometime after 1898. *Port Jefferson Archives.*

a.m. the next morning. The anchor had dragged, leaving the ferry many miles east of its usual track and about seven miles off the Long Island shore. A Coast Guard patrol boat towed the *Park City* back to Port Jefferson with all aboard safe.

During the Great Depression, the company became so financially stressed that it eliminated winter service. The situation became so bad that the company offered itself for sale, but there were no takers. The company survived, and in 1961 it was acquired by McAllister Towing and Transportation. Three ferries now carry approximately one million passengers and about 460,000 vehicles per year.[226]

Ferries have operated from the tip of the North Fork to various locations for two centuries. Seasonal ferry service from Orient Point to New London has existed since the early 1930s. In 1975, John P. Wronowski purchased the New London Freight Lines operation to form Cross Sound Ferry Services Incorporated. The company is the first to offer year-round service on the sixteen-and-a-half-mile route.

The company started with the ferry *Gay Head* and purchased its first new vessel, *Caribbean*, two years later, retiring the *Gay Head*. In 1983,

Steamboats tied up at the Locust Grove recreation area dock on Manhasset Bay. *Courtesy of the Port Washington Public Library.*

Wronowski purchased the *Cape Henlopen*, built in 1941 as a U.S. Navy landing ship tank vessel, the LST 510, from the Cape May, New Jersey–Lewes, Delaware ferry line. The vessel had landed on Omaha Beach during the D-day invasion in 1944. The company built an enlarged Orient Point terminal in 1985. It began the first high-speed ferry operation to Connecticut with the *Sea Jet I* catamaran, capable of more than thirty miles per hour, in 1995. Two years later annual ridership exceeded one million passengers for the first time.

There are currently eleven vessels in the Cross Sound fleet, including the oldest, the recently overhauled *Cape Henlopen*, and *Caribbean*. In the summer, the Viking Fleet operates boats from Montauk to the Cross Sound Ferry dock in New London four days a week as well as running to Block Island.[227]

Besides the vessels providing regular passenger and freight service, some steamboats had specialized in excursion trips from the city to a number of Long Island recreational areas. In addition to traveling to Sea Cliff and Lloyd Neck, excursion steamboats made frequent weekend trips from Manhattan and the Bronx to the Locust Grove recreation area on the shore of Manhasset Bay in Manorhaven in the early twentieth century. Food and entertainment were provided in a pavilion next to the dock until the area was developed in 1925. Cold Spring Harbor was a popular destination. Families came ashore for picnics at Laurelton Grove, located near today's Lloyd Neck Causeway. The facilities included bathhouses, a carousel and a dance pavilion.[228]

LOCAL FERRY SERVICE

FIRE ISLAND FERRIES. Before the early twentieth century, people who wanted to get across the Great South Bay from the South Shore to Fire Island had to take a private vessel. Then small ferry operations began popping up. Ocean Beach Ferry Company ran from the 1920s until 1947. There was a ferry to Saltaire until the late 1940s. Fair Harbor ferry service began in the early 1930. Seaview and Ocean Bay Park was serviced by the Zee Line Ferry Company from the late 1920s until 1983.

When the owner of Ocean Beach Ferry Company lost the contract to run to the village in 1947, the successful high bidders created a new company, Fire Island Ferries Incorporated, that year to take over the service. The owners, Elmer Patterson, Bill White and Ed Davis, scrambled to assemble a fleet. They began operating in 1948 with four vessels, including an ex-rumrunner named *Vagabond* that was renamed the *Fire Island Miss*. An old fishing boat became the freight boat, *Fire Island Maid*. The third was a converted yacht that had already been a Point O' Woods ferry, the *Fire Island Queen*. The fourth was the first purpose-built ferry for the bay, the *Fire Island Belle*.

The company soon acquired contracts for routes to Saltaire, Atlantique and Dunewood. It bought out the Fair Harbor company in the 1970s and Zee Line in 1983. Patterson sold the business to Edwin Mooney, Francis X. Mina and John Van Bree. Mooney eventually became the sole owner in 1989. Today, his son Timothy is president of the company, his daughter Morgan is a captain and his son Brendan manages operations on land.

Fire Island Ferries Inc. is the largest ferry operator on Fire Island. It serves just under one million passengers annually with a fleet of fourteen ferries, not counting the people carried by seven water taxis operated by a business the firm acquired in 2004. The 124-year-old Sayville Ferry Service and the 70-year-old Davis Park Ferry also serve Fire Island.[229]

NORTH FERRY COMPANY. Captain Elisha Griffin Beebe of Orient is said to have operated the first ferryboat between Greenport and Shelter Island after serving as assistant keeper at the Little Gull Lighthouse. A forerunner of the current North Ferry Company, the Greenhill Wharf Company was incorporated in 1830. The Greenport and Shelter Island Ferry Company was incorporated in 1883. And the North Ferry Company was incorporated in 1979.[230]

South Ferry Company. Jonathan Havens started a sailboat ferry soon after he arrived on Shelter Island in 1700. His descendants ran the ferry until Samuel Gibbs Clark purchased the enterprise in 1833 and expanded it beyond a small sailboat and rowboat operation. In 1904, Clifford Youngs Clark introduced the first boat to be powered by a gasoline engine: *Reba* could carry twenty-four passengers. In 1906, he incorporated South Ferry Company. Six generations of the Clark family have now been involved in running the business.[231]

14

SHIPWRECKS IN PEACETIME

Long Island has been the site of thousands of shipwrecks since the mid-seventeenth century. That total might seem surprisingly high until one considers the vast volume of traffic traveling to and from New York City in the era when most transportation was by water.

It's no wonder that captains often did not make it to port in bad weather in the days before Long Island's shoreline development and ring of protective lighthouses. There were headlands and rocky reefs deposited by the glaciers protruding into Long Island Sound and sandbars hidden off the low-lying empty beaches along the Atlantic Ocean barrier islands.

From 1878 to 1888 alone, 250 vessels were stranded along Long Island's coastline. Between 1640 and 1915, more than 600 shipwrecks were recorded just off Fire Island alone. And in a blizzard on December 23–24, 1811, more than 50 vessels sank or were driven ashore in Long Island Sound. It was the worst storm ever recorded for shipping in that body of water.[232]

PRINS MAURITS

Shipwrecks began almost as early as Europeans started coming to America. A Dutch brig, part of a convoy of four ships carrying colonists from Amsterdam to Delaware, was lost off Fire Island in 1657, becoming the first recorded casualty off that barrier beach. *Prins Maurits* had 16 crew members transporting 113 passengers on a voyage from Amsterdam that began on Christmas Day 1656. The passage was rough: storms blew away sails and cannons broke loose and caused carnage. Finally, the crew sighted land on March 6. They thought they had reached the area near Manhattan Island. But with no one aboard familiar with the region, the captain crept toward shore with the crew frequently checking the depth with a weighted line. When the water began to get shallow, *Prins Maurits* attempted to reverse course without success. About 11:00 p.m., the bow plowed into a sandbar a quarter mile offshore.

At dawn, passengers and crew saw they were mired just off a barren beach. A leaky boat was lowered, and after numerous trips everyone reached shore near today's Saltaire on Fire Island without mishap. With no driftwood to make fires, the survivors fashioned tents from salvaged sails and spars. They were discovered on March 12 by Native Americans, two of whom agreed to carry a message to Governor Peter Stuyvesant in Manhattan. The day after learning of the disaster, the governor dispatched a small sloop. Nine other ships followed from New Amsterdam and made the recovery after the Indians showed them Fire Island Inlet. Colonists and crew were carried to Manhattan, where the convoy's three other ships had already arrived. In April, the colonists finally made it to their intended destination, what is now New Castle, Delaware, some by sea and some overland.[233]

Even after President George Washington approved the establishment of New York State's first lighthouse at Montauk Point in 1795, shipwrecks continued. The beacon could help mariners locate the tip of Long Island. But the most direct Great Circle Route followed by vessels headed from Europe to New York bypassed Montauk, with captains aiming for a landfall farther west closer to the city. Before the first Fire Island Lighthouse was constructed in 1826 and the Shinnecock Bay Lighthouse farther east in 1857, there was nothing to guide ships along the shifting coastline between Montauk and New York, a distance of almost 120 miles. The result was that ships continued to be snared by the sandbars hidden beneath the surf.

SAVANNAH

One of the more notable vessels lost was the *Savannah*, bound from that Georgia city to New York when its voyage ended abruptly off Fire Island on November 5, 1821. The 120-foot vessel had been launched on August 22,

1818, on the East River in New York as a transatlantic sailing packet. It was also equipped with a one-cylinder ninety-horsepower steam engine. That allowed *Savannah* to gain fame in 1819. On a run from its namesake city to Liverpool, England, it was propelled by steam alone for eighteen days of the trip—the first use of steam power on a transatlantic voyage.

By the time the vessel approached Long Island on its final voyage in 1821, *Savannah*'s engine had been removed to reduce operating costs, so the ship was propelled by sails alone. The weather on the trip north had been very bad, and Captain N.H. Holdridge was forced to navigate by dead reckoning. The ship, carrying 250 tons of cotton and at least three passengers, was farther north than Holdridge estimated. By the time he heard the sound of breakers at 3:00 a.m., it was too late to reverse course. *Savannah* plowed into a sandbar just east of where Bellport would later be established on the other side of the bay.

Holdridge tried to get help by having two seamen row him to shore in a small boat through the surf. They made it to the beach, where several residents were waiting. One of them was enlisted to go to New York City to seek salvage help. When the captain tried to return to *Savannah*, the boat capsized in the surf. Holdridge nearly drowned before being saved by his two crew members and fishermen on the beach. The captain eventually made it back to his vessel and sent the passengers—two men and a boy from Savannah—and crew ashore when the storm abated. Some of the cargo was salvaged. But a week of pounding by the waves split open the hull, and *Savannah* could not be saved.[234]

BRISTOL

The American barque *Bristol*, with a crew of 16 transporting 127 Irish immigrants and three hundred tons of iron and coal from Liverpool, arrived off the entrance to New York Harbor on the night of November 20, 1836. Captain Alexander McKown ordered the ship's bell rung and lanterns hoisted in the rigging as a signal to the pilot boat usually anchored inside of Sandy Hook to come out and provide guidance for entering the port. When fireworks still didn't bring out a pilot, the captain had the ship's gun fired, but again no pilot appeared, even though pilots traditionally were on station there around the clock. McKown felt he had no choice but to spend the night at anchor.

Around midnight, the weather began to deteriorate, and the captain worried that the ship would be driven ashore. He instructed the crew to weigh anchor and head for open water. McKown ordered First Mate William Tapscott to tack back and forth between Long Island and New Jersey, with the intention of arriving back at Sandy Hook before dawn to try again to meet up with a pilot. As a safety precaution, he ordered continual soundings with a lead line and then went to bed.

Having misunderstood or ignored the captain's instructions about tacking and not reacting to the sound of breaking waves on the beach at Rockaway, Second Mate James Malone continued sailing toward shore. At 3:45 a.m., a crewman yelled from the bow, "Five fathoms! Five fathoms!" (signaling only thirty feet of water). The helmsman tried to reverse course, but the momentum of the ship carried it up on the sandy Rockaway Shoals four hundred yards off the beach, near today's Jacob Riis Park.

The captain rushed on deck and realized his orders had not been followed. Several attempts to free the ship were unsuccessful. So he shifted his focus to getting the passengers to shore. Considering the rough seas, McKown deemed it safer to wait until daylight. He ordered the first mate to fire *Bristol*'s signal gun and rockets to attract help from the thinly populated barrier island. Just before daylight, the storm worsened, and the ship, which had been pointing toward the beach, was shifted so the waves began striking on its beam and increased the pounding it was taking.

Then a tremendous wave struck *Bristol*. It knocked passengers off their feet and swept the deck almost clean, carrying away the lifeboats and ripping off the hatches leading below. The waves inundated passengers seeking refuge on the lower deck. The water rose, trapping and then drowning passengers. The few who reached the deck faced the new danger of being washed overboard. Crew members who had taken refuge up the masts and out on the bowsprit pulled some passengers to safety, but others were swept into the sea. The next wave destroyed the deckhouse, where some first-class passengers had been waiting. "The scene that now presented itself on deck, beggars description," the *Hempstead Inquirer* reported on November 30. "Every spot that could afford shelter from the sea was filled by some of the survivors, who lashed themselves to the sails, the rigging, and the masts."

Luckily, the distress signals from *Bristol* had been seen and heard by two Rockaway Beach fishermen, Oliver Cornell and Stephen Watts. They ran more than five miles inland to the home of wealthy landowner Stephen Rider, who had also heard the distress gun. He dispatched servants to gather the residents of the small hamlet of Rockaway. At daylight, fishermen who had begun to gather on the beach could see *Bristol* with its passengers and crew suspended in the rigging. Watching the waves crash across the deck of the doomed vessel, the observers decided it was too rough to launch rescue boats.

Help came when Rider's servants brought David T. Jennings to the beach. He was the local "wreckmaster," a position created by a 1787 state law that stipulated that the governor would appoint someone in each county along the ocean to protect the cargo from grounded vessels from being looted and direct volunteer rescue efforts. Jennings, a skilled boat handler, persuaded three men to help him launch a surfboat, but they were forced back to the beach. On the *Bristol*, McKown had the shaking mainmast cut free before it could capsize his vessel. Jennings and his team made it almost to the wreck in a larger boat but could not approach the ship because the mainmast hung over the side. One fearless young woman worked her way along the mainmast, jumped into the water and was rescued by the men in the boat, who returned to shore with her while waiting for the mainmast to be cleared away from the side of the ship.

When that work was done, the four men rowed back out in an even larger surfboat. McKown, who announced he would be the last person to leave the vessel, shifted the lowest spar on the mizzenmast to extend it out over the water and rigged safety lines along it. Then he placed women and children along the spar and directed the crew of the boat to take them off first. When no other women and children were nearby, the captain told shipping company owner Arthur Donnelly to take the last seat in the boat, which he did. But then Donnelly saw one of his family's servant girls in the rigging. He gave her his spot. It turned out to be a fatal act of chivalry, because he did not survive. As the surfboat carrying eight women and children and the first mate neared the shore, a huge wave lifted the stern and flipped it end over end, but men on shore saved everyone.

Obtaining a still larger surfboat, the rescuers rowed a fourth time out to the *Bristol* and took off eight or nine male passengers and crew. After making four trips in four boats over four hours and with the sun setting, the worsening conditions prohibited any further rescue attempt until morning. As night fell, a huge wave toppled the foremast and the ship began to break up. Some of those onboard tried to swim to shore, but none made it.

Before midnight, after the four initial rescuers had gone home for some sleep, the tide dropped and conditions improved. That allowed men still on the beach to hear cries for help. Five of them manned the largest surfboat yet used and made three trips out to the *Bristol*. They retrieved all the remaining survivors, including Captain McKown, who had survived by lashing himself to the railing at the stern and was suffering so much from exposure and injuries that he was unable to walk.

In the following days, bodies washed ashore along Rockaway Beach. Despite the best efforts of the wreckmaster and his helpers, the *New York Times* reported years later that many of the bodies were missing fingers or ears because thieves had cut them off to steal jewelry. When everyone was accounted for, one hundred people—ninety-five passengers and five crewmen—had died in the disaster. It was the largest number of deaths in an accident in the history of the country to that point. Within a few days of the wreck, five men were arrested by federal marshals and charged with stealing goods that washed ashore.[235]

MEXICO

Another ship also carrying Irish immigrants and other poor residents of the British Isles was lost in the same area two months later. The *Mexico*, carrying 111 passengers and 12 crew, ran aground off Long Beach Island and broke up on January 2, 1837. While Captain McKown acted with exemplary bravery, the same cannot be said of *Mexico*'s captain, Charles Winslow.

The owner of the aging vessel considered the poor passengers as nothing more than cargo and cut corners where he could. The *Mexico* was overloaded, undermanned and poorly maintained. The ship had few accommodations for the passengers, who were crowded together on one deck without partitions.

The *Mexico* experienced rough seas on its sixty-nine-day voyage to New York, with the rotting hull leaking badly. The barque reached the New Jersey coast just before midnight on New Year's Eve 1836. There Winslow confronted the same problem that had greeted McKown: no pilots were available. A buildup of ice had kept them in New York Harbor. Winslow, his crew suffering from frostbite and considering mutiny while the passengers were starving because provisions had run out, flew distress signals and kept lamps burning in the rigging. But there were no pilots in the area to respond.

Winslow had no choice but to continue sailing through a blizzard with zero visibility and temperatures in single digits. With only four of the crew in condition to sail the vessel, three passengers volunteered to help—a decision that would save their lives but leave them frostbitten. *Mexico* returned to Sandy Hook on the morning of January 2, but again there were no pilots. Meanwhile, ship owner Samuel Broom had received word that the barque was off Sandy Hook with distress flags flying. He responded by chartering a steamboat and put a pilot aboard with instructions "to find and bring up the *Mexico*, at any rate, without regard to cost," the *New York American* reported on January 6. The steamer returned to the pier three hours later and reported conditions were so bad that it could not cross the bar at the entrance to the harbor. The last hope for a safe berth for the *Mexico* and the 123 people aboard had vanished.

Because the ship was so shorthanded and the sails unmanageable, Winslow made each of his tacks longer but ordered that soundings with a lead line be taken regularly. But a faulty sounding at 4:00 a.m. that showed ninety feet of water when there were only fifteen led the *Mexico* to strike bottom with great force off Long Beach Island. Winslow and his crew spent two hours trying desperately to get the ship back into deeper water until a large wave knocked off the rudder, making further attempts to maneuver hopeless. He ordered the ship's gun fired to try to gain the attention of rescuers. Winslow stabilized the listing ship by having the mainmast cut away and then planned to rescue the passengers with the ship's boats. His idea was to have the boats row to shore with a rope attached to their sterns so those remaining on the ship could pull the boats back to ferry more people to the beach. But after launching the longboat, the sailors lost control and it floated away, empty, to shore. After Winslow had the foremast cut down because the ship was listing dangerously, the crew launched a smaller yawl. A female passenger jumped into the boat and would not obey the captain's orders to get out so he could proceed with his rescue plan. Winslow instructed the first mate and a sailor to remove the woman by force. While they were attempting that, a large wave lifted the boat onto the deck, overturned it, dumped the three occupants out and then carried it away to the beach where it was smashed by the surf.

On the morning of January 3, the waves began to separate the ship's planking, and water poured in. Winslow had the passengers come on deck and the crew and male passengers prepare rough shelters there and in the mizzenmast rigging with sailcloth and rope.

No one would have survived if not for Raynor Rock Smith, a boat captain and fisherman. He and his surfboat crew, which included three of his sons, dragged their craft several miles across the frozen bay, likely with the aid of a horse, to the ocean beach. Other boats and crews were already there, but no one had attempted a rescue because it was so cold that the water had turned to a frozen slush by the beach, making launching difficult. The waves were described by one observer as "high as a house."

Raynor, a veteran of several ocean rescues, heard the cries of women and children from the ship two hundred yards offshore and observed passengers trying to find shelter in the mizzenmast rigging. After enduring an hour of this, at 2:00 p.m. he asked his men if they were willing to attempt a rescue, and they agreed. Smith and his six men launched a surfboat with the assistance of other men on the beach and reached the *Mexico* just before 3:00 p.m. The passengers had been out in the open for four hours while the captain and his seamen huddled in the cookhouse and other sailors remained sheltered in the forecastle. Winslow attempted to create order among the panicked passengers by brandishing a saber, but it proved impossible. So the captain and his crew members worked their way out onto the bowsprit and signaled to Smith that he should bring the boat there. As the crew members began climbing down a chain into the surfboat, one fell into the sea and sank. When the boat began to pull away, the cook, Edward Felix, jumped into the water and was picked up by the boat. He was the last person to leave the *Mexico* alive.

Smith barely made it back to the beach with 8 survivors and decided it was too risky to make another trip. But he had attached a line from the stern of the surfboat to the chain dangling from the bow of the *Mexico*, which would allow those still onboard to pull the empty surfboat back out to save more people. Unfortunately, there was no one left on the *Mexico* with enough strength to retrieve the surfboat. With the deaths of 108 passengers and 7 crew members, *Mexico* replaced *Bristol* atop the list of the worst death toll in American disasters.

The three passengers who had volunteered to help the crew manage the ship later condemned Captain Winslow for abandoning the vessel and its passengers and then sitting on the beach warming himself by a fire without even looking back at the *Mexico*. By the next day, January 4, the decks were awash, and the remaining rigging pointed toward the beach almost horizontally. Frozen bodies washed into the sea and up on the beach. When the weather abated, surfboats made it out to what was left of the ship, and frozen bodies were pried from the mizzenmast rigging.

Only eight—the captain, four other crew members and the three passengers—survived. The widely vilified captain was required to testify before a grand jury but was never charged with a crime. Winslow continued to command vessels until he died onboard the *Minerva* off Gibraltar in 1842.

Of the 115 victims, 62 were placed in donated coffins and buried in a donated plot in Sand Hill Cemetery located between today's villages of Lynbrook and Rockville Centre. It became known as the Mariners Burying Ground until it was renamed the Rockville Cemetery in the last century. In 1839, the victims of the *Bristol* were removed from temporary graves at Rockaway Beach and reinterred next to those who died on the *Mexico*. With local contributions and $300 found in the clothing of the victims, an eighteen-foot-high memorial obelisk was purchased and erected at the cemetery in 1840 to mark the mass grave of 139 of the 215 who died in the two wrecks.

Long Island–born poet Walt Whitman, who described himself vaguely as "almost an observer" at several shipwreck sites, would immortalize the *Mexico* in his poem "The Sleepers," first published in 1855:

> *The beach is cut by the razory ice-wind…the wreck-guns sound,*
> *The tempest lulls and the moon comes floundering through the drifts.*
> *I look where the ship helplessly heads end on…I hear the burst as she strikes…*
> *I hear the howls of dismay…they grow fainter and fainter.*
> *I cannot aid with my wringing fingers;*
> *I can but rush to the surf and let it drench me and freeze upon me.*
> *I search with the crowd…not one of the company is washed to us alive;*
> *In the morning I help pick up the dead and lay them in rows in a barn.*[236]

ELIZABETH

The wreck of the *Elizabeth* on a sandbar off Fire Island on July 19, 1850, garnered international headlines because of the death of one passenger: Margaret Fuller, a women's rights advocate, author and writer for the *New-York Tribune*. The barque sailed from Livorno, Italy, in mid-May, bound for New York City with a cargo that included oil paintings, silks, almonds and a marble statue of John C. Calhoun, the former vice president and secretary of state. Seven days out, as the ship was about to leave the Mediterranean, the captain died of smallpox. First Mate Henry Bangs assumed command and proved to be a poor navigator. He was far off course when he sighted the Fire Island Lighthouse and confused it with the beacon at Cape May, New Jersey, in a gale.

About 3:30 a.m., *Elizabeth* crashed onto a sandbar three hundred yards from the beach and about three miles from the lighthouse near Point O' Woods. The impact ejected passengers from their bunks. The next wave lifted the stern and pushed the ship broadside to the breakers. The rolling of the ship caused the cargo of marble to shift and the statue of Calhoun to be propelled through the side of the hull, allowing it to flood.

As the ship began to disintegrate under the assault of breaking waves, all of its lifeboats were crushed or carried away. Two sailors successfully used planks to float to the beach, but when one passenger tried to replicate their feat he quickly sank. That prompted the rest of those onboard to wait for help. The crowd that gathered was more intent on salvage than helping those stranded on the *Elizabeth*. A volunteer lifeboat crew based near the lighthouse learned of the ship's plight and prepared to help. But when the surfmen arrived, they could not launch their boat into the heavy surf.

After two more hours and no sign of an attempted rescue, the acting captain urged everyone to save themselves and jumped overboard. Most of the crew followed. Because she was unable to swim, Fuller, wearing only a nightgown, remained onboard with her husband, Giovanni Ossoli, an Italian count; their infant son, Angelo; and four sailors, all huddled around the mainmast. Finally, more than ten hours after the grounding, the ship began to break up. The steward grabbed Fuller's son and jumped overboard; both drowned. Ossoli and the family's Italian maid were swept out of the rigging. Fuller remained in place as the remaining mast toppled and the ship disappeared. Only thirteen survived.

About $15,000 worth of silk was carried off by the crowd that had gathered on the beach; six were arrested later for theft. Writer Henry David Thoreau came to Fire Island to search in vain for Fuller's body. A pavilion with a memorial plaque to Fuller was erected in Point O' Woods in 1901, but it was destroyed in a storm a dozen years later. The statue of Calhoun was later salvaged from seven feet of water at low tide. It was installed at the capitol in Columbia, South Carolina, where it remained until it was destroyed when General William T. Sherman's Union troops arrived in the closing days of the Civil War in 1865.

Horace Greeley, the influential editor of the *Tribune*, wrote Fuller's obituary, which guaranteed that the news of the disaster was reprinted in publications around the world. "America has produced no woman who in mental endowments and acquirements has surpassed Margaret Fuller," Greeley stated. Poet Ralph Waldo Emerson wrote that "it is a time that the United States, instead of keeping troops and forts, should keep a coast guard of lighthouses to defend lives and property." The death of Fuller provided the impetus needed to replace the original 1826 Fire Island Lighthouse with a taller, improved structure in 1858.[237]

CIRCASSIAN

The *Circassian* was a square-rigger sailing from Liverpool, England, to New York when it ran aground on December 11, 1876, near the Mecox Life-Saving Station in Southampton. The 280-foot iron-hulled ship carried 1,400 tons of cargo, including bricks, chemicals and hides. Captain Richard Williams commanded a crew of thirty-four.

The *Circassian* had been built in Belfast, Ireland, in 1856. It had carried passengers and cargo on the Irish Sea before serving as a Confederate blockade runner during the Civil War. The vessel was captured by the Union navy and pressed into service as a troop and supply ship. After the war, the government sold the ship. The new owners removed the engines and smokestack as an economy measure, and the *Circassian* resumed transatlantic service under sail.

On the last voyage, the ship encountered several gales. As the vessel approached New York, it picked up a pilot, Captain James Sullivan, to guide it along the South Shore and into New York Harbor. Engulfed in another storm, the pilot suggested to Williams that they take soundings to determine how far offshore they were. The vessel pointed up into the wind so the crew could throw a lead line overboard. Just then, the *Circassian* struck a sandbar a dozen miles east of the Shinnecock Lighthouse and just west of the Mecox Life-Saving Station.

The captain, who later blamed a compass error for the grounding, ordered cargo jettisoned in hopes of refloating the ship. Flares were fired. Surfman Samuel H. Howell was on patrol and had seen the ship much too close to shore through the snow and sleet. He answered the *Circassian* with a red flare, indicating the ship's distress signal had been seen, followed by a blue flare, alerting the stricken vessel that help was available. Crowds gathered on the beach, bringing blankets, clothing, food and hot tea for the rescued and rescuers. School was canceled. When the weather improved the next day, the surfmen rescued the forty-nine passengers and crew in seven trips out to the stricken vessel. (It was the second shipwreck in two days for twelve passengers, who had been taken aboard *Circassian* from another wrecked ship named the *Heath Park* a day or two earlier.) The captain sent a telegram to the owners' agent in New York for assistance with salvage, and late that day a tug arrived and helped position the ship with its bow out to sea in preparation for refloating it.

As the seas calmed, the salvage company put the ship's former captain, John Lewis, sixteen crew members and a dozen local workers, including

The wreck of the *Circassian* in 1876 with the loss of twenty-eight salvage workers, including ten Shinnecock Indians. *Courtesy of the East Hampton Library, Long Island Collection.*

ten Shinnecock Indians, aboard to remove cargo and attempt to save the vessel. When another storm struck on December 29, eighteen days after the *Circassian* was wrecked, Lewis refused to remove the workers to shore. "We'll float tonight or go to hell!" he screamed before ordering the lifesaving crew's line from the rigging to shore cut because he feared some of the salvage workers would try to use it to get to the beach. As the wind and waves grew in intensity, the next morning the lifesavers attempted to shoot out another line to the ship with a mortar, but the distance was too far in the hurricane-force conditions.

Those onboard clung to the rigging, and the Shinnecocks could be heard singing hymns and praying. The ship broke up the next night. Four men—the first and second officers, the carpenter and a seaman employed by the salvage company—reached shore by clinging to a five-foot-long cork fender from a lifeboat. One of them subsequently died. In all, twenty-eight perished, including all of the Shinnecocks.

The Indians, who left behind nine widows and twenty-seven children, were buried on the Shinnecock Reservation, where a monument was erected. Fourteen of the sailors were buried in the Old South

End Cemetery in East Hampton. Lewis and three others were buried privately. Theodore Roosevelt of Manhattan, father of the future twenty-sixth president, sent a check for $217 to the Hildreth general store in Southampton to pay for supplies for the bereaved Indian families and provided other monetary support.[238]

USS *Ohio*

The ship of the line USS *Ohio* was launched in 1820 at the Brooklyn Navy Yard, the first warship to be constructed there. It was 197 feet long, designed to carry sixty-eight guns and featured an eight-foot-tall figurehead of Hercules. The vessel served as flagship for Commodore Isaac Hall in the Mediterranean Squadron, participated in the Mexican-American War in 1847 and was based in Boston during the Civil War to defend against Confederate raiders.

In 1883, the government sold the aging *Ohio* for $17,000 to Israel L. Snow of Rockland, Maine, who resold the vessel to a group of men from Long Island for $20,000. The ship was towed by two tugboats from the Boston Navy Yard to Greenport, surviving a severe storm along the way. After arriving on November 1, the *Ohio* was docked at the main wharf for many months as a tourist attraction.

The following summer, after being stripped of valuable wood, metal and the figurehead, the *Ohio* was towed to nearby Conklin's Point to be demolished with dynamite. Some people thought the spirit of the ship may have resented the planned inglorious end because of the way it turned out: After lighting a fuse, Robert N. Corey, one of the supervisors of the project, ran to join other workmen crouching about eighty feet away. When the dynamite detonated, an iron bolt from the ship struck Corey in the head; he died three hours later. The warship settled into the dark water of the harbor.

Scrap metal recovered from the vessel was cast as a bell for the Greenport Methodist Church. The Hercules figurehead was sold for ten dollars to the Aldrich family of Aquebogue and resold for fifteen to Miles Carpenter, owner of the Canoe Place Inn in Hampton Bays, where it remained on display for decades. Businessman and philanthropist Ward Melville acquired Hercules in 1954 and deeded it to what became the Ward Melville Heritage Organization in Stony Brook. It remains there in a pavilion on Main Street

USS *Ohio* in Greenport prior to its demolition in 1884. *Courtesy of Naval History and Heritage Command.*

near the harbor next to an anchor from the ship. Legend has it that anyone who kisses the brow of the massive bust will be married within a year.

The remains of the *Ohio* lay undisturbed in Greenport Harbor until discovered in 1973 by scuba divers, who began to map the site and recover artifacts.[239]

LOUIS V. PLACE

The three-masted schooner *Louis V. Place* was wrecked on February 8, 1865, in the Atlantic Ocean off Sayville. By the time the 163-foot vessel reached Long Island, the crew of eight bringing a load of 1,100 tons of coal from Baltimore to New York had been battling a storm for four days, and the vessel was coated with ice, making it unmanageable. The ship was leaking so badly that the pumps could not keep up with the flow. Captain William H. Squires believed he was near Sandy Hook, New Jersey, but the snow was so heavy it was impossible to determine a position. Squires cast a lead line, showing 42 feet of water, and decided to anchor to ride out the storm. But the anchors were encased in ice and could not be lowered. The crew cut the halyards of the sails hoping they would drop and slow their progress toward land. But the sails were rigid with ice and refused to budge. So the captain called the crew aft and told them he had decided the best chance of survival was to run the ship up on the beach. "Boys, I guess we have to go ashore and trust in a kind of Providence to save our lives," he said, according to a *New York Times* report. "Eat all you can, drink what brandy you think you need, and when we strike take to the rigging."

When the schooner ran up on a sandbar an eighth of a mile east of the Lone Hill Life-Saving Station on Fire Island, the crew did as instructed and clambered up the rigging as waves broke over the deck. Minutes before it hit bottom, a surfman from the lifesaving station spotted the ship in distress. He ran to the station, which put out a call to two adjacent stations for assistance.

With heavy surf and the water turned into icy slush, the rescue crew could not launch their lifeboat. So they used a small cannon called a Lyle gun to shoot ropes out to the *Louis V. Place*. The schooner's crew was so debilitated

The *Louis V. Place* encased in ice in 1865. *Courtesy of Long Island Maritime Museum.*

by the cold and precipitation that they could not handle the rescue lines. So the eight men on board climbed back into the rigging and lashed themselves to the masts to escape the waves crashing over the deck. The storm lasted another two days.

When rescuers were finally able to row out to the hulk, only two crewmen remained alive, and one of them died in a Staten Island hospital. The lone survivor, Claus Stuvens, recounted that he had clung to the rigging for thirty-nine hours while one by one other sailors froze to death or washed away. Stuvens said he survived because he and Soren J. Nielson, the seaman who was rescued but later died, were able to crawl inside a furled sail for shelter and kept each other awake by kicking and hitting each other.

As the ship disintegrated in the following weeks, its cargo of coal washed ashore and was salvaged by local residents, who took it home across the frozen Great South Bay. The Village of Patchogue purchased one of the masts and set it up in the middle of the community as a flagpole.

After the disaster, a local woman purchased cemetery plots, and eight headstones were erected as a memorial to the crew in Lake View Cemetery in Patchogue. But only five bodies were buried under them. The captain, whose body washed ashore two weeks after the tragedy not far from the Shinnecock Bay Lighthouse, where he had been assistant keeper as a young man, was buried in Southold. Nielsen was buried in Brooklyn. The body of the cook, John J. Horton, was never recovered. Stuvens lived until 1902. Photos of the ice-shrouded wreck with the crew suspended in the rigging were widely circulated. Artifacts from the *Louis V. Place* are displayed at the Long Island Maritime Museum in West Sayville.[240]

OREGON

It might seem that a much smaller coastal schooner could not cause serious damage in a collision with a huge transatlantic steamship. But when the Cunard Line's *Oregon* and a wooden sailing vessel tried to occupy the same space off Fire Island in 1886, both vessels went to the bottom.

The *Oregon*, built in 1883 for the Guion Line, was 518 feet long. That made it one of the largest vessels of the era. Constructed in the transition period between sail and steam, the vessel was powered by a three-cylinder steam engine but also fitted with four masts and sails. In the spring of 1884, it broke records for westbound and then eastbound transatlantic voyages with

The Cunard liner *Oregon* before its sinking in 1886. *Courtesy of the Dan Berg Wreck Valley Collection.*

average speeds of more than eighteen knots. When Guion went bankrupt later that year, the ship was sold to rival Cunard.

On March 6, 1886, the *Oregon* sailed from Liverpool for New York. At 4:30 a.m. on March 14, the ship was traveling at full steam in clear weather five miles off Fire Island. It collided with what is believed to have been the three-masted schooner *Charles R. Moss* of Maine, which was reported missing that night.

Passenger John Hopkins of Brooklyn told the *New York Times* that "I heard a crash and felt a shock that shook the *Oregon* from end to end." He observed crewmen looking over the port rail near the bow at a hole large enough to accommodate a horse and wagon. It was one of three holes that had been punched through the iron hull. The vessels drifted apart, and those on the *Oregon* heard the schooner's crew calling for help. That vessel sank so quickly that no one aboard could be rescued.

Oregon captain Philip Cottier ordered distress rockets fired while the crew tried to stem the flooding in the largest watertight compartment below the dining salon. The pumps managed to keep the ship afloat for eight hours.

Left: A diorama at Nassau County's Garvies Point Museum shows a Native American burning, adzing and scraping a tree to make a dugout canoe. *Courtesy of Lisa Nordstrom 2017.*

Below: A reproduction wigwam and dugout canoe at the Shinnecock Museum in Southampton. *Courtesy of David Martine.*

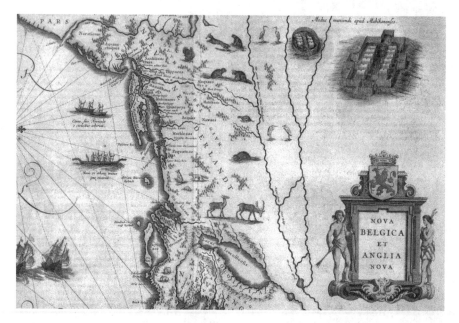

Dutch cartographers William Janszoon and Joan Blaeu based this 1640 map—unusual in that it is oriented with west on top—on the 1613–14 exploration of Adriaen Block. *Courtesy of Special Collections, Stony Brook University Libraries.*

Painting of whaleship *Alice* and whaleboat. *Courtesy of the Whaling Museum & Education Center of Cold Spring Harbor.*

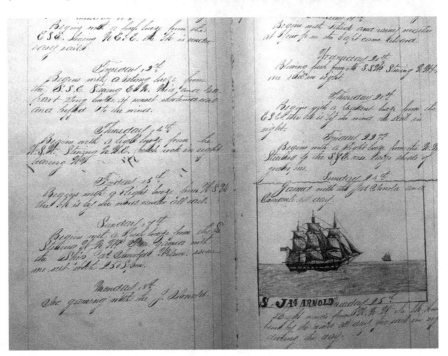

Right: The whaling ship *Lucy Ann* painted by a crewman. *Courtesy of the New Bedford Whaling Museum.*

Below: James R. Foster of Southampton, second mate on the barque *Washington*, illustrated his entry in the ship's log after "gamming," or visiting mid-sea, with another vessel's crew. *Courtesy of the Southampton Historical Museum.*

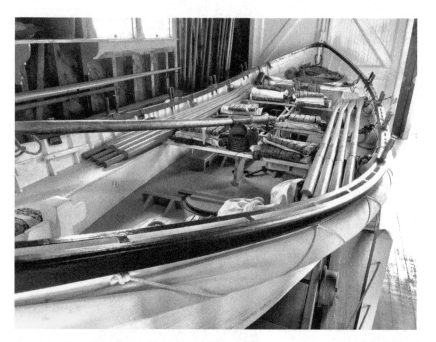

An original Beebe-McLellan surfboat on display at Sleeping Bear Dunes National Lakeshore in Michigan. *Author photo.*

Left: Navy captain David Porter painted by Charles Wilson Peale, 1818–19. Porter completed an epic journey by small sailboat after being captured off the coast of Chile by the British in the War of 1812. *Courtesy of Independence National Historical Park.*

Right: Commodore Stephen Decatur by Gilbert Stuart, 1806. Decatur commanded American vessels that planned to break the British blockade of Long Island Sound during the War of 1812 but never made the attack. *Courtesy of Independence National Historical Park.*

The 1937 WPA mural of the War of 1812 battle over the American revenue cutter *Eagle* painted by Aldis Brown in what was then the library for the Coast Guard Academy cadets in New London, Connecticut. *Aldis Brown,* Battle of the Eagle, *1937, Coast Guard Academy Art Collection.*

Rockaway Beach, New York, with the Wreck of the Ship "Bristol," by Thomas Chambers, circa 1837–40. *Morton and Marie Bradley Memorial Collection, Eskenazi Museum of Art, Indiana University 98.44. Photograph by Kevin Montague.*

Wreck of the Mexico, 1837 by James Fulton Pringle (1788–1847). *Courtesy of Art and Nori Mattson and the Long Island Museum.*

Amistad trial study by Hale Woodruff. *The New Haven Museum.*

Schooner Yacht WANDERER as a Slaver by William G. and Mary Yorke, circa 1888. The image shows the topsail schooner flying the post-1847 Spanish merchant ensign being chased by a naval warship believed to be USS *Vincennes*. The *Wanderer*, built in East Setauket, was the last vessel to carry a large cargo of slaves from Africa to the United States—a half century after the trade was outlawed. *Courtesy of the Kelton Foundation, Los Angeles.*

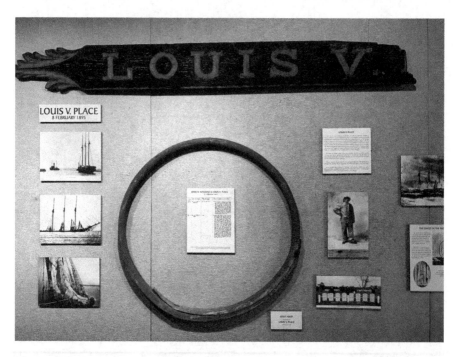

The name board and a mast hoop from the *Louis V. Place*, wrecked off Sayville in 1865, at the Long Island Maritime Museum. *Photo by the author.*

U. S. SHIP OF THE LINE OHIO, *104 Guns.*

Currier and Ives image of the USS *Ohio* under sail before being demolished in Greenport in 1884. *Library of Congress.*

The sinking of the USS *San Diego* depicted by Frank Litter. *Courtesy of the artist.*

Postcard of the U.S. Life-Saving Service Station at Point O' Woods on Fire Island. *Author's collection.*

A postcard of Fort H.G. Wright on Fishers Island. *Author's collection.*

A model of the Prohibition rumrunner *Lizzie D.* and liquor bottles salvaged from the wreck by Captain Dan Berg. *Courtesy of the Dan Berg Wreck Valley Collection.*

Right: Postcard view of the Shinnecock Bay Lighthouse before its demolition in 1948. *Author's collection.*

Below: The tugboat *Gwendoline Steers* before its sinking, depicted in *Last Moments*, by Long Island artist Jo-Anne Corretti. *Courtesy of Ed Carr.*

Above: Billy Joel and the Shelter Island Runabout he helped design. *Courtesy of the Billy Joel Archive.*

Left: The restored oyster sloop *Christeen* under sail in Oyster Bay. *Photo by the author.*

The historic oyster sloop *Priscilla* sailing on the Great South Bay. *Photo by John Vahey, courtesy of Long Island Maritime Museum.*

Long Island Maritime Museum volunteers build a dory in the Penney Boat Shop at the Long Island Maritime Museum. *Copyright 2018 by Audrey C. Tiernan.*

Volunteer Peter Richichi planing the keel of a dory under construction at the Long Island Maritime Museum. *Copyright 2018 by Audrey C. Tiernan.*

Shipwright Joshua Herman (*center*) led a group of volunteers who put in 2,500 hours of work over a dozen years to restore the Gil Smith–designed P-Class sloop *Elvira* at the Carmans River Maritime Center in Brookhaven. *Photo by Thomas B. Williams.*

The restored *Elvira* is launched in Patchogue in July 2018. *Photo by Thomas B. Williams.*

Elvira under sail on her way to her new mooring in Bellport. *Photo by Philip Alling.*

The replica of the oyster dredge *Ida May* under construction in Oyster Bay in the fall of 2017. *Photo by Jamie Deming.*

Restoration projects underway at the Bayles Boat in Port Jefferson. In the foreground is the frame of a 1928 historic "SS" class sloop designed by Benjamin Hallock circa 1906. *Photo by Nancy Solomon, 2011.*

That was sufficient time for all 845 passengers and crew to be rescued by three vessels. There was even enough time for the crew to serve the passengers hot tea and toast before abandoning ship. Officer John Huston jumped into the ocean to save two children who fell in while being transferred to lifeboats. Captain Cottier was the last to leave before *Oregon* sank bow-first.

The top twenty feet of the masts and smokestacks remained above the surface, posing a hazard to other vessels. So the government dispatched lightship LV *20*, which was serving as a relief vessel for New York Harbor light vessels undergoing repairs, to mark the site. The lightship, essentially a floating lighthouse, left Fire Island late in the year when the steamer's stacks and masts were removed. After a board of inquiry in Liverpool held the *Oregon*'s captain responsible for the collision, Cunard relieved him from duty.

Today, the broken-up remains of the *Oregon* lie in about 130 feet of water about twenty-one miles southeast of Fire Island Inlet. It is considered the premier Long Island wreck site to explore by divers, who still find artifacts from the ship and its passengers.[241]

GWENDOLINE STEERS

Shipwrecks became less frequent in the twentieth century with improved navigation devices and safety equipment, but they still occurred. One of the vessels lost was the *Gwendoline Steers*. The ninety-six-foot tugboat sank in Long Island Sound between Lloyd Neck and Eatons Neck during a storm with winds that exceeded ninety-five miles an hour on the night of December 30–31, 1962. All nine crew members died.

The vessel, built in 1888, was used by the Steers Sand and Gravel Company of Northport to transport barges. The *Steers* left New York Harbor about 11:30 a.m. on December 30, 1962, to head for Northport to pick up barges of sand and gravel. Captain Herbert Dickman, who had three decades of experience on tugs and other vessels, was joined by eight other men.

As the *Gwendoline Steers* headed east on the sound, the weather deteriorated. About 4:30 p.m., the Eatons Neck Coast Guard Station heard a radio call from the tug that it was an hour overdue for arrival in Northport and taking on water, but the bilge pumps and engines were functioning properly. The Coast Guard commanding officer, Chief Warrant Officer George C. Bannan, replied that he would attempt to launch rescue craft if the *Steers*'s situation worsened. He and Dickman agreed to talk in an hour. After that

The tugboat *Gwendoline Steers. Courtesy of Monmouth County Historical Association.*

interval had passed, the radio operator attempted to contact the tugboat, but there was no response. Because of the severe weather, the Coast Guard could not launch a search until the next morning.

Coast guardsmen and members of the Suffolk County Police marine unit discovered a metal lifeboat with damage around its keel on the sand spit at Sand City south of the Coast Guard station. On its side, the words *Gwendoline Steers* stood out in black letters. Inside was the body of a man wedged under the seat with his left wrist lashed to the boat, the corpse totally encased in a solid block of ice. He was later identified as Hugh Reid, an engineer on the tug. *Life* magazine ran a widely discussed picture of U.S. Coast Guardsmen chipping away at the ice that filled the lifeboat to remove Reid. Other bodies washed up on beaches nearby, including that of Dickman on January 4 in Nissequogue.

In April, the crew on the tugboat *Judith Steers* spotted a hawser, or heavy rope, floating in the area where the *Gwendoline Steers* had last been seen. A piece of an aluminum mast like the one that had been mounted on the lost tug was attached to the heavy line. A buoy was dropped to mark the location. On April 13 divers followed the line down and discovered the remains of the tug sitting upright on the muddy bottom in forty feet of water one hundred yards from where the hawser had been discovered. There was no damage that indicated why the tugboat sank and no bodies were found inside the wreck. On May 26, the last body, that of deckhand Roy L. Burnett, was found floating in the sound off the tip of the North Fork.

After completing its investigation, in October 1963 the Coast Guard published a 1,200-page report. It found no evidence of negligence or violation of navigation regulations. The agency offered possible reasons for the sinking but could not establish the cause.

In the following years, as the *Gwendoline Steers* sank farther into the mud, the wreck became a popular destination for fishermen and scuba divers.[242]

Photographs, artifacts and other information on the numerous shipwrecks around Long Island can be found at museums, including the Long Island Maritime Museum in West Sayville, the East End Seaport Museum and Marine Foundation in Greenport, the East Hampton Town Maritime Museum in Amagansett and the lighthouses at Montauk Point, Fire Island and Horton Point.

SLAVE SHIPS

Although slavery had been abolished in New York in 1837, Long Island played a part in the stories of two infamous slave ships in later years of the nineteenth century.

AMISTAD

The arrival of an old black schooner off Montauk in 1839 sparked a debate over slavery that would reach all the way to the Supreme Court.

The schooner was the *Amistad.* On August 25, 1839, it anchored on the north side of Montauk off Culloden Point, where a group of starving black men paddled to shore seeking food and fresh water. The men had been captured from Sierra Leone in West Africa and transported against their will across the Atlantic to Havana, Cuba. There they were purchased at a slave auction and loaded onto the ironically named *Amistad*—"friendship" in Spanish. They were chained together in the hold of the Portuguese ship until forty-nine men and four children freed themselves in a bloody uprising. They sailed the ship to Long Island, and soon after they went ashore, the U.S. Navy brig *Washington* appeared. *Amistad* and the Africans were seized and taken to New London, Connecticut, a state where slavery would not be outlawed until nine years later.

José Ruiz and Pedro Montes, two Spanish-speaking slaveholders held by the Africans on the ship, told authorities they had bought the enslaved

Amistad, watercolor on paper, circa 1839, artist unknown. *The New Haven Museum.*

men in Havana. After being loaded on the *Amistad* for transportation to another part of Cuba, the captives, led by their leader Cinque, broke free of their shackles and killed the captain and the cook. Montes and Ruiz survived by promising to sail the captives back to Sierra Leone. They headed east during daylight and at night steered to the northwest without the Africans realizing it.

After being captured by the *Washington*, the Africans were charged with murder and piracy. But eventually, the legal case segued into whether the captives should be returned to the two Spanish slavers. The litigation ended up in U.S. District Court in New Haven, Connecticut. Abolitionists in New York formed a committee to defend the Africans, and Connecticut attorney Roger Baldwin, a future governor, agreed to be their chief counsel.

At the trial in January 1840, the government cited a 1795 agreement between Spain and the United States under which both countries pledged to return any ships or goods from the other party found on the high seas. They were supported by the Spanish embassy in the contention that the U.S. courts had no jurisdiction and the captives should be returned to Ruiz and Montes. Baldwin countered with an 1817 treaty between Spain and Great Britain outlawing importation of slaves into Spanish colonies after 1820. He said that the *Amistad* captives were illegal imports, making them free men.

After a week of testimony, District Court Judge Andrew T. Judson ordered the captives freed.

However, the case did not end there. President Martin Van Buren, seeking reelection, did not want to alienate the South. He appealed to the Supreme Court. Former president John Quincy Adams, now a seventy-three-year-old member of the House of Representatives, agreed to assist Baldwin on the appeal. Arguments before the court began on February 22, 1841. After the government and Baldwin reiterated their arguments from New Haven, Adams took over and excoriated Van Buren, arguing the case was simply a matter of justice versus injustice. The justices upheld the lower court ruling and freed the *Amistad* captives.

Their abolitionist supporters were determined to turn the Africans into missionaries. For nine months, they had the *Amistad* captives study the Bible, singing hymns in English so they could spread the Christian faith in Africa. Finally, on November 27, 1841, Cinque, some friends and Christian missionaries sailed for Freetown, Sierra Leone, on the *Gentlemen*.

Adams performed one more favor for the Africans. He had the marshal of the District of Connecticut revise the 1840 census so that the *Amistad* captives would be listed as free men and not slaves.[243]

WANDERER

In constructing the *Wanderer* a generation after the *Amistad* saga, East Setauket shipbuilders became an unsavory historical footnote. They had built what became known—incorrectly—as "the last American slave ship."

In 1858, half a century after the United States had banned the importation of African slaves, the schooner carried five hundred to six hundred slaves from the Congo across the Atlantic to Georgia. About seventy of the Africans died before the schooner reached Jekyll Island.

But, contrary to its nickname, *Wanderer* was not the last American slave ship. That distinction belongs to the eighty-six-foot schooner *Clotilda*, which in 1860 transported 110 slaves from the Kingdom of Dahomey on the Atlantic coast of Africa to Mobile Bay in Alabama.[244]

Wanderer was built in 1857 by Joseph Rowland at his yard on Bayview Avenue in East Setauket for Louisiana sugar magnate John D. Johnson. It was designed as a pleasure yacht that would be bigger and faster than comparable vessels. But a year after its completion, New York Yacht Club

Cover illustration of the *Wanderer* from *Harper's Weekly* on January 15, 1859. *Courtesy of the Three Village Historical Society.*

member William Corrie and Charles Lamar, a Savannah, Georgia cotton planter, purchased the schooner and had it altered in Port Jefferson. The retrofitting, which included extra-large water tanks capable of holding fifteen thousand gallons, made a customs official suspicious. The *New York Times* questioned whether the yacht was being converted to transport slaves but dismissed the possibility "that a vessel so costly, and so well adapted for a gentleman to spend his elegant leisure in, should be selected as a slaver." Government officials ordered the ship to New York City for a more in-depth inspection. Although they found the alterations "showed that an extraordinary voyage of some kind was contemplated," customs inspectors had no grounds to detain the vessel. It sailed to Charleston, South Carolina, and on to Africa to collect its human cargo.

After the six-week return trip to Georgia, the organizers of the *Wanderer* enterprise were arrested and charged with slave trading, piracy and other offenses. At the trial in federal court in Savannah in the summer of 1860, the members of the jury refused to convict their peers. Corrie received the most severe sanction of any of the conspirators, albeit not from the legal system:

he was expelled from the New York Yacht Club. Lamar bought back *Wanderer* for 25 percent of its value. But after the outbreak of the Civil War, Union forces seized the schooner in May 1861 and converted it into a gunboat. The USS *Wanderer* became part of the blockading fleet off Confederate ports. It survived the war and was employed in the fruit trade. The end for *Wanderer* came in 1871, when it ran aground in Cuba and was declared a total loss.[245]

THE U.S. LIFE-SAVING SERVICE

S hipwrecks were common before Long Island was ringed with lighthouses and the development of electronic navigation technology. And when a vessel was in distress in the Age of Sail, there was no Coast Guard or any other organized effort to help victims before the mid-nineteenth century. Because it generally fell to volunteers to respond to a ship aground, the number of deaths could be staggering.

The death toll brought demands from shipping interests and the public for government action, both for construction of lighthouses and a rescue network. Congress responded in 1848 by appropriating $10,000 to build eight small lifesaving huts along the New Jersey coast to be utilized by volunteers. The next year, Walter Restored Jones, the Cold Spring Harbor businessman and whaling company investor, led a group of other New York philanthropists who were so appalled by shipwrecks such as the *Mexico* that they organized the Life Saving Benevolent Association of New York. Its goal was to build and maintain stations along the Long Island and New Jersey coasts. Aided by $10,000 in federal funds, the association constructed ten stations on Long Island at Eatons Neck, Fishers Island, Amagansett, Bridgehampton, Quogue, Moriches, Mastic, Fire Island, Long Beach and Barren Island in Jamaica Bay. The structure at Eatons Neck north of Huntington is believed to have been the first on Long Island and began operating on March 3, 1849. The association subsequently selected fourteen additional sites on Long Island, with operations of the volunteer effort overseen by the new U.S. Life-Saving Service.[246]

The work of the surfmen, as they were called, had immediate results. They saved nearly 300 lives on Long Island in the winter of 1850 alone. Over the ensuing decades, the lifesavers nationwide rescued more than 100,000 people from shipwrecks.[247]

With no managers to oversee the all-volunteer crews, efficiency suffered. As a result, Congress in 1854 approved hiring paid keepers at a salary of $200 per year. Some of the keepers hired were already the keepers of nearby lighthouses, such as Fire Island.[248]

Because of continual problems with volunteers not being available and theft of equipment from the huts, Congress in 1869 approved funding to hire surfmen for every alternate station in New Jersey. After many shipwrecks in the severe winter of 1870–71, it became clear to all that the system of huts, permanent keepers and volunteer crews was inadequate. In 1871, Congress appropriated $200,000 for paid crews at all stations along with new buildings and upgraded equipment. Eventually, there were thirty-two stations around Long Island.[249]

The salary made it easier to attract experienced men for a dangerous and difficult job. Even though they had waterproof oilskin suits, the surfmen were usually drenched in any rescue, even when the boats did not swamp. But only one Long Island lifesaver is known to have died in the line of duty, a crewman at Southampton who drowned while crossing an inlet in a rowboat at night.

Early on, the stations were equipped with a galvanized metal lifeboat or surfboat, a mortar and shot for shooting lines out to ships on the sandbars, a manila hawser that would be dragged out to the ship by its crew, lanterns, shovels, axes, a speaking trumpet for communicating with the stricken vessel and a wagon to carry all of the equipment. Later, the crews were equipped with a more advanced mortar called a Lyle gun for shooting a projectile out to the ship. A line attached to the projectile would be used to pull out a heavier hawser to support a breeches buoy, which was basically a pair of canvas shorts suspended from a life ring that would be attached to the hawser so the wearer could be pulled to shore, hopefully above the waves but sometimes through them. If the ship was too far from the beach or conditions were too severe, it would be impossible to get a line out to the stricken vessel. Then the surfboat was the only option.

The surfmen had mixed results using the breeches buoy. Bellport lifesavers responded in January 1891 to the stranded schooner *Otter*. One crewman was saved using the breeches buoy. And then, according to the official Life-Saving Service report, things didn't go so well for the second crewman. "He

Postcard of the U.S. Life-Saving Service Station in Southampton. *Author's collection.*

had placed himself snugly in the buoy, when his weight caused the hawser to slip down." After the line jammed, the surfmen tried to pull the seamen back onto the ship so they could free the line. "This was repeated two or three times….Meanwhile the poor fellow in the buoy, unable to climb out, was being smothered by the seas tumbling onboard in rapid succession, until at last he was dashed out of the buoy." The inundation proved fatal. Another crewman died when after getting one leg into the buoy a large wave washed him into the ocean.[250]

When not rescuing endangered sailors, the surfmen stood watches at their stations, patrolled the shore at night, maintained their equipment and conducted practice drills on the beach.[251]

The Life-Saving Service continued to operate until 1915, when it was merged with the Revenue Cutter Service to form the U.S. Coast Guard. As the need for lifesaving crews waned with improved navigation technology, some old stations were demolished while others were repurposed on-site or moved to serve as homes, stores or museums. For example, the original 1850 Southampton station was sold and became the nucleus of St. Andrew's Dune Church after a new station was erected in 1878. The Napeague station, reconstructed in 1888, was moved to Star Island on Lake Montauk by barge and remains part of the Coast Guard station there. And the Amagansett Life-Saving Station opened as a museum in the summer of 2017.[252]

The Beebe-McLellan Surfboat

In 1876, Frederick Chase Beebe, the son of a ship captain and a former apprentice to a veteran Greenport boatbuilder, opened his own shop in the village.

Beebe designed an improved self-bailing boat for surf rescues by crews of the U.S. Life-Saving Service and sold one of them to the Mecox station in Southampton. When C.H. McLellan of the U.S. Revenue Marine was planning a test of different surfboat designs in Bridgehampton, he ordered a boat from Beebe. When it surpassed all of the others, the federal government ordered twenty of the boats and over the years purchased four hundred.

The white cedar boat was twenty-five feet, four inches long, seven feet wide and weighed 1,300 pounds. Previous lifeboats that took on water needed to be bailed by hand or, if completely flooded, brought back to the beach to be emptied. Even if completely filled with water, Beebe's surfboat would empty itself within twenty seconds because it had a dozen square tubes fitted with one-way valves that allowed any water to drain out on either side of the oak keel. The boat also had air chambers on either side to improve buoyancy. And it was equipped with a water ballast tank that could be filled with three hundred gallons through a valve in the stern to add stability. The boat was usually propelled by eight men rowing with oars, but it also came with a removable mast, mainsail and jib for longer trips if conditions allowed. The surfboat came with a horse-drawn wagon for transporting it along the beach to the site of a shipwreck. An experienced crew could launch the boat in forty-five seconds. The boats were manufactured until 1918.

After retiring from government service, McLellan became Beebe's partner. In addition to manufacturing the original surfboat, they teamed up to build a thirty-four-foot model based on an English design for use on the Great Lakes. They manufactured 184 of them. In 1906, the partners introduced a variation of the original surfboat powered by a gasoline engine. It was not self-bailing and could not be launched from the beach. But a later model came with a retractable propeller for launching through the surf and was used until World War I.[253]

17

CIVIL WAR

After the outbreak of the Civil War in 1861, the Confederacy deployed a number of "commerce raiders" to prey on Union shipping. These converted merchant vessels armed with cannons and crewed by navy officers and sailors sought to disrupt Union trade and seize cargoes of value to the South. And some of the vessels targeted sailed just off the coast of Long Island.

The schooner *Thomas Potter* out of Greenport narrowly eluded capture by the *Jefferson Davis*, namesake of the Confederate president, only eight miles off Montauk Point in 1862. *Mary Gardiner* of Sag Harbor and other vessels were able to bluff their way past the Southern raiders by flying English or Brazilian colors, but not all local craft were that fortunate.

Jefferson Davis snared the Brookhaven-based coastal schooner *S.J. Waring* on July 7, 1861, southeast of Long Island and 150 miles off Sandy Hook, New Jersey. The Southerners put a five-man crew of their own aboard *Waring*. They removed most of those on board as prisoners, retaining only four to help run the vessel: two sailors, a passenger and the steward, William Tillman. The Rebels told Tillman, a free African American raised in Delaware and Rhode Island, that he would be sold as a slave when the vessel reached Charleston, where he would earn them $1,000 or more. After several days, Tillman convinced the passenger and one of *Waring*'s sailors to help him take back the ship. On the night of July 16, the seemingly compliant steward, who had the run of the vessel, grabbed a hatchet and bashed in the heads of the Confederate captain and two officers. Tillman

Above: The schooner *S.J. Waring* depicted in *Harper's Weekly*. *Courtesy of Harrison Hunt.*

Opposite: William Tillman, steward on *S.J. Waring*, taking back control of the schooner from Confederate raiders in a *Harper's Weekly* engraving. *Courtesy of Harrison Hunt.*

and his accomplices were then able to turn *Waring* northward, arriving at New York on the July 21. Tillman's fight to recapture the ship and preserve his freedom was celebrated throughout the North, which at that point in the war had few victories to celebrate.

In August 1864, the raider *Tallahassee*, a blockade runner built in England and then armed for raiding duty, slipped out of Wilmington, North Carolina. It sailed along the northeast coast before heading back to its home port in September, having destroyed at least twenty-six ships, some of them near the entrance to New York Harbor. Along the way, the *Tallahassee* accumulated two hundred prisoners. The captain put them ashore on Long Island.

The presence of Confederate raiders on the high seas had a dramatic effect on Long Island's whaling industry. Whaling ships were prime targets: they were slow and filled with valuable cargo. *Myra* from Sag Harbor was chased by the raider *Alabama* off Cuba in 1862. *Shenandoah* pursued Sag Harbor's *Jirah Perry* in the Northern Pacific in 1865. The threat of the Rebel ships kept some of the whalers idle in Sag Harbor.

In December 1861, the Federal government purchased several old unused whale ships, transported them to Charleston Harbor in South Carolina, filled them with rocks and scuttled them at the entrance to the port to try to make the blockade more effective. But the so-called Stone Fleet, which included *Timor* and *Emerald* from Sag Harbor, failed because the currents soon cut a new channel past the sunken vessels.

The war, along with the California gold rush and the discovery of crude oil in Pennsylvania, put the Long Island whaling industry into a final death spiral that ended with the last, uncompleted voyage of the *Myra* in 1871.[254]

18

DEVELOPING TECHNOLOGY

S ubmarines and the torpedoes that would be fired from them were developed in Suffolk County starting in the late nineteenth century.

TORPEDO TESTING

In 1891, the E.W. Bliss Company of Brooklyn began experimenting with torpedoes in Noyac Bay near Sag Harbor. The company selected the waterway because of its depth, lack of current and protection from wind and waves. The torpedoes were manufactured at a Brooklyn factory and then shipped to Sag Harbor in four sections for assembly.

Having secured the patent rights to build the Whitehead-Schwartzkopff torpedo, the company acquired the steamboat *Sarah Thorpe* to test the eighteen-foot-long cigar-shaped devices. The vessel had carried passengers and freight between Sag Harbor and New London, Connecticut, for several years. Bliss arranged for Captain Thomas Corcoran and a crew of thirteen to live and work on the steamer. The testing was supervised by Robert A. Hannah, a retired army officer and the government's top torpedo expert, who lived on Main Street in Sag Harbor.

After Frank W. Leavitt developed a new torpedo for the company, the *Thorpe* was too small to accommodate it. So the company acquired a 140-foot-long steel barge, the *E.W. Bliss*, and the *Thorpe* was then used

The Bliss Torpedo Company tested its weapons at its Sag Harbor facility. This pre–World War I photograph shows a torpedo being loaded onto a battleship. *Courtesy of Richard F. Welch.*

to supply it. The barge was positioned with four anchors, each weighing more than a ton. Leavitt's "dirigible" torpedoes—minus their explosive charge—were fired from the barge with compressed air, speeding toward a target at forty-five miles an hour. A launch would retrieve the weapon and tow it back to the barge. The company would often test-fire twenty torpedoes in a day. Sometimes, the testing had unintended consequences. In the spring of 1909, an errant torpedo struck the steamboat *John B. Dallas* while it was discharging coal alongside the *Bliss* in Noyac Bay. The badly damaged steamboat had to be towed to shore to keep it from sinking. In another incident in 1914, a torpedo struck one of the company launches.

During World War I, Bliss received a $2 million order from the federal government, requiring the company to expand its facilities. Bliss leased the east side of Long Wharf in Sag Harbor from the Long Island Rail Road and erected an office, storehouse and machinery there. Bliss tested torpedoes for thirty years in the waters around Sag Harbor until the business tapered off after World War I.[255]

Submarine Testing

At the close of the nineteenth century, pioneering submarine builder John P. Holland needed a new test site. He chose the North Fork hamlet of New Suffolk.

Holland had been testing his vessels in the busy waters of New York Harbor, which was calm enough for his new boats not to be swamped while on the surface. But heavy ship traffic, curious bystanders and spying by officers on U.S. Navy ships and foreign operatives continually interrupted his work.

In response, in the spring of 1899 Holland dispatched the chief engineer of the Holland Torpedo Boat Company, Charles Morris, to the end of the North Fork to look for a new location. Morris suggested the company move to the tiny resort community of New Suffolk on Cutchogue Harbor. Holland leased a shipyard there, making the hamlet America's first submarine base.

Holland was born in Ireland in 1840 and immigrated to the United States when he was thirty-three. A small man who wore rimless glasses and bowler hats, he was constantly in motion. Holland became a parochial school teacher in Paterson, New Jersey, and while there began developing plans for submarines.

His first, called simply *Boat No. 1*, was launched in Paterson in 1878. Failing to interest the U.S. Navy in his creation, Holland reached out to the Irish Republican Brotherhood, an organization striving for Irish independence. It handed over $6,000 for the fourteen-foot, one-man submarine. The launching for the first test run was inauspicious. No one remembered to reinstall the drain plugs and the boat sank, luckily without injuries, but it was salvaged.

Subsequent designs followed, but it was not until the sixth one—named for the inventor—that Holland made a breakthrough. That submersible was 53.3 feet long and could travel at eight miles per hour submerged and nine on the surface. Equipped with a single torpedo tube and a gun for shooting dynamite charges, it was manned by a crew of five. Surface propulsion was provided by a gasoline engine, while an electric motor moved the vessel underwater. This dual-power system invented by Holland was copied in subsequent submarines until the nuclear era.

The *Holland* was launched at Elizabethport, New Jersey, on May 17, 1897. The inventor began to test it early the next year from his base in nearby Perth Amboy. According to chief engineer Morris, "She goes like a fish and dives better than one." As a war with Spain was looming, U.S. Navy vessels and Spanish spies observed the sea trials. Theodore Roosevelt, then assistant secretary of the navy, recommended that the *Holland* be purchased for use in the anticipated war. The navy, however, was not interested, so the designer continued testing from a new site in Brooklyn.

Morris came up with a critical suggestion for improving performance of the craft: placing the rudder behind the propeller instead of in front of it. An entrepreneur named Isaac Rice then went for a test ride and was so impressed that he bought out Holland to establish the Electric Boat Company. Holland remained with the new entity.

The vessel was towed down Long Island Sound on its way around Orient Point to New Suffolk. Passing Greenport, "many pairs of curious eyes gazed at the strange craft as she came up the harbor," the *Long Island Traveler* reported on June 8, 1898. Remembering the spies hovering around New York Harbor, Holland insisted on secrecy. "The members of the crew have strict orders not to allow any visitors on board," the local newspaper noted.

The new base for the *Holland* was the Goldsmith and Tuthill Shipyard, which Morris had leased for ten dollars a month. The name Holland Torpedo Boat Co. was painted in white letters on the roof of the white wood-frame shipyard building. The arrival of the submarine company generated an economic boom in Southold Town. Morris grumbled that "the folk of this sleepy little town saw a chance to make some quick money by raising the rates on room and board."

The *Holland*, which would become the U.S. Navy's first submarine, on a test run off New Suffolk. *Department of the Navy.*

In the early days, Holland had always been at the controls for the sea trials of his submarine designs. But Rice put an end to that, either because the inventor was too valuable to risk or possibly because of his absentmindedness. Rice may have known about Holland's failure to insert the drain plugs on the inglorious early trial or was aware the designer could be so mentally diverted that he once got lost walking the two miles from the Cutchogue train station to New Suffolk. Whatever Rice's reason, Frank Cable, a young electrician, was trained by Holland to become the new captain.

For the testing at the new base, Holland and his crew placed buoys to mark a three-mile course in Little Peconic Bay. The inventor then took naval officers and other VIPs on demonstration trips. The most famous passenger was Clara Barton, the indefatigable seventy-seven-year-old founder of the American Red Cross. Barton did not like what she saw. Having witnessed the horrors of Civil War battlefields, she criticized Holland for inventing "a deadly instrument of war." He responded—naïvely, in retrospect—that he envisioned his submarines as a deterrent to future wars.

Two U.S. senators, while less famous than Barton, experienced a more memorable sea trial. During their October 11, 1899 voyage, a gasket failed in the exhaust system and fumes overcame crew and guests. Like a horse that knows its way back to the stable, the *Holland* glided back to the dock without guidance. Crew members on shore secured the vessel and revived those aboard. Following that close call, Cable began to carry mice in a cage on each trip. "When the mice died, it was time to go ashore," he remarked impassively.

Despite the occasional mishap, the submarine performed admirably. Still, the U.S. Navy was not convinced and refused to place a purchase order. Rice decided to send the *Holland* to the capital to see if it could sell itself to the government. The vessel made the five-hundred-mile trip through inland waterways—no insurance company would underwrite a more direct voyage offshore—without incident. Once in Washington, the submarine garnered banner headlines and large crowds of curious civilians. At the Washington Navy Yard, the submersible was overhauled and then put through trials in the spring of 1900 in front of dignitaries, including Admiral George Dewey, the hero of the Spanish-American War. The *Holland* performed so impressively that the navy purchased it for $150,000. It was a costly sale for Electric Boat, which had already invested $236,615 in the submarine.

The navy put its own crew aboard and pitted the submarine against surface vessels in maneuvers off Northport, Rhode Island. When the craft again proved its value, the navy commissioned the vessel as USS *Holland* on October 12, 1890. Lieutenant Harry Caldwell had the distinction of becoming the U.S. Navy's first submarine captain.

Despite its initial ambivalence, the navy was so enamored of the submersible that the service agreed to purchase six additional submarines. Five of them—the *Adder*, *Moccasin*, *Porpoise*, *Shark* and *Fulton*—were tested in New Suffolk until Electric Boat moved to Groton, Connecticut, in 1905. Eventually, it became part of General Dynamics, which still builds nuclear submarines at the site.

As for the groundbreaking *Holland*, the U.S. Navy later renamed it SS1 and used it as a training vessel until 1910. It eventually became a traveling exhibit and park display before being purchased for $100 in 1930 and demolished for scrap.

The submarine's namesake left Electric Boat in 1904 to set up a new company. He managed to build two submarines for Japan that year, but continued opposition from Rice and the U.S. Navy thwarted additional sales. He lived in obscurity in East Orange, New Jersey, until his death in 1914.

But Holland's achievements were never forgotten in naval circles. He was hailed as the "Father of the Modern Submarine," and his design principles were copied by not only the U.S. Navy but also by England, Germany, Russia and Japan.

In New Suffolk, only one building used by Holland remains at the boatyard he leased at First and Main Streets, which is now a private marina. A granite monument and historical marker there tell the story of America's first submarine base.[256]

THE SPERRY GYROSCOPE

The gyroscope, an instrument that made navigation on the seas much safer, was commercially developed by a Long Island company.

The Sperry Gyroscope Corporation of Brooklyn perfected the device invented by Professor W.R. Johnson in 1832. It consisted of a heavy spinning wheel mounted within rings so only its center of gravity was fixed. Once the wheel was spinning at high speed, it continued to point in the same direction no matter which way the ship was headed.

Inventor Elmer Sperry began thinking about gyroscopes in the 1890s after he endured a rough trip across the Atlantic. He envisioned a gyro-stabilizer that could prevent ships from rolling from side to side in heavy

An early Sperry gyroscope. *Courtesy of Hagley Museum & Library.*

seas. He was able to interest the U.S. Navy in the concept and was awarded a contract to install a prototype on a destroyer in 1914. Eventually, another forty-three navy ships would be equipped with the Sperry Gyro-stabilizer. But because the initial devices were heavy and expensive, they were not accepted for general use. Sperry continued to perfect the concept.

He had also given a lot of thought to problems with ship compasses. Navy vessels with their heavy steel superstructures created huge errors in the readings of their magnetic compasses. So Sperry developed the Gyro-compass, which would point to true north regardless of its surroundings. The first of his Gyro-compasses was installed on a navy destroyer by 1911. The device proved so successful that orders flowed in, and the company built a new plant near the Brooklyn Navy Yard. By the outbreak of World War I in 1914, Sperry Gyro-compasses had been installed on most navy vessels.

After the war, Sperry developed a way to make the gyrocompass control a ship's steering and keep it on any set course. What he called the "Gyro-pilot" was initially installed on a merchant vessel in 1922. These auto-pilots are still in use in most merchant vessels.

In 1942, Sperry relocated to Lake Success in Nassau County. Sperry merged with Burroughs Corporation in 1986 to form Unisys Corporation. That company does not operate on Long Island.[257]

19

COASTAL DEFENSES

E fforts to prevent foreign enemies from invading New York by sea date
back to the American Revolution.

The fortifications erected by order of General George Washington
failed to keep the British out of Long Island and New York during the Battle
of Brooklyn in 1776. But that did not stop construction of future military
projects along the shorelines.

Following the Revolution, the first coastal fortifications built on Long
Island to protect New York City were Fort Hamilton in Brooklyn in 1825
and Fort Totten at Willets Point in Queens in 1850. Both were of brick
construction. During the Civil War, it became clear that brick forts could
not withstand the power of rifled naval guns, so the next generation of forts
relied on lower-profile separated concrete emplacements hidden behind
earthen embankments. These were designed to be less visible and less
vulnerable to enemy shells. The concrete used to protect the huge naval guns
in the emplacements could be more than twenty feet thick. The military
also developed "disappearing" cannons and mortars, designed to fire and
then use the force of the recoil to drop back out of sight for reloading and
protection against return fire.[258]

In 1896, in response to concerns voiced by the public and some
military planners about the vulnerability of the New York City region, the
government decided to construct a string of forts to protect the eastern
approaches to Long Island Sound. Smith S. Leach, head of the New
London District Office for the U.S. Army Corps of Engineers, was placed

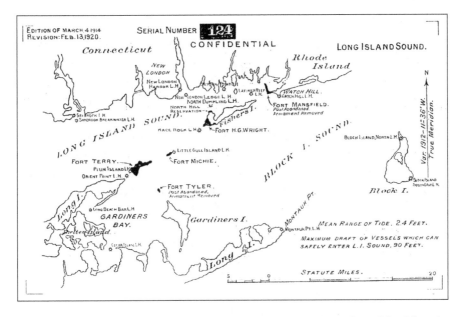

Map showing the location of forts defending the eastern approaches to Long Island Sound in 1920. *Courtesy of Bolling Smith and the Coast Defense Study Group.*

in charge of obtaining land and creating the fortifications. Great Gull Island was transferred to the War Department to become Fort Michie. Land on Plum Island just off Orient Point was acquired to become Fort Terry. And the site of an abandoned lighthouse on a sandbar northwest of Gardiners Island would become Fort Tyler.[259]

In hindsight, it seems absurd that Americans would worry about an attack by the subpar Spanish navy. But by the spring of 1898, as war with Spain loomed, historians Pierce Rafferty and John Wilton note that "the need for seacoast fortifications had become a national obsession. Fear and panic of grand proportions gripped the East Coast. Rumor circulated widely that a fleet of Spanish warships was loose on the Atlantic, intent on attacking and bombarding American coastal cities....Leases for Long Island house rentals included bombardment clauses."[260]

Leach's initial step was creation of a chain of signal stations connected by telephone as an early warning system. He chose Mount Prospect on Fishers Island as the first one. Smith also suggested removing all buoys and lightships (floating lighthouses) in Fishers Island Sound to confound an invading armada. And he even had eighty-nine submarine mines planted in New London and New Haven harbors.[261]

By the time Spain was defeated on August 13, 1898, the forts still were not in a position to offer any effective defense. Military officials considered themselves lucky that there had been no attack and pushed hard to complete the forts. Great Gull Island was acquired to become Fort Michie, the smallest of the coastal fortifications, in 1896. The largest of these installations was Fort Terry, constructed on Plum Island in 1898. The western end of Fishers Island, to the northeast just off the Connecticut shore, became Fort H.G. Wright the same year. Also in 1898, Fort Tyler was built on the site of a former lighthouse on a sandbar northwest of Gardiners Island. The line of fortifications was anchored on the mainland by construction of Fort Mansfield at Napatree Point in Rhode Island. The last of the East End forts, Camp Hero in Montauk, was not constructed until World War II.[262]

Details on each of the fortifications on the East End follow.

FORT MICHIE

Despite the grandeur its name implies, Great Gull Island totals only seventeen acres. Fort Michie (pronounced "my-key") would occupy the entire island after construction began in 1897.

To reassure nervous coastal residents after the United States declared war on Spain in 1898, one company of the First Connecticut Volunteer Infantry Regiment was sent to Great Gull in June of that year. The infantry encountered 250 workmen—largely Italian immigrants—constructing the fort. With little to do, the soldiers left a month later. In 1899, the fort received its name; it honored First Lieutenant Dennis Michie, who had been killed in the Battle of San Juan Hill in Cuba the previous year.[263]

A small artillery unit was transferred to the island, while the eastern end facing the entrance to the sound became the site of concrete and steel gun emplacements, tunnels and underground ammunition storage magazines. Two batteries with two twelve-inch and two ten-inch disappearing guns were ready in May 1900. By that year, the fort had a barracks, officers' quarters, a fourteen-bed hospital, a guardhouse that could accommodate six prisoners and other structures. More housing was added by 1905 and three batteries between 1905 and 1908. But the fort rarely had a full complement of soldiers.[264]

When the United States entered World War I, one of the emplacements, Battery Davis, was reconstructed to accommodate a single sixteen-inch

Fort Michie on Great Gull Island in a photo postcard postmarked 1911. *Courtesy of Henry L. Ferguson Museum, Fishers Island, New York.*

disappearing gun, the largest weapon in the American arsenal. The huge gun was brought by barge to the island in late 1923, lifted by a derrick onto a railroad car and pulled by a locomotive down the island on tracks. Its shells weighed more than a ton, required more than eight hundred pounds of powder to fire and could hit a target more than fifteen miles away. When it was first fired, the gun's shockwave reportedly broke windows on the North Fork and in New London. The proximity of Little Gull Island—about a half mile away—with its lighthouse presented a particular problem. Whenever the soldiers at the fort planned to fire the huge weapon, they had to notify the lighthouse keeper so blankets could be hung over the windows around the lantern room at the top of the tower to keep the concussion from shattering the glass. But the gun was rarely used.[265]

Between the world wars, the property was manned only by a small caretaker force. When World War II was looming, most of the buildings were scrapped because they had deteriorated. Temporary buildings were erected to replace them. Between 1934 and 1945, three batteries, their guns considered obsolete, were dismantled. The sixteen-inch gun was brought back by railroad car to the dock, sawed in half and sold for scrap.

Fort Michie was manned until 1948, three years after the end of World War II. The following year, the property was declared surplus and offered for sale at auction. The American Museum Natural of History in New York, which had watched with dismay as construction of the fort and its operation decimated the tern population, submitted a bid to establish a wildlife research station and bird sanctuary. The museum was given the island free of charge. The battery emplacements—minus their guns—remain along with three brick buildings used by the museum staff.[266]

Fort Terry

The War Department purchased 193 acres on Plum Island in 1897 and established Fort Terry. It was named for Major General Alfred Terry, a Union general in the Civil War and a prominent commander in the later Indian Wars. Two companies of soldiers arrived in May 1898 while six hundred men—half of them Italian immigrants—were still building four batteries and other structures. The batteries equipped with long-range guns and mortars were augmented by minefields laid in Gardiners Bay.

In 1901, the War Department bought the rest of the island other than the land surrounding the lighthouse on the west end. Seven rapid-fire gun batteries were constructed on those additional 690 acres between 1903 and 1906. As with Fort Michie, the firing of the largest guns cracked windows in Orient and East Marion, so a siren was placed at Orient Point to alert residents of impending firing so they could open their windows to minimize the concussive force.

The first 250 men stationed at the fort lived in tents. The first ten buildings, completed in 1899, included barracks, officers' quarters, a guardhouse, a storehouse, stables, shops and a bakery. A hospital, post exchange and gymnasium were added between 1904 and 1906. The final construction, which occurred between 1909 and 1912, included brick barracks, officers'

Postcard view of Fort Terry on Plum Island. *Author's collection.*

quarters and a power plant. For a brief period before World War I, Fort Terry served as a military prison. It also was the site of a training camp for would-be soldiers aged fifteen to eighteen in the summer of 1916.

When the United States entered the war, the primary focus of Fort Terry shifted in 1917 to provide basic training of recruits for service in Europe. The first wave, consisting of National Guardsmen and regular army artilleryman, left the island for France in March 1918. Some of the fort's artillery was shipped to Europe when it became clear that there was no threat to the American coastline.

Operations were scaled back after the war, although Fort Terry was chosen as the site for a new army balloon unit. A new landing field was created south of the parade grounds, and a hangar 127 feet by 77 feet was completed for the one airship assigned to the fort in 1921. During the Great Depression, Fort Terry was almost closed as an economy move, but the army decided the location was still needed for training. In the 1930s, the Department of Justice looked at Plum Island as a site for a new federal penitentiary, but nothing came of the plan.

After the attack on Pearl Harbor brought America into World War II, the soldiers manning the batteries at Fort Terry were kept on active alert for several days. But when it soon became clear that no attack was coming, the army again began to cannibalize the installation's artillery for service elsewhere. Although the war would continue for more than a year, there was little activity at the fort after the end of 1943. With its remaining armament obsolete, the fort was decommissioned in 1948 and Plum Island was offered for sale. But the government decided to keep it, and by 1956 the Department of Agriculture was operating a foot and mouth disease research lab on the western end.

The Plum Island Animal Disease Center is slated to be closed with the research transferred to a new complex in Iowa. The federal government is obligated by law to sell the island to the highest bidder, but congressional representatives from New York and Connecticut are trying to reverse that mandate and save the property as a wildlife refuge.[267]

Fort H.G. Wright

Fishers Island was first put to military use in 1704 when a beacon was erected atop Mount Prospect to notify authorities in New London of the approach of an enemy vessel.[268]

Creation of Fort H.G. Wright began with the federal government's acquisition of about ten acres on Race Point on the southwestern corner of the island in 1871. In 1885, the army leased land on the western end of the island and rifle squads from Fort Trumbull in New London were brought over for training.[269]

Residents of the region voiced some concerns about having a multitude of soldiers in their midst. The *Day*, the newspaper in New London, Connecticut, the nearest city, tried to reassure its readers on July 4, 1888, that "no difficulty is anticipated preserving the best discipline among the men. They cannot get away from the island without difficulty and although there is lager, etc., on sale at the hotels it will not be furnished to others than guests of the hotels."[270]

On the positive side, the increased military activity boosted Fishers Island's appeal as a tourist attraction. The presence of the soldiers, the *New York Times* reported on July 22, 1888, "has completely revolutionized life on this hitherto quiet spot. The soldiers' visit promises to be a godsend to the Summer hotels and cottages which already flourish here." The article said thousands of people were coming from the mainland to visit the area around the camp housing three hundred soldiers to the point that it had become "The Coney Island of the East." Special excursion trains were traveling from as far away as Springfield, Massachusetts, to New London, where three ferries shuttled them to the island.[271]

After the United States declared war on Spain in April 1898, the government began construction of gun emplacements on Fishers Island in December. Early the next year, Silver Eel Pond was dredged open to the sea to create a protected harbor.[272]

The new post was named in 1900 in honor of Major General Horatio G. Wright, a Civil War corps commander and former chief of the Corps of Engineers. The first troops to man the fort arrived in February 1901, and in March artillerymen took over completed batteries of six-inch, ten-inch and twelve-inch disappearing guns. Quartermaster Corps crews began arriving in large numbers in 1901 to erect buildings, including barracks, six wooden officers' quarters (five of which still stand as private homes) and a hospital.[273]

Most of the manual labor was done by immigrant laborers from New York City and Philadelphia who lived in tarpaper shanties in what was known as "Little Italy" near the harbor. The site picked for Fort Wright was not entirely ideal. There were twenty stagnant ponds of fresh or brackish water covering an estimated 1 million square feet, plus about more than twenty acres of marsh. The wetlands "furnishes breeding places for hordes

Aerial view of Fort H.G. Wright on Fishers Island in 1944. *National Archives and Records Administration, courtesy of Henry L. Ferguson Museum, Fishers Island, New York.*

of mosquitoes, which interfere greatly with the comfort and health of the garrison stationed here," wrote Captain John Cree of the Artillery Corps on June 8, 1901. The construction crews dumped more than 100,000 cubic yards of fill to eliminate the swamp in the middle of the parade ground, and most of the ponds were obliterated. The work was done under military secrecy because Leach found news stories filed by a few reporters who had snuck onto the island early on to be inaccurate and inflammatory. In 1908–9, the government acquired additional land, including the west side of the Hay Harbor peninsula and land on Mount Prospect.[274]

Training on the island didn't agree with everyone stationed there. On New Year's Day 1910, sixty-seven members of the 131st Company, Coast Artillery, were placed under arrest for refusing an order to make a fifteen-mile march around the island. Then in July, militia soldiers got into a brawl with the regulars after being called "tin soldiers."[275]

With the declaration of war against Germany in 1917, the fort became the headquarters for all the coastal defense sites protecting Long Island Sound.

The following year, troops began leaving the island for service in France, and the government bought more land, 18.37 acres on North Hill.[276]

The armistice ending the war did not end the military activity at the fort. Around 1920, a hangar was built to house observation balloons. The following year, experiments were conducted on how sounds traveled underwater.[277]

After President Franklin Delano Roosevelt created the Civilian Conservation Corps as part of his New Deal, a unit was assigned to Fort Wright to work on projects there as well as at Fort Terry on Plum Island.[278]

In 1942, after the outbreak of World War II, Fort H.G. Wright became a major center for processing coast artillery units for service. The government also leased a hill on the east end of the island to establish fire-control and radar stations.[279]

The following year, the government purchased more than 94 acres at Wilderness Point to construct new batteries, bringing the size of the fort to approximately 419 acres. Also that year, members of the Women's Army Corps (WAC) were assigned to the fort.

In 1944, an airship detachment arrived at the fort's airfield, Elizabeth Field, named for Elizabeth Nugent, daughter of the fort commander, Colonel George A. Nugent. Also in 1944, emplacements were completed at Wilderness Point for sixteen-inch guns that were never mounted because it was unlikely the United States would be attacked by German sea forces.

At the end of May 1949, the fort was placed on inactive status, and the following year the government decided it no longer needed the site. The Race Point Corporation purchased the fort property at auction for $350,000 in 1958. The land and its buildings were eventually used for public purposes such as a school and private housing.[280]

FORT TYLER

After erosion caused the Gardiners Island Lighthouse to be decommissioned in 1894 and later fall into the sea, the Treasury Department transferred the site to the War Department in 1898. Work began the next year to construct Fort Tyler, named for President John Tyler, whose second wife was Julia Gardiner. It was designed for two batteries but was never completed because the ground underneath it was quickly eroding.[281]

In 1924, the property was turned over to New York State. Gardiner's Point State Park was created in 1927 and a dock, picnic areas and bathrooms

Fort Tyler under construction on Gardiners Point Island. *Courtesy of Bolling Smith and the Coast Defense Study Group.*

installed. But three years later, all of these facilities were washed away by a storm, so the state returned the property to the War Department. The remnants of Fort Tyler were used for target practice by bombers stationed at Mitchel Field in Nassau County before and during World War II. What's left today is known locally as "The Ruins." The site is part of the Long Island National Wildlife Refuge system and is used by the American Museum of Natural History, along with nearby Great Gull Island, for bird studies.[282]

CAMP HERO

The site of Fort Hero near Montauk Point had been utilized for military training from the Revolutionary War through the War of 1812, Spanish-American War and World War I. With the outbreak of World War II and German U-boats threatening the East Coast, Montauk was considered vulnerable. The army upgraded Fort Hero and renamed it Camp Hero in 1942. The navy took control of land and water in the area, including Montauk Manor and Fort Pond, and built docks, seaplane hangars, barracks and other buildings. A torpedo testing facility was also established.

The fort, the final link in the eastern Long Island defense chain, was equipped with four sixteen-inch guns that could fire a shell weighing a ton almost thirty miles out to sea. These and other weapons were placed in three batteries hidden in artificial dunes that covered thirteen feet of concrete. The openings for the guns were protected with six inches of steel. The army designed the fort to be mostly invisible from offshore. The cluster of a few buildings that were visible was disguised to resemble a fishing village. The whole facility, with U.S. Army, Navy and Coast Guard components, was officially known as the U.S. Military Reservation, but the locals just called it Camp Hero.

After the war, the base was temporarily shut down and used as a training facility by the U.S. Army Reserves. The naval facilities were largely abandoned. In 1951, the property was designated as a firing range and field exercise area for an antiaircraft unit from Fort Totten in Queens. In 1952, the 773rd Aircraft Control and Warning Squadron was transferred

A gun emplacement at Camp Hero in Montauk. *Courtesy of Bolling Smith and the Coast Defense Study Group.*

to the 26th Air Division and operated as an Air Defense Direction Center. That same year, the air force tract was renamed the Montauk Air Force Station and occupied by the 773rd. Training with antiaircraft weapons was carried out until 1957. In November 1957, the army closed the Camp Hero portion of the site.

The facility was inactive until October 1958 when the 773rd was re-designated as the 773rd Radar Squadron with a new mission to provide surveillance data on air traffic in the area. The radar operations ended in the early 1980s. The huge radar antenna was left behind to shift position with the wind to prevent it from being torn off its base in a storm. A Ground Air Transmitter Receiver facility remained in service at the site to direct military aircraft operating within the region until 1984.

Between 1974 and 1984, all of the land was transferred to local, state and federal agencies. The majority of the site—468.69 acres—was given to the New York State Office of Parks, Recreation and Historic Preservation. It became Camp Hero State Park, where the exterior of the gun emplacements, historic buildings and huge radar antenna still can be seen.[283]

THEODORE ROOSEVELT

Theodore Roosevelt, the only commander in chief to call Long Island home, is best known for hunting, ranching and other terrestrial activities. But the twenty-sixth president also had a deep love for the water. And his choice of a home site, Sagamore Hill in Cove Neck, reflected that.

But even before TR became a resident of the Oyster Bay area, activity on the water was one of his major pastimes. Initially, his family spent time at the Oyster Bay summer house rented by his grandfather Cornelius van Schaack Roosevelt, beginning during the Civil War. After Cornelius died in 1871, Theodore's father, Theodore Senior, rented another house in Oyster Bay for six summers. And after he died in 1878, the family continued to come to the quiet hamlet.

Even as a small child, Theodore loved Oyster Bay, where his father would sometimes take him on an all-night carriage ride when he had a crippling attack of asthma. When he was a teenager, the daily routine included afternoons on the water in rowboats or a sailboat. Theodore Senior joined other Roosevelts as a member of Long Island's oldest yacht club, Seawanhaka, founded in Oyster Bay in 1871.

When TR was seventeen, Edith Carow, a fourteen-year-old family friend, made an extended visit with the Roosevelts at Oyster Bay. Theodore had known Edith since he was three and she was an infant because her family lived next to his grandfather on Union Square in Manhattan. He spent hours rowing her around Oyster Bay so they could talk about wildlife, books and poetry.

Theodore Roosevelt with rowboat on the shore at Sagamore Hill with swimming platform in the distance. *Houghton Library, Harvard University, 560.52 1905-153.*

Theodore married college sweetheart Alice Hathaway Lee in 1880, the year he graduated from Harvard. Later that year, he bought 155 acres in what is now Cove Neck. The site offers views of Oyster Bay and Cold Spring Harbor as well as Long Island Sound.

On Valentine's Day 1884, Alice died of kidney disease two days after giving birth to the couple's first child, Alice. To ensure the child would have a proper place to live, just two weeks later TR signed a contract to build a Queen Anne–style home on the land he called Sagamore Hill. Edith Carow would live there after becoming Roosevelt's second wife in 1886.

Once Roosevelt became president in 1901 and Sagamore Hill became the summer White House, the water continued to play a prominent role in his life. In a 1905 story in the *Country Calendar*, TR explained his love of rowing: "I like it because it is something Mrs. Roosevelt and I can do together. We take our lunch and two or three boats. I row down to Lloyd's Neck, where there is a portage, and we spend the day in Lloyd's Harbor. In all, it gives me a fifteen-mile row and some good exercise."[284]

In a 1913 article in the *Outlook*, Roosevelt described Sagamore and his nautical life there:

The Sound is always lovely. In the summer nights we watch it from the piazza, and see the lights of the tall Fall River boats as they steam steadily by. Now and then we spend the day on it, two of us together in the light rowing skiff, or perhaps with one of the boys to pull an extra pair of oars; we land for lunch at noon under wind-beaten oaks on the edge of a low bluff, or among the wild plum bushes on a spit of white sand, while the sails of the coasting schooners gleam in the sunlight, and the tolling of the bell-buoy comes landward across the waters.[285]

His eldest son, Ted, wrote later about the house that "on three sides runs a broad verandah....The Northwest looks towards the Sound....In the evening we gather there in the restful dark and talk to the creak of the rockers....When the lights of the [Fall River] boat from New York had passed out of sight behind Lloyd's Neck, it was the rule that the young ones should go to bed."

Roosevelt had a bathhouse and boathouse built on the shore by 1888 and a dock constructed out into Cold Spring Harbor in 1890. There also was a floating wooden platform anchored off the beach. TR's method for teaching the children how to swim was simple: he dropped them off the end of the pier into the deep water. The children knew better than to resist because of the family tradition of taking on strenuous activity without complaint.[286]

Before and after he became president, TR would take his children and their cousins—initially only the males—on what the family called the annual "camping out" adventure. They would pick a destination usually five or six miles away along the sound shore and row there. They would camp on the beach overnight, and TR would fry chicken or steak before telling stories around the campfire. After a schooner wrecked just off the beach, it became a dormitory for girls so they too could go on the camping trips.

Two years after Eleanor Butler Alexander married Ted in 1910, she was subjected to one of the nautical picnics as well. TR suggested they take her on an outing on what she later described as a "boiling hot day." After taking her place in one of five rowboats, "under the blazing sun, we rowed and rowed. There was not a vestige of breeze....Some two hours later, we landed on a beach precisely like the one from which we had started....There was not the least shade." She had envisioned eating a variety of delicious food but instead was confronted with a menu of ham sandwiches and baked clams. After being given the first bivalve as the guest of honor, Eleanor wrote that "at first, although gritty with sand, it was delicious; but that soon wore off and it became like a piece of old rubber hose."[287]

When Roosevelt became president, the 273-foot presidential yacht *Mayflower* came to Oyster Bay with him. The president also had a smaller vessel at his disposal, the USS *Sylph*. That craft had previously been the presidential yacht until the navy acquired the larger *Mayflower*, relegating *Sylph* to other duties during the year but still available for Roosevelt's use in Oyster Bay during the summer. *Sylph* was 123 feet, 8 inches long and could cruise at fifteen knots. Because it could float in only seven and a half feet of water, *Sylph* was more practical for local trips. Roosevelt could be picked up right off the dock at his cousin Emlen's Cove Neck estate. Edith Roosevelt also used the *Sylph* for entertaining and even meetings of the Needlepoint Guild of Christ Church.[288]

The *Mayflower* was the president's platform of choice for two important events while in residence at Oyster Bay. On August 5, 1905, he brought Japanese and Russian diplomats together on the yacht before they headed north to a peace conference at Portsmouth, New Hampshire, for negotiations to end the Russo-Japanese War.

TR also used the *Mayflower* to review forty-five vessels of the U.S. Navy's Atlantic Fleet in Long Island Sound off Oyster Bay on September 3, 1906. As the presidential yacht sailed between the rows of ships—the largest gathering of American warships in history to that point—each vessel fired a twenty-one-gun salute in honor of the commander in chief.[289]

While the negotiations to end the Russo-Japanese War were dragging on in Portsmouth, TR made headlines and shocked editorial writers by heading out on Oyster Bay Harbor on a wet, gusty August 25, 1905, to visit the *Plunger*, one of the navy's six submarines. The commander in chief had summoned the craft from Newport because he wanted to see its capabilities. The plan had been for TR, his wife and guests to view the submarine from the deck of *Sylph*. But that arrangement was scuttled because it turned out to be a rainy, blustery day. Instead, the president proceeded out in a launch on his own, protected by an oilskin suit.

The *Plunger*'s commander, Lieutenant Charles F. Nelson, assumed the president would examine his vessel on the surface, but he probably should have known better. TR boarded the submarine and squeezed through an eighteen-inch hatch into the conning tower, where he was received by the captain. Nelson steered the *Plunger* out to Long Island Sound and brought the submersible to periscope depth as divers waited on the navy tugboat *Apache* nearby in case of emergency. Roosevelt eagerly explored the entire vessel like a schoolboy and interrogated the crew, expressing special interest in the torpedo-firing mechanism. After watching the captain control the

Left: Theodore Roosevelt reviewing the Atlantic Fleet from the presidential yacht *Mayflower*. *Courtesy of Sagamore Hill National Historic Site.*

Below: USS *Plunger* partially submerged with four members of the crew standing on deck in Oyster Bay, 1905. *Library of Congress.*

submarine from the conning tower, TR took over and steered the submarine down to the bottom, about forty feet from the surface. Then Nelson put *Plunger* through a series of maneuvers.

After about three hours onboard and almost an hour submerged, Roosevelt was content. He thanked the captain and crew, stating he was "very much impressed with the submarine boat." On his way back to shore on *Apache*, the president reportedly said: "I've had many a splendid day's fun in my life, but I can't remember ever having crowded so much of it into such a few hours."

Back on shore, Roosevelt wrote his son Kermit—with unusual understatement for TR—that he had been on the submarine "for 50 minutes; it was very interesting." The reaction of the rest of the world was less muted. The *New York Times* ran a front-page story the next day with the headline "President Takes Plunge in Submarine." The sub-headlines added more detail: "Remains Below the Surface for Fifty-five Minutes, ONCE 40 FEET UNDER WATER, He Manoeuvres the Vessel Himself and Is Greatly Pleased—Divers Were at Hand." There was much grumbling in the newspapers about the risk the president had taken. "Curiosity got the better of discretion," the *Constitution* editorialized in Atlanta. But Roosevelt characteristically shrugged off the criticism.

Once out of the White House in March 1909 and a full-time resident of Sagamore Hill, Roosevelt continued to spend enjoyable hours rowing on the local bays and the sound until his health flagged in the years before his death in January 1919. [290]

WORLD WAR I

Only one large American warship was sunk by the enemy in World War I, and it happened off Long Island. The vessel was the USS *San Diego*, a navy cruiser that sank in 1918 only eight miles off Fire Island after running into a mine laid by a German U-boat.

When the United States declared war on Germany in 1917, the German navy developed larger submarines capable of crossing the ocean. The following year was the first time a foreign navy attacked American shipping along the U.S. coastline since the War of 1812. During a six-month campaign, six U-boats destroyed ninety-one vessels between Newfoundland and South Carolina. Some of the attacks took place within sight of shore.

The 503-foot, 11-inch *San Diego* was commissioned as USS *California* in 1907. After sailing as part of Theodore Roosevelt's Great White Fleet, on September 1, 1914, the warship was renamed *San Diego* and became the flagship for the Pacific Fleet. In July 1917, it was ordered to the Atlantic to escort convoys through the first dangerous leg of their journey to Europe.

On July 8, 1918, the *San Diego* left Portsmouth, New Hampshire, for New York. The next day, the cruiser was steaming along Long Island's South Shore at more than fifteen knots with the crew at battle stations. About 10:00 a.m. a lookout spotted a small object moving on the surface. The gun crews thought it might be a submarine periscope and fired several rounds at the target until it disappeared. It was the first time the *San Diego*'s guns had fired at a suspected enemy. At 11:05 a.m., there was a huge explosion believed to have been caused by a German mine laid by the

The USS *San Diego*, which sank in 1918 off Fire Island after hitting a mine laid by a German U-boat. *Navsource.org.*

U-156. It ripped a huge hole in the port side amidships, and the *San Diego* immediately listed ten degrees to port.

C.E. Sims, an eighteen-year-old seaman who would later become an engineer in Islip, wrote years later that he was on the bridge at the time of the explosion. "I looked aft and saw a huge column of smoke about 100 feet high. There was no panic. There was an officer who stood on the ladder with his hand on his holster. I remember he said 'If anyone jumps before [the] abandon ship [command] is given, I'll shoot him.'" The explosion destroyed the port engine room, killing two seamen instantly. Another crewman oiling the port propeller shaft was never seen again. Captain Harley Christy immediately ordered the closing of all watertight doors, rang for full speed on the undamaged starboard engine and ordered the helmsman to steer for shore, hoping to save the ship by running it aground. But soon there were two more explosions, later determined to have been caused by the rupture of a boiler and ignition of the ammunition magazine. Flooding knocked out the remaining engine, leaving the ship without propulsion or power to send out an SOS. As the vessel continued to list, guns were fired at what the crew thought might be a submarine periscope. But by this time the *U-156* was already off the New England coast.[291]

With the ship settling into the sea and some guns already awash, Christy shouted the order "All hands abandon ship!" The crew struggled to manually launch the lifeboats as the ship continued to list. The four smokestacks broke loose, one of them fatally landing on a sailor in the water. Another crew member died when a life raft dropped from the deck landed on his head. The sixth fatality was a sailor who drowned after becoming trapped inside the crow's nest. At 11:51 a.m., *San Diego* sank, twenty-eight minutes after the initial blast. In accordance with tradition, Christy was the last man off the vessel. As the vessel was rolling over, he made his way down from the bridge on a ladder and then a rope and then walked over the rolling hull like a lumberjack on a log. He paused to salute his doomed vessel and then jumped eight feet into the water. The more than 1,200 crew members in the lifeboats and rafts cheered him and sang "The Star-Spangled Banner" and "My Country 'Tis of Thee." The captain dispatched a small boat to shore in an effort to contact the navy. Two hours later, it landed through the surf at Point O'Woods. Vessels were quickly dispatched to rescue the rest of the crew and hunt for the submarine. Explosive canisters known as depth charges were dropped on a target that turned out to be the sunken *San Diego*. Most of the sailors were picked up by other vessels, but at least four lifeboats were rowed ashore, three at Bellport and one near the Lone Hill Coast Guard Station, located seven miles east of the Fire Island Lighthouse.

In what some would call poetic justice, the *U-156* was sunk by an American mine in the North Sea on its way home.

In 1957, the navy awarded a salvage contract to a company that planned to cut up the *San Diego* for scrap. But divers, fishermen and environmentalists persuaded the navy to cancel the contract four years later after the contractor had started to remove the propellers. Today, the *San Diego* lies upside down in 110 feet of water, 13.5 miles southeast of Fire Island Inlet, where it is considered one of the premier shipwrecks off the South Shore visited by divers and fishermen.[292]

Another ship involved in the war came to grief off Long Island as well. On January 1, 1919, the troopship USS *Northern Pacific*, bringing 1,671 wounded doughboys back from the conflict, ran aground off Fire Island. Despite stormy conditions, Coast Guard crews brought everyone off the ship the safety the next day.

Long Island boatyards mobilized during the war to build small craft for the military. The United States' entry into World War I in 1917 brought a resurgence in American shipbuilding, including the companies in Port Jefferson. The government paid to upgrade the yards in the village so they could construct steel-hulled vessels. From 1917 to 1919, the number of shipyard workers there exploded from 250 to more than 1,100, and they built dozens of new ships. In Northport, the Carll shipyard was leased to a company that built scows for the navy. In Freeport, the Scopinich family was able to open the renowned Freeport Point Boatyard with the revenue from military contracts to build patrol boats.[293]

The federal government established several seaplane bases on the shores of Long Island during the war to train pilots. Their story is told in the next chapter.

22

LANDING ON WATER

A Long Island bay was the departure point for the first commercial transatlantic flight—one of many aviation firsts for the region. As aviation began to take off in the early twentieth century, Long Island was a natural place for it to blossom. It was located adjacent to America's largest city and was a natural jumping-off spot for aircraft attempting to cross the Atlantic. The southern two-thirds of the island was pancake-flat glacial outwash plain; the Hempstead Plains and mostly empty terrain to the east were perfect for sprawling assembly plants and runways.

Long Island also had plenty of protected waterways suitable for seaplane bases. And some of the aircraft manufacturers who set up shop on the island used those waterways to develop seaplanes and equipment for them.

The Fairchild Company of Farmingdale operated a seaplane base at the Hulse Brothers Boatyard in Amityville from 1927 to 1932. The company used the base to install planes on floats and test new designs for flying boats. The Bayport Seaplane Base operated from 1930 to 1935, taking advantage of the calm waters of the Great South Bay. Its planes provided summer rides for tourists or ferried people back and forth to Fire Island. Other seaplane bases operated in Babylon (1935–47), Island Park (1946–59) and Port Jefferson (1934–42).

The Long Beach Seaplane Base, which operated from 1921 to 1959, was a stop for the Aeromarine Company of New Jersey commuter airline

A Curtiss MF flying boat in Port Washington in 1918. *Cradle of Aviation Museum, Garden City, New York.*

service between New York City and destinations in the Northeast in the early 1920s.

The Port Washington Seaplane Base on Manhasset Bay was established in 1916 and continued to operate commuter service until 1993 because of its protected site and proximity to New York City. The American Aeronautical Corporation, a division of Savoia Marchetti, constructed a large seaplane base on sixteen acres of the Manhasset Isle peninsula in 1929. It operated through 1931, until American Aeronautical went bankrupt. Then the site became New York Seaplane Airport until 1937 when Pan-American Airways took over and operated Sikorsky S-42 seaplanes to Bermuda and two years later Boeing 314 Clippers across the Atlantic.[294]

Manhasset Bay was the departure point for the first commercial transatlantic flight. The Pan-American Airways Boeing 314 *Yankee Clipper* left from Port Washington for a flight to Marseille, France, on March 20. 1939. Carrying only mail, it arrived twenty-six hours and fifty-four minutes later, including a refueling stop in the Azores. The first commercial passenger flight followed on June 28 with the Pan Am Boeing 314 *Dixie Clipper* carrying twenty-two passengers from Port Washington to France for a one-way ticket price of $375, the equivalent of more than $6,000 today.[295]

Pan American Boeing 314 *Atlantic Clipper* at its dock in Mahasset Isle on Manhasset Bay getting ready to receive passengers in 1939. *Cradle of Aviation Museum, Garden City, New York.*

To prepare for these commercial trips, in the summer of 1937 Pan-American and London-based Imperial Airways—the forerunner of British Overseas Airlines—made joint survey flights to study the feasibility of transatlantic passenger service by flying boats. On July 9, an American Sikorsky S-42B flew from Port Washington to Foynes, Ireland, while the Imperial Airways Short G-class flying boat *Caledonia* made the trip in reverse. A monument at the Port Washington town dock commemorates the accomplishment.[296]

Pan-American operated out of Manhasset Bay successfully for a year and then moved to New York City Municipal Airport, now LaGuardia.

Gold Coast millionaires maintained private hangars on the shores of Manhasset Bay for seaplanes they used to commute to Manhattan or for racing. Farther east in Centerport, William K. Vanderbilt II built a large stucco seaplane hangar featuring state-of-the-art hydraulic doors at his Eagles Nest estate. In operation from 1936 to 1947, it was the base for Vanderbilt's large amphibious aircraft that he used to shuttle back and forth between Long Island and his estate in Florida.

Not all seaplane bases were established for commercial purposes. The military also realized Long Island was a good base for amphibious aircraft. During World War I, there were three naval air stations. The Bayshore Naval Air Station, in operation from 1917 to 1919, was the site of advanced training and a base for coastal patrol aircraft. In a 1917 federal construction spree, forty-six buildings were erected, including five hangars and a hospital. The base supported forty seaplanes and flying boats. Approximately eight hundred naval aviators were trained or based there during the war. When hostilities ended, the base was closed and many of the buildings were sold for civilian use.

During the war, the U.S. Naval Aviation Reserve was created on Long Island. In 1917, the Yale Unit organized by F. Trubee Davison enlisted college students who hoped to fly for the navy. They trained on Curtiss flying boats in Huntington Harbor. Within a year, a seaplane base was up and running with hangars and workshops all paid for with private funds. There were at least eight flying boats stationed there. The training allowed the volunteers to go overseas for combat.[297]

The third World War I naval air station on Long Island was situated in Montauk. The complex—dominated by a huge 250-foot-long hangar

First Yale Unit floatplanes on ramp in Huntington Bay, circa 1918. *Cradle of Aviation Museum, Garden City, New York.*

Dirigible controlled by ground crew at Montauk Naval Air Station in World War I. *Courtesy of Montauk Public Library.*

for airships—contained a hospital and housing for four hundred men. Its location on thirty-three acres on the shore of Fort Pond allowed aviators in dirigibles and seaplanes to monitor shipping to and from New York and patrol for German submarines.[298]

23

SAILING AND POWERBOATING

S ailing on Long Island initially was a means of transportation and a tool for making money, not a source of recreation. Sailing was how people got to where they needed to be, how goods got to market or how fishermen more efficiently deployed their nets or dredged for shellfish. The idea of sailing for fun developed later, in the nineteenth century, as people began to have leisure time.

When powered vessels were developed later, they also initially were used for commerce and transportation before becoming a recreational sport.

As affluent residents began to purchase sailing yachts to cruise and race in the 1800s, initially they didn't handle the vessels themselves. They relied on professional crews and just went along for the ride or, during some races, even watched from afar. The professional captains typically had begun their careers as fishermen or harbor pilots, while their crews were recruited from the ranks of local fishermen. The owners paid the bills and entertained their guests but likely had no clue about how their boats worked. As the *New York Herald* wrote on June 8, 1860, "It is a singular fact that half the yachtsmen of the present day do not know how to sail their yachts themselves in a match."

The concept of organized yacht racing traces back to the 1820s, when some members of the Royal Yacht Squadron in Great Britain began buying and racing boats. In the 1840s, as amateur yachtsmen began to take a greater interest in the designs of their boats and how they sailed, the term "Corinthian" began to emerge in sailing literature as a synonym for amateur.

It referred to the idle rich of ancient Corinth, but in terms of sailing it meant owners who liked to sail their own vessels.[299]

The New York Yacht Club tried the concept in 1846 when it held the first Corinthian race in America. The rules stipulated "only members to sail and handle their yachts." Apparently, the members were not pleased with the results because the club did not repeat the experiment. The country's next Corinthian race would not take place for twenty-six years. It would be sponsored by the first yacht club organized on Long Island: Seawanhaka.[300]

In the early days of American yachting, the vessels sailed were sloops similar to early working vessels. But after the Civil War, the wealthy owners began sailing large schooners that required bigger crews. Before the advent of yacht clubs and organized races, they would organize private matches with sizable stakes. In one ocean race off Long Island in 1866, each of the three competing owners put up $30,000 toward the prize money. As yacht clubs formed and began to hold regattas, there was so much public interest that the daily newspapers covered them in great detail.[301]

In 1871, with the concept of Corinthian racing becoming increasingly popular in England, Manhattanite William L. Swan, who kept a sailboat in Oyster Bay, began to promote the idea in this country. At the time, most of the racing was done by "sandbaggers." These variations on working sloops were fifteen to thirty feet long with a wide beam and a flat planing hull that could skim over the water. Because they were equipped with oversized sails, the only thing that kept them from tipping over—most of the time—was the dozen or so fifty-pound sandbags that the crew moved across the wide cockpit every time the boat tacked, or changed direction. Taverns, clubs and villages backed their local favorites, so the rivalries often led to post-race barroom brawls.[302]

In September 1871, Swan invited Manhattan friends who also vacationed on Long Island to meet aboard his sloop *Glance* in Oyster Bay to discuss organizing a Corinthian yacht club with racing by different types of boats than sandbaggers. He wanted to form a purely amateur organization in which the members would know all about their boats and sail them without professional help in races open to all yacht clubs. The initial sixteen members included prominent local names such as Townsend and Weeks as well as three Roosevelts: Cornelius, Hillbourne ("Hilly") and Alfred. Swan was elected the first commodore. Most of the members owned sailboats, but H.L. and Cornelius Roosevelt shared a steamer named *Fearless*.

The name they selected for their club, Seawanhaka, was found in old Indian deeds dating back to 1636 for land bought by the Dutch in what is

Seawanhaka Corinthian Yacht Club in an antique postcard. *Author's collection.*

now Brooklyn. Seawanhaka was said to be mean "wampum shell land" in the Algonquin language and was also used to describe Long Island. The new club's constitution stipulated that members should be encouraged in "becoming proficient in navigation" and "in the personal management, control and handling of their yachts." The "sailing regulations" also stipulated that sandbags and other movable ballast would be prohibited, forcing a significant shift in the type of boats that could compete.[303]

Seawanhaka held its first Corinthian race at Oyster Bay on July 4, 1872. Because most of the members lived in the city and wanted to race there, the club established a "station" on the shore of Staten Island in 1881. The shift alienated members, including Swan and other founders, interested only in racing on Long Island. They would split off to organize the Oyster Bay Yacht Club in 1885.[304]

At Seawanhaka's annual meeting at Delmonico's restaurant in Manhattan in January 1882, the members voted to change the name to better reflect what the club was all about. Seawanhaka Yacht Club became Seawanhaka Corinthian Yacht Club. The club also instituted another major change that would upset the established order and revolutionize sail racing. It decreed that the sail area of a boat would be a factor in the measurement of boats for handicaps during races to take into account the differences in boat designs.[305]

In 1887, Seawanhaka leased a clubhouse in Manhattan to replace Delmonico's. But four years later, the club's board decided that changing conditions in New York Bay made a permanent home on or near Long Island Sound the best option for the future. The shore of Oyster Bay on Centre Island was selected because it had sufficient land available at a reasonable price along with a good anchorage.[306]

The clubhouse was completed in the spring of 1892, and on Memorial Day weekend, 350 people gathered to witness flags raised and cannons fired to mark its opening. At the ceremony, the Oyster Bay Yacht Club officially merged back into Seawanhaka.[307]

The club continued to set precedents. In 1895, the Seawanhaka Cup was created as an international match race—one boat against another—series for small craft. It is the oldest active yachting trophy originating in America. Before the start of the twentieth century, Seawanhaka was the first club in America to organize a junior sailing instruction program for young people.[308]

Seawanhaka has produced many competitive sailors over the years. The most prominent was C. Sherman Hoyt, who began racing as a teenager. He would win races around the world in everything from dinghies to a huge America's Cup boat in 1934. "Hoyt was the first world-class yachtsman in America," former Seawanhaka commodore P. James Roosevelt wrote in a 1994 history of the club. "He remained a prime personage in yachting until his death in 1961."

The Oyster Bay club served as a model for other yacht clubs that followed as more wealthy men with abundant leisure time moved to Long Island. Three years after Seawanhaka was established, the Knickerbocker Yacht Club, which had been formed in Manhattan, moved to Port Washington, in 1874. (Long Island's second-oldest yacht club closed in 2010, and the property was developed.) In 1891, four new clubs appeared: Hempstead Harbor in Glen Cove, Sea Cliff, the West Hampton Country Club Yacht Squadron and one that would become Manhasset Bay. The latter started out as the Douglaston Yacht Club on Little Neck Bay. But lacking a clubhouse and with Little Neck Bay silting up, the club members relocated to Port Washington. Eight years later, the club's name was officially changed to Manhasset Bay Yacht Club.

Huntington Yacht Club was organized in 1894 by wealthy summer and year-round residents. They included pharmaceutical titans August Heckscher, Frederick L. Upjohn and George McKesson Brown. Sag Harbor followed in 1897.

Sayville Yacht Club, now located in Blue Point, began operation in 1901. It has an interesting history. Some of the sailors who created Seawanhaka later moved to the South Shore and formed the Bayport-based Southside Yacht Club. The founders included Robert B. Roosevelt, uncle of Theodore Roosevelt, and his sons John E. and Robert B. Jr. The first commodore was John E. Roosevelt, who served from 1901 to 1907, and meetings were held at his home, Meadow Croft, now a historic site owned by Suffolk County. In the beginning of the twentieth century, the twenty-sixth president would travel to the South Shore to race with his uncle and cousins.

The club disbanded during World War I and was reorganized in 1920 as Sayville Yacht Club. The club became inactive again during the Depression. After World War II, a group of local residents and veterans reclaimed the charter and relocated the club to its present location. Land was acquired, and the club's first clubhouse, a Victorian bathhouse, was floated across the Great South Bay from Cherry Grove on Fire Island.

Port Washington Yacht Club was established in 1905 and Centerport in 1907. Northport was organized in 1908, Bay Shore in 1910, Ketewomoke in Halesite on Huntington Harbor in 1913 and the Cold Spring Harbor Beach Club in 1924.[309]

The New York Yacht Club—the first winner and then defender of the America's Cup, the world's most prestigious sailing race series, held periodically between boats from two nations—established a station on the shores of Hempstead Harbor in Glen Cove in the 1890s. The club barged its original clubhouse from Hoboken to the new location in 1904. Station 10, as it was known, was a popular rendezvous spot. Members also used it as a place to board their powered yachts for the trip to the club's station at Twenty-Sixth Street on the East River. Station 10 was closed in 1949. The building was donated to the Mystic Seaport Museum in Connecticut and transported there by barge.[310]

HUGE ESTATES WITH HUGE YACHTS

As the North Shore became the Gold Coast in the early twentieth century, newly made millionaires with surnames including Vanderbilt, Belmont and Gould built large and lavish summer homes from Great Neck to Centerport. Others created estates along the Great South Bay. Between 1860 and 1940, more than 950 of these country houses, as they were called, were built.

The owners commissioned extravagant sail and steam vessels as a complement to their grand properties. Of the list of 212 yachts owned by Seawanhaka members in 1900, most of the boats, as one would expect, were sailing vessels. But there also were 45 steamers.[311]

Corsair IV is considered by most experts to be the most perfect power yacht ever built. The 343-foot vessel was built for J.P. Morgan in 1930 by the Bath Iron Works in Maine as the fourth of his series of floating palaces. Morgan sold the steam-powered vessel, the largest private vessel in America when it was launched, to the navy for one dollar in 1940 for service during the coming war. It survived the conflict but sank off Acapulco, Mexico, in 1949 while on a cruise.[312]

Besides competing to have the most luxurious yacht, the owners also engaged in speed trials. William K. Vanderbilt II of Centerport, scion of the railroad and steamboat fortune, and Howard Gould, the mining magnate from Sands Point, held a series of races between their steam yachts on the sound. On one race they wagered $5,000.

The era of Long Island's mega-yachts began to fade with the stock market crash of 1929 and the America's Cup competition moving from New York

J.P. Morgan's *Corsair* in 1889. *Library of Congress.*

to Newport, Rhode Island, the following year. Many of the millionaires' great yachts were loaned to or requisitioned by the navy during World War II and never returned. *Viking*, owned by George F. Baker, who had an estate on the northern edge of Glen Cove, sank off Cape May, New Jersey, after being rammed on convoy duty in 1943. William K. Vanderbilt II's *Alva* was torpedoed off North Carolina.[313]

COMMUTER YACHTS

To augment their mega-yachts, many of the millionaires commissioned smaller and faster "commuter yachts" or "business boats." Also known informally as "commuters" or "flyers," their purpose was to get their owners quickly and comfortably to their Manhattan offices. Many of the commuter owners, including financier Otto Kahn, who built Oheka, the largest Gold Coast mansion on Long Island in Cold Spring Hills, were not yachtsmen. By the 1920s, the already fast boats became even faster when they began to utilize high-powered World War I surplus aircraft engines.[314]

The popularity of the commuter yachts was spurred in part by extensive press coverage of the phenomenon in newspapers and magazines. *Country Life in America* magazine, which derived from and thoroughly covered the country house boom, wrote numerous articles about the commuters. That's not surprising, as publisher Nelson Doubleday owned one himself.[315]

The first express cruiser was built in England in 1869 for an iron magnate. The first American commuter yacht was built for financier J.P. Morgan to travel across the Hudson River from his estate to the Garrison train station from 1873 to 1882.[316]

"Commuters were an extravagance in every way," C. Philip Moore wrote in his definitive history of the vessels.

Most of them were built and finished to the highest yacht standards. They were big speedboats engineered and powered with torpedo-boat sophistication. They burned extraordinary quantities of fuel and cost shocking amounts to maintain. They were tended by crews whose only business was to run them at wild speeds for a few hours each day and spend the time in between cleaning, polishing, oiling, and tuning these wonderful conveyances devoted to the whims and working routines of the titans of finance and industry. Commuters were anywhere from 25 to 300 feet or more in length. Their

Aphrodite, the famous and beautiful commuter yacht built by the Purdy Boat Company Shop on Manhasset Bay. *Courtesy of Alan Dinn and the Port Washington Public Library.*

accommodations were generally minimal but plush. Speed was the foremost consideration, and speeds were sometimes astonishing.

They were essentially civilian versions of the navy torpedo boats being developed in America and Europe. More than three hundred commuter yachts were built by about seventy firms, including Purdy Boat Company on Manhasset Bay.[317]

The *New York Herald* reported in 1902 that "an enormous fleet of private yachts" could be observed "at racing speeds twice a day from their great estates to the wharf on Manhattan Island nearest their offices."[318]

Owning a flyer made possible a pampered commuting routine. Usually, the owners were picked up at their docks or from their yacht clubs, sometimes clad only in their nightgowns because they would dress for business onboard. James D. Mooney, a vice chairman of General Motors, would walk to the end of the dock of his Centre Island home at 7:30 a.m. every weekday morning wearing only a bathing suit. His captain would have *Rosemarie*, powered by twin Liberty aircraft engines, waiting with his mail and daily newspapers onboard. Halfway to the city, the captain would stop so Mooney could take a morning swim before dressing for work. George F. Baker would summon his commuter *Little Viking* to the dock of his home in northern Glen Cove by pushing a button on the wall of his bedroom. It activated a signaling device on the roof that would summon his business boat or launches from his 272-foot yacht *Viking* or his 72-foot sloop *Ventura*.[319]

There were so many commuter yachts coming from Long Island's northern and southern shores, Connecticut, the Hudson River and the Jersey Shore that during rush hours the East River in Manhattan would be jammed and the boats would have to tie up three or four deep at the docks, wait at anchor in the river or stop at piers in Brooklyn or New Jersey to land their owners.[320]

The commuter yachts may have offered speed and luxury, but the trips were not problem-free. Debris in the East River regularly fouled and damaged propellers. One owner had to replace his propellers twenty-seven times in one season. More worrisome was the tendency of the boats to explode because of built-up fuel fumes in enclosed spaces.[321]

The peak period for the commuters was after World War I, when taxes were low and magnates had fortunes to enjoy. Then several factors brought an end to the commuter yacht era: the Great Depression beginning in 1929; completion in 1936 of the Triborough Bridge, which allowed faster automobile travel into Manhattan; the New York Yacht Club giving up its dock on Twenty-Sixth Street in Manhattan in 1938; and the increasing use of seaplanes by millionaires, including Marshall Field III of Caumsett on Lloyd Neck.[322]

The builders of the commuters did not fare well during or after World War II. They suffered from shortages of manpower and materials but most of all from the decline in customers. The existing boats were transformed into family recreational vessels or were abandoned to rot on riverbanks or in boatyards. The more than fifty that survive were saved by the wave of interest in old boat restoration that began in the 1960s.[323]

Sail Racing

North Shore harbors were the scene of national and international racing championships starting in the early twentieth century.

International competitions in the Six Meter Class were held off Oyster Bay between the world wars and attracted some of the best international sailors. The British-American Cup of 1922, contested in Long Island Sound off Oyster Bay, was the first international team sailing race held in American waters. It attracted so much public interest that when the competition returned two years later, the navy had to dispatch three destroyers to control the spectator fleet. The 1927 Scandinavian Gold Cup races in Oyster Bay brought together the largest fleet of foreign yachts to ever compete in the United States. And off Port Washington, the Manhasset Bay Challenge Club Cup, which began in 1903, continues to this day.[324]

The most prestigious local race is the Around Long Island Regatta. It has been run on varying courses since 1977. For the 2018 edition, the course covered 205 nautical miles—a distance that typically takes from one to three days to complete. Beginning in 2017, the starting point was in New York Harbor near the southern tip of Manhattan rather than the Verrazzano-Narrows Bridge as in previous years to allow more spectators to see the action. The finish line has remained in Hempstead Harbor near the host Sea Cliff Yacht Club.[325]

Sailboat racing continues to be popular on Long Island. Most yacht clubs organize their own race series and provide racing junior racing programs for young people. And there are open-to-all weeknight races in many harbors.

Not all sailing training is provided by yacht clubs. There are commercial sailing schools in Port Washington and a few other harbors as well as municipal and nonprofit programs.

The most prominent nonprofit operation is the WaterFront Center in Oyster Bay. It offers a range of racing and cruising sail training courses for students and people of different ages, veterans and those with disabilities. It also rents kayaks and other watercraft. The WaterFront Center was incorporated in 2000 under the leadership of local philanthropist Fritz Coudert to serve primarily as an education organization that developed shore programs for local schools and groups to learn about the habitat of the estuary. Then in 2001, Jamie Deming raised funds to purchase the Oyster Bay Sailing School and a fleet of dinghies and support boats as an environmentally friendly way to increase the public's access to the bay and to complement the education programs. Over the next few years, more boats were added. Then in 2002, the historic oyster sloop *Christeen* was acquired for taking groups out on the bay. By 2018, the center had provided hands-on education and recreational activities to more than twenty thousand people.[326]

America's Cup Connections

Long Island has several connections to the America's Cup, the most famous racing competition.

In 1851, Port Jefferson sailmaker Ruben Wilson sewed the sails for the schooner *America*, commissioned by the New York Yacht Club to race against British yachts in England. *America* won a trophy that became known as the America's Cup. The international competition continues to this day.

Captain Henry "Hank" Haff was the captain or tactician of four Cup winners between 1881 and 1895, a record matched by Nathanael G. Herreshoff, C. Oliver Iselin and Dennis Conner but never surpassed. Haff, born in 1837, began working as a bayman at age twenty and became proficient handling catboats on the Great South Bay. Developing an interest in racing, he began taking out sailing parties, worked as captain on yachts owned by wealthy men and served as superintendent of the Olympic Club in Bay Shore for seven years.

America's Cup skipper Hank Haff of Islip. *Courtesy of Long Island Maritime Museum.*

Haff's reputation as a skilled and savvy racing skipper led him serving as "advisor"—a position later known as tactician—on two America's Cup winners: *Mischief* in 1881 and *Mayflower* in 1886. In 1887, as captain of *Volunteer*, he held off a serious challenge by the Scottish yacht *Thistle*. After serving as skipper of the unsuccessful 1893 defender candidate *Colonia*, he won the Cup again in 1895 as captain of *Defender*, crewed by professional fishermen he recruited from Deer Isle in Maine. It was the first time the series had been won by an all-American crew. Haff was fifty-eight, making him one of the oldest winning skippers in Cup history. He briefly came out of retirement in 1901 for his sixth Cup season to serve as captain of the defense candidate *Independence*. Two of his five sons later sailed aboard Cup defenders.[327]

Greenport also had connections to the America's Cup. A village resident, Captain George S. Monsell, son of a Long Island Sound cargo schooner captain, was a three-time Cup-winning skipper. He selected and trained the crews that sailed to victory aboard three of Harold S. Vanderbilt's yachts: *Enterprise* in 1930, *Rainbow* in 1934 and *Ranger* in 1937. During the competition, however, Vanderbilt steered his own boats.

Between 1928 and 1937, boatyards in Greenport built ten of the huge J-Class yachts for the America's Cup series at an average cost, in Depression-era dollars, of $500,000 (more than $9 million today). J-Class yachts were twice the length of America's Cup Twelve-Meter boats that replaced them. The 135-foot *Ranger*, nicknamed "Super J," had a staggering 7,546 square feet of sail area. It also flew an 18,000-square-foot spinnaker, the largest sail ever made.[328]

Long Island residents have competed for the cup in recent years. The most prominent among them is Dawn Riley, the founding executive director in 2010 of the Oakcliff Sailing Center in Oyster Bay, a nonprofit center for race training. She moved to the island after becoming the first woman to sail on an America's Cup yacht, in 1992; the first woman to be the skipper of an America's Cup boat, in 1995; and the first woman to run an America's Cup racing syndicate, in 2000.[329]

Powerboat Racing

With their well-protected bays, Huntington and Port Washington became popular sites for speedboat racing in the early twentieth century. The competition for the British International Trophy for Motorboats, informally known as the Harmsworth Trophy, was held in Huntington Bay in 1908 and then again from 1910 to 1912. International speed records were set as large spectator fleets gathered. Competition for the prestigious Gold Cup were held in Manhasset Bay in 1915 and 1925. The races were watched by the occupants of 1,500 spectator vessels and others in floating grandstands.[330]

Early in the twentieth century, racing in Freeport began with sailing competitions when the village became a summer getaway for New York City residents. Powerboat racing soon followed because Freeport had several boatyards that specialized in constructing speedy small craft.

In the 1930s, the famous boat builder and racer Gar Wood competed in his wooden speedsters off Long Island. Another celebrity boater was band leader Guy Lombardo, who organized powerboat races from his home in Freeport. Lombardo's *Tempo* broke all speed records from 1946 to 1952. He also competed in annual races in Long Beach.

The Around Long Island Marathon offshore powerboat race was based in Freeport from its creation in 1959 through 1965. In the first 271-mile race, Jim Lacey won in 8 hours 30 minutes in a seventeen-foot Hunter powered by a seventy-horsepower Mercury outboard. Later races featured larger boats powered by multiple outboard and inboard engines. Subsequently, a Freeport Grand Prix was organized in 1985 and ran for at least five years. The boats raced two miles offshore in Jones Inlet or off Long Beach at speeds of up to 120 miles per hour.[331]

The "Japansky," fastest of the Auto-boats, covering the Nineteen-and-a-half-mile Course in 1.06.29

"Fiat II." Winning the Class 8 Contest over the Nineteen-and-a-half-mile Course in 1.13.23

POWER-BOAT RACES ON LONG ISLAND SOUND

A speed test of power-boats was held at Manhasset Bay on May 30 in a regatta of the American Power-boat Association. Twelve boats competed, four of them being of the auto type. Of this class the "Japansky," owned by F. H. Wakkorf, proved the fastest, covering the nineteen-and-a-half-mile course in 1.06.29 (corrected time). Winners in other classes were C. H. Tangerman's "Fiat II," and Alexander Stein's "Allure." Mr. W. K. Vanderbilt, Jr.'s, "Hard Boiled Egg"—so named because it "couldn't be beat"—was injured by an accident to her rudder and obliged to retire from the contest.

Photographs by Pesfield

Harper's Weekly illustration from 1904 showing speedboat races sponsored by the American Power-boat Association on Manhasset Bay. The magazine noted that twelve boats competed and that William K. Vanderbilt Jr.'s *Hard Boil Egg*, "so named because 'it couldn't be beat' was damaged by an injury to its rudder and obliged to retire from the contest." *Author's collection.*

Band leader Guy Lombardo standing in front of his *Tempo VI* raceboat in Freeport. *Courtesy of the Freeport Historical Society.*

Offshore powerboat races were also held for several years off Patchogue starting in 2006. The Battle on the Bay event was marred by the deaths of two racers in one boat in 2008.[332]

Some racing boats and commuter yachts were put to other uses during Prohibition. That story is told in the next chapter.

RUMRUNNING

Hijackings at sea. Shootouts between U.S. Coast Guard patrol boats and vessels transporting illegal liquor. Cases of whiskey carried ashore at secluded coves late at night. Bribery of public officials. Smugglers of booze murdered by competitors.

All of this took place around Long Island during the federal government's ill-fated experiment with Prohibition.

This was the era of rumrunning: trying to avoid the authorities while smuggling illegal liquor from ships offshore to customers ashore.

With its proximity to the large and thirsty population of New York City, it's not surprising that the island became a major center for rumrunning when Congress passed the Volstead Act in 1920, a year after the Eighteenth Amendment to the U.S. Constitution authorized banning most production of alcohol.

For thirteen years, Long Island was the setting for so much rumrunning activity that the Atlantic Ocean along the South Shore earned the nickname of "Rum Row." Besides its location adjacent to the city, sparsely populated Long Island had 1,180 miles of coastline with secluded bays and creeks along with deserted beaches. And law enforcement generally wasn't a problem: there were plenty of policemen, local officials and even Coast Guardsmen on the take willing to look the other way. Some of them even helped unload the illegal cargo or facilitate its transportation.[333]

Since the liquor was still legal in Canada and the Bahamas, entrepreneurial crooks purchased it there and transported it by schooner, freighter and other powered vessels to just outside the three-mile territorial limit, where their cargo was still legal. Their prices were posted on signs.

This floating marketplace was the inspiration of William McCoy. After a Florida boatbuilding business he ran with his brother failed, the graduate of the Philadelphia Maritime School started rumrunning with a small boat and used the profits—$15,000 from his first trip alone—to purchase a schooner named *Arethusa*. He wanted to register it in England to avoid problems with American law enforcement, but there was already a vessel of the same name on the registry so he renamed it *Tomoka*. After installing a more powerful engine, McCoy converted it into a floating liquor warehouse complete with free samples and anchored the vessel off Long Island in May 1921. He protected the merchandise with a hidden machine gun mounted on deck.

While many suppliers watered down their liquor, McCoy, a teetotaler who never sampled his own merchandise, was known for selling unadulterated product for fair prices. So buyers flocked his vessel to get "the real McCoy," giving rise to the still-used expression. His schooner could carry five thousand cases of liquor, giving him a profit of $50,000 for each trip. His immediate success allowed him to quickly buy five more boats and hire additional crews to load up in the Bahamas and then return to Rum Row.

McCoy's success quickly attracted the attention of the authorities. When the federal government arrested him in 1923, he became a folk hero whose following even included federal agents and congressmen. At his trial, the rumrunner was sentenced to nine months with the unusual provision that he was able to leave jail every morning as long as he returned by 9:00 p.m. He gave up Rum Row and resumed the Florida boatbuilding business with his brother, continuing in that trade until his death in 1948.

The first customers of McCoy and the other suppliers were local fishermen who transported the liquor back to shore in their boats to make some extra cash. Soon, however, they were pushed aside by professional smugglers. Until 1924, the only enforcement threat they faced was a small group of federal agents using a few old navy boats. The Prohibition agents were greatly outnumbered and frustrated by the many routes that the rumrunners could take. But they did have their successes. On one day in July 1922, three large vessels carrying rum were captured off Long Island.[334]

Two years later, things began to change. The Coast Guard was brought into the enforcement effort, and Congress appropriated funds for the agency to greatly expand its personnel and number of vessels. Also in 1924, Congress ratified treaties with Canada and European nations that moved the territorial limit out from three miles to twelve and allowed vessels registered in those countries and suspected of smuggling liquor to be stopped and searched within the expanded territorial zone.

Now competing with the Coast Guard, the rumrunners commissioned ever faster boats to outrun the patrols. Eventually, they began purchasing surplus World War I four-hundred-horsepower Liberty military aircraft engines to maintain their advantage. If a patrol boat came too close, the smugglers would pour oil onto their hot exhaust manifolds to create a smokescreen to mask their escape.[335]

This speed war proved profitable for local boat builders. Freeport Point Boatyard, founded in Freeport in 1922 by Fred Scopinich and his brother Mike, built more than thirty rumrunning boats. Playing both sides, it also built fifteen Coast Guard vessels designed to catch them. "They knew the Coast Guard boats were going about twenty-six miles an hour, so they made the rum-running boats to go near thirty loaded," recalled Fred Scopinich Jr., whose father and uncle ran the boatyard. "They were making rumrunners for *everybody*"—from cops to elected officials to gangster Dutch Schultz, who operated out of Patchogue. Initially, they built forty-foot skiffs such as the *Wanda*, launched in 1926 with a single five-hundred-horsepower Liberty engine. But eventually the Scopinich brothers began building boats like *Maureen*, a fifty-two-footer completed in 1929 and powered by three Liberty engines. There was no attempt to hide the purpose of these boats. *Maureen* was built with a bulletproof pilothouse. The boat's owner, Bill Kleb of Baldwin, told a federal census canvasser that he was a plumber when interviewed in 1930.[336]

Some of the rumrunners were far from being old salts. Fred Pitts of Montauk was only fourteen when a "benefactor" put him at the helm of an eighty-five-foot speedster equipped with three Liberty power plants. His crewman was just twelve years old. The intrepid Pitts made forty-five-mile runs out to Rum Row and back for three years. He did not have to worry about the price and quantity of his load. That had already been decided by crime bosses ashore. To ensure that the right load went on the right boat, the young driver was given half of a $2 bill to match with the other half being held by the supply ship captain. After Pitts dropped the cases on the beach, usually they were trucked to what is now Deep Hollow Ranch in Montauk. Pitts' share was $400 per trip—about $6,000 in current dollars.[337]

Smuggling illegal liquor carried risks beyond hijacking of the cargo and interdiction by the Coast Guard. The tugboat *Lizzie D* sank off Long Beach on October 19, 1922, carrying all eight crewmen with it. The vessel's owner filed a marine casualty report with the Department of Commerce's Bureau

Gala was built as a rumrunner by the Scopinich family at Freeport Point Boatyard in Freeport. *Courtesy of Long Island Traditions.*

of Navigation stating that the eighty-four-foot tug was on a "cruise of the Narrows" at the entrance to New York Harbor and was carrying no cargo. The *Lizzie* remained missing until July 1977, when the vessel—along with its true mission—was discovered by diveboat captain John Larsen in eighty feet of water, eight miles southeast of Atlantic Beach Inlet. Along with the ship's bell and other artifacts, the divers brought up full cases of 100-proof Kentucky bourbon and Canadian rye whisky—still suitable for drinking.[338]

The owners of the bay houses out on the marsh islands along the South Shore often supplemented their fishing and waterfowl hunting income with rumrunning during Prohibition. Their remote shacks made great hiding places for illegal liquor. It could be stored there until it was brought ashore for delivery or dropped off at nearby hotels where it joined dancing and the views as attractions at places such as Scott's or Charlie Johnson's on Meadow Island. Besides delivering liquor, some of the baymen also made their own in stills out on the marshes.[339]

Rumrunning wasn't limited to the South Shore and the East End. Long Island Sound was used by smugglers as a conduit to New York City. That was the route being taken by the lumber schooner *William T. Bell* of Norfolk,

Rumrunner *William T. Bell* ashore in Bayville in 1927. *Courtesy of Nassau County Photo Archives Center.*

Virginia, on February 20, 1927, when it encountered a nor'easter. With the sails, rigging and steering wheel coated with ice, the 119-foot, two-masted vessel was being driven ashore on the beach of the Winslow S. Pierce estate at Oak Point in Bayville early in the morning. Bayville Fire Department chief Howard E. Taylor and his brother Sam witnessed the vessel's predicament and called for their uncle, T.B. Smith. When the *Bell* grounded, the six crew members shouted for help from the three observers and then rigged a boatswain's chair—a plank with ropes on the corners that can be attached to a pulley or line above it—so they could be hauled to the beach by the onlookers. Once the men were safely ashore, the Taylors and Smith took them to nearby homes to recuperate. But as soon as the men had warmed up and eaten something, they slipped away.

The reason for their hasty departure became clear the next morning. Bystanders made their way onto the *Bell* and discovered the lumber schooner was not carrying a cargo of wood; it was filled with illegal whiskey. For the rest of that day and into the middle of the following day, residents and members of two local gangs of bootleggers carried off about 250 kegs containing 5,000 gallons of malt whiskey worth more than $250,000.

It was only then that the first law enforcement officer showed up. Village police officer Howard DeMott shooed away the looters before they could pilfer the entire cargo and notified the Coast Guard. The episode garnered much newspaper coverage locally and internationally over several days. The *New York Times'* first story on February 21, 1927, carried the tongue-in-cheek headline "Rum Ship Wrecked, Townsfolk Save Crew, Then Brave Raging Sea to Share in Liquor."

The remaining 125 kegs of liquor aboard the *Bell* were removed by the authorities. Then the Coast Guard dispatched two cutters to attempt to tow the schooner off the beach. When they were unsuccessful, on March 26 one hundred pounds of dynamite was placed in the hull and the *William T. Bell* was blown into splinters. The *Times* ran a picture of the explosion the next day with the headline "Davy Jones's Locker Loses a Lot of Booze."[340]

Artemis was another infamous rumrunning boat operating in the Sound. Built in Greenport in 1929, it also had three twelve-cylinder Liberty engines that allowed the boat to exceed forty-five miles per hour. In August 1931, *Artemis* rammed a Coast Guard patrol boat that previously had been the rumrunner *Black Duck* off Orient Point and then sped away under fire. Authorities eventually caught up to the boat in Port Jefferson, where the bullet-riddled craft was undergoing repairs. After the repeal of Prohibition, *Artemis* was rebuilt with an enclosed deck and became a Fire Island ferry with the new name of *South Bay Courier*.[341]

Enterprising rumrunners would remove the bottles from their wooden cases and transport them ashore wrapped in straw placed inside burlap bags to make them easier to handle—and easier to get rid of if the authorities showed up. Sometimes, they would put salt and cork inside the bag. If they saw law enforcement approaching, they would throw the bags overboard so they would sink. When the salt dissolved, the cork in the bags brought the bags back to the surface for recovery.

As with young Pitts's Montauk loads, typically the liquor was brought to a dock or beach and then placed on a truck. Some went to openly operating speakeasies on Long Island. These included Frank Friede's in Smithtown, Texas Guinan's in Lynbrook and the Canoe Place Inn in Hampton Bays, where the smugglers would hang out with notables, including New York governor Alfred E. Smith. Claudio's restaurant in Greenport, which sits on pilings at the harbor's edge, retains the trapdoor behind the bar that allowed rumrunners to bring their boats underneath the structure and hand up illegal liquor to the employees. The alcohol that wasn't consumed locally traveled into the city, sometimes by seaplane or on Long Island Rail Road freight trains.

While rumrunning was prevalent all along the South Shore and the North Fork, the busiest hub was Long Beach. One reason was that the police commissioner, Moe Grossman, organized all rumrunning activity in the city. Municipal workers reportedly used the light in the clock tower of the old city hall to signal the rumrunners when the coast was clear. Not everybody was in on the operation. In 1930, five city police officers were charged with offering a bribe to a Coast Guard officer to allow liquor to land.

But enforcement of the Volstead Act remained spotty. Out in Greenport, former village historian Jerome McCarthy related that "there were several rum-running boats tied up at the railroad dock, and the Coast Guard boats would be tied up on the other side of the dock and the crews would talk to each other." In Freeport, the rumrunners and prohibition agents were particularly chummy. They gathered every afternoon at Otto St. George's restaurant to chat and drink illegal liquor. Coast Guard captain Frank Stewart was charged with accepting $2,000—the equivalent of a year's pay—to let fishing boats land liquor in Montauk. And the Coast Guard officer in charge of the Georgica Coast Guard Station in East Hampton was sentenced to a year in jail in 1932 for cooperating with the rumrunners.

But like the Coast Guard officer refusing the bribe in Long Beach, some enforcement agents did their jobs faithfully. "There were a lot of bootleggers around here," retired Patchogue cop Roland Baker remembered. "They would offer police officers $25 when they were off duty to come at night and help unload liquor at a creek, but I did not get involved in that." Life could be dangerous for honest law enforcement personnel like Baker. A headline in the *Center Moriches Record* of May 12, 1932, reads, "Coast Guard Shot in Rum Seizure."

Hijacking of liquor on its way to shore or on the roads leading away from the landing spots was a recurring problem for the highly competitive rumrunners. Dutch Schultz and other lesser-known gangsters were quick to retaliate when their merchandise was hijacked. Gangster Sam Grossman of Brooklyn was dumped on a quiet road in Brightwaters with three bullets in his head. And then there was Arthur "Happy Whalen" Waring, found by a clammer in the same area. He had been tied to a lawnmower that failed to keep his corpse submerged.[342]

Even before the Twenty-First Amendment repealed Prohibition in 1933, so much liquor was coming into the country that the price had dropped significantly.[343] With drinking legal again, the waterways around Long Island calmed down—at least until 1941, when the area became a different type of battleground.

WORLD WAR II

T he United States faced immediate challenges, not only in the Pacific Ocean but the Atlantic as well, after the nation was drawn into World War II by the Japanese attack on Pearl Harbor on December 7, 1941. The German navy dispatched U-boats to attack Allied shipping along the Eastern Seaboard and in the Gulf of Mexico. And in the early months of the war, the U.S. Navy and Coast Guard struggled to mobilize from peacetime status with few resources to counter the submarine threat.

One of the first vessels near Long Island to experience the U-boat peril—and luckily survive it—was a lightship. Light Vessel 114, basically a floating lighthouse, was stationed six miles offshore from the Fire Island Lighthouse. Military leaders initially did not grasp that the highly visible lightships augmenting lighthouses along the coastline were highly desirable targets for German captains. Not only were they stationary sitting ducks, but sinking them would complicate navigation for other vessels as well. So LV 114 remained on its station out in the Atlantic despite the outbreak of hostilities.

On Christmas night in 1941—eighteen days into the war—LV 114's logbook recorded that a lookout had spotted flares on the horizon. The crew knew that no Allied shipping was in the area and came to the unnerving conclusion that the flares were probably fired by a prowling U-boat looking to sink the lightship. The government got the hint and ordered LV 114 into Bay Shore on January 11, 1942. Although it was fitted out for military service with armament and radar, the vessel spent the duration of the war at the dock.[344]

Despite the lurking U-boats, initially the government did not order seaside cities to extinguish their lights at night, so vessels traveling along the coast were backlit for submarine captains to easily spot. Tankers and freighters were sunk with shocking rapidity, sometimes within view of the beaches. Debris and oil from stricken ships regularly washed ashore on Long Island's ocean beaches. The casualties included the tanker *Coimbra*, turned into a fireball and sunk by a single torpedo twenty-five miles off Quogue on January 15, 1942. Later that same month, the tanker *Norness* went down sixty miles off Montauk. The tanker *Resor* was targeted in February off Fire Island by *U-578*; all but two of the fifty crew members died. The freighter *Tolten* was dispatched on March 13 by *U-404* off East Rockaway with only one survivor from the twenty-eight aboard.[345]

Soon after the United States entered the war, the navy selected Fort Pond Bay in Montauk as a torpedo testing site. It leased property from the Long Island Rail Road and bulldozed the fishing village that had developed there illegally. About forty structures were demolished, including a general store, restaurant and post office. The navy relocated the Montauk School and gave the residents two options: move your home or abandon it. Those who chose to leave their buildings behind were given $300. In March 1942, the navy announced plans to build a Coast Guard base—which remains today—on Star Island. During the war, more than five hundred acres of private and state land was taken over by the military. The army commandeered the Montauk Point Lighthouse and established a radar station there. After the war, some of the structures erected by the navy were taken over by the New York Ocean Science Laboratory and others were converted to recreational use. The rest of the torpedo testing station was demolished in the mid-1980s.[346]

Zaida and the Picket Patrol

With the U.S. Navy and Coast Guard short on warships and desperate to combat the U-boats, the Coast Guard took an unorthodox action: it organized a fleet of about 120 civilian sailboats longer than fifty feet into the Picket Patrol. Only sailing yachts were used, because their lack of engines allowed them to patrol silently without detection by the crews on submerged U-boats. The yachts were painted battleship gray and crewed by Coast Guard Reserve personnel unable to qualify for active service because of disabilities or age. Protected only by small arms, they patrolled out as far as two hundred miles from shore on cruises lasting from two to three weeks in search of submarines. Thirty-three of the sailing vessels, crewed by 350 volunteers, were based in Greenport from July 1942 until the Picket Patrol was disbanded in October 1943, when the navy decided it had enough regular vessels to hunt submarines.

Picket Patrol vessels recorded numerous U-boat sightings but no confrontations. A Coast Guard report stated that "the *Edlu II*, patrolling south of Montauk Point, N.Y., on September 15, 1942, spotted a surfaced U-boat less than 100 yards away....The small craft began to close, hoping to take the U-boat under machine gun fire. The Nazi vessel spotted the small boat and immediately dove." While the sailboats posed little direct threat, their ability to summon help from warships and aircraft encouraged U-boat skippers to avoid them.

Zaida was the most famous of the Picket Patrol vessels. The 1937 Alden cutter based in Greenport gained renown for battling nature rather than a U-boat. On a December 1942 patrol, the fifty-seven-foot vessel, re-rigged as a yawl and carrying a wartime designation of CGR 3070, was caught in a near-hurricane-force nor'easter off Nantucket. The boat almost capsized and lost its mizzen mast and power. The sails were shredded. The crew of nine bailed nonstop with buckets and burned wood torn from the cabin to keep warm as the vessel was tossed so violently that the potbellied stove was ripped from its mounting. *Zaida* did manage to broadcast an SOS, and HMS *Caldwell* managed to find it despite the driving snow and mountainous waves. The British destroyer pumped fuel oil over the side to calm the seas enough to rig a towline. But the waves splashed the oil onto *Zaida*, where it coated the beleaguered crew. Several hours after the destroyer began the tow, the line snapped and *Zaida* disappeared into the storm.

The navy mounted an extensive search with several sightings and near-rescues. A B-17 bomber dropped supplies by parachute, but the crew on the disabled yacht could not retrieve them. The sailors jury-rigged a sail to propel the boat and then encountered a convoy headed for North Africa three hundred miles offshore. It was too rough for the escort vessels to take off the crew, as they were pounded by forty-foot waves. Eventually, *Zaida* reached the North Carolina coast and encountered a patrol boat offshore when the crew was down to its last five cans of food. But another storm blew the yacht back offshore before the men could be rescued. Finally, several days later salvation came in the form of an airship that spotted the yacht, dropped supplies and summoned help. A patrol boat towed *Zaida* into

Zaida, shown here as it appeared during its service with the anti-submarine Picket Patrol in World War II, still sails out of Greenport. *Courtesy of David Lish.*

Ocracoke Inlet in North Carolina twenty-one days after the initial storm. Its owner, George Ratsey, a famous yachtsman and sailmaker from City Island in the Bronx, died of his injuries the next day, making him the only fatality. The rest of the crew was flown home in time for Christmas. The ordeal of *Zaida* and its crew was recounted in the 1944 book *The Navy Hunts the CGR 3070* by Lieutenant Lawrance Thompson (USNR).

As of 2018, *Zaida* was owned by David Lish and still sailing out of Greenport. But the sixty-seven-year-old owner, who bought the boat in 1978 and spent countless hours and tens of thousands of dollars on restoration and maintenance, had listed the craft for sale.[347]

MOBILIZING THE SHIPYARDS

The United States' entry into the global conflict brought a mobilization of Long Island shipyards to support the war effort. The yards were too small to build warships, but they did turn out auxiliary vessels.

At Greenport Basin and Construction Company, "they were building… mine sweepers every thirty days," said Steve Clarke, who has owned the yard since 1973. "They also built small landing craft at the rate of one every three or four days. It was a 24-hour-a-day, seven-days-a-week operation. Twelve hundred men worked here." The company built 39 of the 481 wooden minesweepers made for the navy during the war. The Greenport yard fabricated more of the 136-foot-long vessels than any of the other thirty-two shipyards around the country mobilized for the work. Three of the Greenport boats were sunk by mines in the Mediterranean and one by a torpedo in the English Channel. One of the minesweepers, YMS 183, was christened in June 1942 by singer Kate Smith. Before smashing a bottle of champagne on the stern and drenching herself in the process, she said, "I christen you YMS 183, and I pray to God that you may always float, that you have a good crew and that you will always bring your crew back to shore safely." Then she sang her famous rendition of "God Bless America," bringing many of the onlookers to tears.[348]

On Huntington Harbor, the Thomas Knutson Shipbuilding Corporation built submarine chasers, rescue and patrol boats and landing craft to carry troops onto enemy beaches. Approximately 1,200 men worked at the yard during the war. After the wooden craft were constructed, they were placed in Huntington Harbor so the hull seams would swell up to stop leaks.

Jakobson Shipyard in Oyster Bay also built submarine chasers. In addition, it constructed thirteen tugboats for the army starting in 1942, two navy minesweepers in 1942 and three navy rescue tugs. More than six hundred people worked at Jakobson during the height of production during the war. One of the Jakobson tugs was ATR-15, which was launched in 1943 and participated in the campaigns in Africa and the Middle East before being

Landing craft built by Thomas Knutson Shipbuilding Corporation in Huntington during World War II await delivery to the navy. *Courtesy of Torkel Knutson.*

lost when it went aground in Normandy on June 19, 1944, after the D-day landings. On the South Shore, the Scopinich family had more than seventy men working at the Freeport Point Shipyard and the Nassau Boat Basin building rescue patrol boats. The Purdy Boat Company in Port Washington built eighty-eight boats for the navy, including thirty-six-foot aircraft rescue boats designed to retrieve downed pilots and forty-five-foot "picket" or patrol boats. Some of the Purdy-built luxury yachts, including the famed commuter yacht *Aphrodite*, saw service during the war as patrol craft.[349]

"THE NAZI INVASION"

The most bizarre and fascinating wartime episode on Long Island was the Nazi "invasion" of 1942. It began when the *U-202* arrived off Amagansett on the evening of June 12 after a fifteen-day journey across the Atlantic. It settled to the sandy bottom a few hundred yards offshore to wait. After midnight, it surfaced and edged toward the beach. Rather than torpedo Allied shipping, the submarine's mission was to put ashore four saboteurs with explosives and tens of thousands of dollars in American money. The saboteurs' mission was to destroy industrial sites.

The Germans paddled ashore at just the wrong time. They had the misfortune of running into Coast Guardsman John Cullen, who was walking the beach as part of his routine six-mile midnight patrol out from and back to the Amagansett Life-Saving Station. After walking for about fifteen minutes and covering less than a half a mile in heavy fog, Cullen, armed only with a flare gun, saw the shadows of three men holding a dark object in the surf. He was immediately suspicious because no one not in the military was supposed to be on the beach because of wartime regulations.

"Who are you?" he yelled.

One of the men approached him and shouted, "Coast Guard?"

"Yes. Who are you?"

"Fishermen. From East Hampton. We were trying to get to Montauk Point, but our boat ran aground. We're waiting for the sunrise."

After Cullen asked more questions about what they had been doing and received cagey answers, he suggested the men come to the station and stay there for the night. The men started to follow him and then stopped, with the stranger saying he had no identification card and no permit to fish, so he didn't want to get in trouble.

Cullen tried to grab the man's arm and said, "You have to come." He had grown increasingly suspicious because the stranger spoke fluent English but seemed out of place. He was wearing a red wool sweater, a gray mechanic's coat, gray-green dungarees, white socks, tennis shoes and a dark-brown fedora—hardly the outfit of a local fisherman.

Then the stranger began asking questions: "Now listen, how old are you, son?"

"Twenty-one."

"You have a mother?"

"Yes."

"A father?"

"Yes."

"Look, I wouldn't want to kill you. You don't know what this is all about."

Reaching into his pants pocket and pulling out a tobacco pouch with a thick wad of bills, the man said, "Forget about this and I will give you some money and you can have a good time."

Cullen responded, "I don't want your money."

Just then, another man—wearing only a wet bathing suit—appeared out of the fog from higher on the beach. He was dragging a canvas bag that was also wet.

"Clamshells," the man in the fedora said. "We've been clamming."

The man dragging the bag said something in a language that sounded like the German that Cullen heard in the movies. The man in the hat responded by putting his hand over the other man's mouth and instructing him in English to shut up and "get back to the other guys."

The stranger took more money from the tobacco patch and shoved what he said was $300—but was actually $260—into Cullen's hands.

The stranger removed his hat and instructed Cullen—twice—to look into his eyes. "Would you recognize me if you saw me again?" he asked.

"No sir, I never saw you before."

There was more conversation along the same lines, with both men giving the other a false name, before Cullen backed away into the fog and then ran, fearing he might be killed. He was back at the life-saving station in less than five minutes. He woke his colleagues by shouting, "There are Germans on the beach!" and "Let's go!"

His supervisor, Boatswain's Mate Second Class Carl Jennett, was skeptical of Cullen's account until the younger man displayed the crumpled money from his pocket. Jennett handed out .30-caliber Springfield rifles and ammunition to the seven men. None had ever handled a gun before, so he spent two minutes loading their rifles and showing them how to shoot before leading them back down the beach. It was almost 1:00 a.m., half an hour after the first encounter, when they reached the spot and fanned out across the beach to search.

Further proof of Cullen's account came when the men began smelling diesel fumes from offshore. Peering through the fog, they made out the shape of a submarine, blinking a signal light through the mist. Periodically, they would hear its engines revving. The *U-202* was hard aground with the tide dropping, and its captain, Hans-Heinz Lindner, struggled with different techniques to free it. When none was successful, he prepared his crew to abandon the ship and had explosives placed to blow it up.

Meanwhile, the man with the fedora, George Dasch, and his colleagues Richard Quirin, Ernest Burger and Heinrich Heinck buried their supplies in the sand. Avoiding the increasing activity on the beach, they made their way inland.

Cullen found more proof for his story when he plucked a pack of German cigarettes from the sand. And with dawn approaching, three of the coast

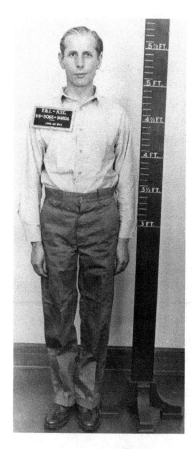

Arrest photo for George Dasch, leader of the Nazi saboteurs who landed in Amagansett. *Courtesy of the FBI.*

guardsmen followed tracks along the beach to the top of the dunes and discovered a freshly piled mound of sand. Poking with a stick, they came across four wooden crates filled with explosives, cash and other supplies. Nearby, they uncovered a canvas sea bag and clothing.

After almost three hours of being stuck on the sandbar, at 3:00 a.m. the *U-202* began to float on the rising tide. Lindner ordered all of his crew aft so the bow would rise from the sand. He used the diesels and electric motors to rock the vessel and finally freed it at 3:10 a.m. The captain wrote in his logbook: "After about four tries she came free. Hurrah!"

Meanwhile, the four German saboteurs, all in their thirties, knew they had to get away from the beach and the men looking to find them. They stumbled upon tracks and followed them to the Long Island Rail Road's Amagansett station, arriving there about 5:00 a.m. They cleaned themselves up as best as they could and got rid of their wet clothes. They looked at a timetable and determined the first train, from Montauk to Jamaica, was due at 6:59 a.m. Dasch bought four one-way tickets, telling stationmaster Ira Baker that "we were going fishing but it's a nasty foggy morning, and I guess we will go back home." They were the only passengers to board in Amagansett. After they left, Baker discovered wet clothes in the hedge by the station. Because the men had aroused no suspicion, he threw the clothes into the incinerator.

After going on a shopping spree for new clothes in Jamaica, the four Germans took another train to Manhattan's Pennsylvania Station. They split up and checked into two hotels by the terminal. Government agents had no clue where they were.

And then inexplicably, two days after coming ashore, Dasch—apparently disenchanted with the Nazi government—contacted the FBI's New York office. He said he had recently arrived from Germany and would call FBI headquarters when he was in Washington, D.C., the following week. Agents in New York dismissed him as a crank and did not follow up. On the morning of June 19, Dasch, who was registered at a Washington hotel, called the FBI. The agent in charge of countering sabotage happened to take the call and sent men to pick him up. Over six days of interviews that produced a 254-page typed statement, Dasch provided details about his mission and also tipped off the agents to another landing that had occurred undetected in Florida four days after the saboteurs landed in Amagansett. Two weeks later, all eight of the Germans, who had been born in Germany but spent time living in the United States, were in custody.

President Franklin D. Roosevelt ordered the men tried by a military tribunal, hoping for the death penalty. He got it. All eight were found guilty and sentenced to die in the electric chair. But Attorney General Francis Biddle and FBI director J. Edgar Hoover appealed to Roosevelt to commute the sentences of Dasch and Burger because of their cooperation with the prosecution. Dasch received a thirty-year sentence and Burger was sentenced to life in prison. On August 8, 1942, the six condemned men were executed and their bodies buried in a paupers' graveyard on the southern edge of Washington. Dasch and Burger were paroled in 1948 by President Harry Truman and returned to their homeland, where they were treated as traitors.[350]

A final incident of the war with Germany occurred just as it was coming to a close. After Adolf Hitler committed suicide, Grand Admiral Karl Dönitz began to arrange Germany's surrender. On May 4, 1945, Dönitz ordered all U-boats to cease hostile action. The *U-853*, cruising east of Long Island, either did not receive Dönitz's radio transmission or its captain, Commander Oberleutnant Helmut Frömsdorf, refused to obey the order.

The following day, *U-853* encountered the freighter *Black Point* carrying 7,595 tons of coal northeast of Block Island while en route from New York to Boston. The submarine fired a torpedo that blew off 40 feet of the merchant vessel's stern. Stewart Whitehouse, a twenty-nine-year-old oiler aboard the *Black Point*, saw a man hanging upside down by one foot in a fouled rope. Whitehouse managed to free the man along with a jammed life raft. That prevented more casualties when fifteen minutes after the torpedo hit, *Black Point* capsized and sank in 130 feet of water, taking with it twelve crew members.

Unfortunately for the submarine's crew, lookouts on the SS *Kamen*, a Yugoslav freighter, witnessed the attack and radioed an alert. Even more unfortunate for the *U-853*, a U.S. Navy task force of destroyers was in the area on its way to Newport following the supposed end of hostilities. Within an hour, the destroyers were hunting for the submarine. The *Atherton* found it within three hours, and the attack began. The navy employed three ships and two blimps dropping depth charges and firing Hedgehog rocket-launched projectiles. Debris, including a life jacket and the U-boat captain's hat floated to the surface, but this proved to be subterfuge, as sonar detected the sub moving east. The attacks continued into the next day until the *853* was declared officially sunk. The navy vessels headed for Newport flying straw brooms at their mastheads, the symbol for a fatal clean sweep.[351]

The encounter between the *U-853* and the American destroyers was the last time the waters around Long Island were the scene of naval warfare.

MARITIME COLLEGES

Acatastrophic 1934 fire aboard SS *Morro Castle* spurred the creation of the first of two unique Long Island institutions of maritime higher education.

The blaze on the passenger liner off the New Jersey coast with the loss of 134 lives and several other maritime disasters prompted the federal government in 1936 to authorize the creation of the U.S. Merchant Marine Academy. But it would take seven more years to open the doors on its campus in Kings Point.

There were already some state maritime academies after Congress authorized their creation in 1874. New York's opened that year. In 1891, Congress established the first of several federal programs for on-the-job shipboard training. But these suffered from a lack of clear criteria for student selection, inadequate pay and no established standards. So by the 1930s, the government had decided that a federal academy open to applicants from every state was important to the nation's security. The resulting federally funded, four-year college prepares its graduates for seagoing careers on U.S.-flagged merchant vessels, service as officers in the American military or business and engineering careers in the maritime industry ashore.

Kings Point, as it is informally known, is one of five federal military academies. It was the fourth to be founded—the Air Force Academy was established in 1954—but the fifth to receive permanent status. That came on February 20, 1956, with the signature of President Dwight D. Eisenhower

U.S. Merchant Marine Academy midshipmen in formation at the Kings Point campus in the 1980s. *Courtesy of the American Merchant Marine Museum.*

after the academy and its alumni mobilized to fight a government proposal to return maritime training to state schools.

The Merchant Marine Act of 1936, which was signed on June 29, 1936, by President Franklin Delano Roosevelt, established the U.S. Maritime Commission and authorized creation of a Merchant Marine Academy. The commission, chaired by Joseph P. Kennedy, father of the future president, established the training program that would result in the academy. Initially, there was only a ship-based training program known as the U.S. Merchant Marine Cadet Corps with some temporary onshore facilities in San Francisco; New London, Connecticut; Biloxi, Mississippi; and Fort Schuyler in the Bronx. But the institution found a permanent home in Kings Point in January 1942. Administrators had been looking for such a location before the December 7, 1941 attack on Pearl Harbor, but the United States' entry into World War II made the change even more important.

On a frigid day in January 1942, dozens of young men boarded large wooden boats at Fort Schuyler and rowed south across the western end of Long Island Sound. They were moving—in a nautically appropriate way—from their temporary home at New York State's maritime college to the new permanent location of the U.S. Merchant Marine Academy.

The school expanded out from the large white mansion, now known as Wiley Hall, built in 1916 for fashion designer Henri Bendel and later purchased by auto magnate Walter D. Chrysler as a country home. His heirs sold the twelve-acre estate to the maritime commission. Wiley Hall's dining room became a mess hall, and the second floor and garages were filled with mattresses to serve as dormitories. The billiard room and playroom became makeshift classrooms.

With additional funding from Congress, the commission purchased several adjoining estates, bringing the campus up to forty-six acres. And over two years, it erected six new barracks, housing 2,700 cadets, a mess hall that could seat 1,200, several academic buildings and other structures, bringing the total to 53 permanent buildings. The academy was dedicated on September 30, 1943, with 2,500 students and 9,000 guests in attendance. The students were known as cadet-midshipmen, now shortened to just midshipmen. Later, a chapel, library and extensive waterfront facilities were added. Today, the North Shore campus is larger than eighty-two acres.

During World War II, the academy condensed its four-year program to meet the burgeoning need for trained merchant officers. The course of instruction shrank first to twenty-four months and then to eighteen, including at least six months at sea. At the same time, enrollments skyrocketed from 136 in 1939 to 2,857 in 1944. By the time the war ended in 1945, the school had graduated 6,634 officers. Kings Point is the only service academy that places its students in war zones during their training. During World War II, 142 cadets were killed while training at sea. After the war, the school resumed the four-year curriculum. It received full academic accreditation in 1949.

Throughout its existence, the academy has periodically had to fight for funding and sometimes even for its survival. The first threat came when President Franklin D. Roosevelt signed an executive order in 1942. The document transferred responsibility for all federal maritime training to the Coast Guard. That agency quickly halted construction at Kings Point, concluding that the academy was only a temporary wartime installation. But the school's supporters successfully lobbied the president, who ordered the Coast Guard not to interfere with the academy.

But funding for new facilities remained an issue. Lauren McCready, the first head of the engineering program, gained a reputation for improvising equipment for training. He begged for handouts from shipyards and even acquired the emergency generators from the French luxury liner SS *Normandy* after it burned and capsized in February 1942 at a Manhattan pier.

In 1946, Kings Point acquired a surplus ship, the four-hundred-foot *Devosa*, and rechristened it *Kings Pointer*, the first in a series of training vessels to carry that name.

The Korean War and the Vietnam conflict boosted the need for merchant officers and hence enrollment. But the U.S. involvement in Vietnam from 1959 to 1975 divided the student body. When antiwar midshipmen were assaulted, the FBI came to the campus to investigate.

The first African American midshipman, Joseph Banks Williams, graduated in 1944. Thanks to federal civil rights legislation, Kings Point was the first federal service academy to admit women: in July 1974, fifteen female midshipmen enrolled. Eight of them graduated four years later.

Another threat came in 1977 when President Gerald Ford proposed a budget with severe cuts for the academy that were to be made up by charging tuition as well as room and board fees. The other service academies were not facing the same requirements. President Jimmy Carter, a navy veteran, torpedoed the plan when he took office. The last challenge to the academy's survival came in the 1990s when a government efficiency commission recommended closing the school. The alumni rallied again and kept the doors open. In the last few years, the school has been criticized by an accreditation agency for not meeting academic standards. And some midshipmen and federal officials accused Kings Point of not properly safeguarding students from sexual harassment during their year at sea. The academy and the federal government have been making changes in response to those criticisms.

To graduate, the midshipmen must complete the educational requirements of the academy, fulfill the requirements for a Coast Guard license as an officer in the U.S. Merchant Marine and qualify to serve in a reserve component of the armed forces or in the National Oceanic and Atmospheric Administration. After graduating, Kings Pointers have an obligation to maintain a license in the Merchant Marine for at least six years, serve for five years in the Merchant Marine or the maritime industry and to serve in the U.S. Naval Reserve or any other reserve unit of the armed forces for eight years. Approximately 20 percent of the graduates enter the armed forces.

Today, the Regiment of Midshipmen numbers approximately 950. In recent years, about 13 percent of the graduates have been women. The students come from every state and U.S. trust territories and possessions. Foreign governments also send students to the school.

The Kings Point campus is also the home of the American Merchant Marine Museum. It preserves, displays and interprets artifacts and artwork

Webb Institute in Glen Cove. *Courtesy of Webb Institute.*

related to the Merchant Marine Academy and the U.S. Merchant Marine. Among the museum's holdings are the archives of the United States Lines, including photographs and other materials relating to the famed ocean liner SS *United States*. The museum, which opened in 1979, also owns a large collection of ship models and navigational instruments.[352]

WEBB INSTITUTE

Located seven miles to the east of Kings Point in Glen Cove, Webb Institute is America's first naval architecture college. It moved to Long Island from the Bronx in 1947, but its story began in 1894 when shipbuilder William H. Webb opened Webb's Academy.

In the nineteenth century, Webb was the foremost shipbuilder in New York City, where the nation's most important shipyards lined the banks of the East River in Manhattan and Brooklyn. Born in 1816, Webb learned shipbuilding from his father, Isaac Webb. When the elder Webb died in 1840, his son took over the shipyard located on the Lower East Side of Manhattan between Fifth and Seventh Streets. From that year until 1869,

William Webb designed and supervised the construction of 135 wooden vessels: fishing schooners, ferryboats, fast sailing packets and clipper ships. He also turned out large oceangoing steamships and ironclad warships for European navies. In Webb's twenty-nine years of ownership, his yard built more vessels with greater tonnage than any other American facility. During and after his years as a shipbuilder, he was involved in the creation of a number of steamship lines.

As wooden ships gave way to iron in the 1870s and steamships grew larger and more powerful, it became clear that the apprentice system under which Webb and other builders of his era learned their trade needed to be replaced by a more formal education system for naval architects and marine engineers.

Webb decided to create a school and obtained a charter from New York State for Webb's Academy and Home for Shipbuilders on April 2, 1889. The school and the retirement home located on Sedgewick Avenue at 188th Street in the Bronx opened in 1894. The academy, which began with three faculty members, graduated its first class of eight men in 1897. The course of study was increased from three to four years in 1909. The University of the State of New York in 1933 granted the academy the authority to award bachelor of science degrees.

In 1947, the institution whose name had become Webb Institute of Naval Architecture moved to its current location in Glen Cove. The relocation came after a board member who lived on Crescent Beach Road learned that the Braes, the nearby twenty-six-acre former estate of Herbert L. Pratt, the son of one of the founders of the Standard Oil Company, was for sale.

Including the mansion, academic and support services are now housed in six buildings. The Alumni Gymnasium was added the year of the move. The Robinson Model Basin building was completed in 1948. Haberle Laboratory came in 1964, the Livingston Library and Henry Auditorium in 1973 and the Motley Residence Hall in 1995.[353]

Until 1974, no women are known to have applied to attend Webb. But in the spring of that year, Karen Hansen wrote the president, Rear Admiral William A. Brockett, seeking admission. The school's charter and William Webb's will made no mention of women students receiving scholarships, so the president sent Hansen a note stating that the school was restricted to male students. When she wrote back, Brockett admired her persistence and realized she had all the qualifications for success at Webb. So he approached the board of trustees, which agreed the school should begin to admit women. Webb applied to the New York Bard of Regents to amend its charter, and

Webb Institute founder William Webb. *Courtesy of Webb Institute.*

the request was approved quickly. So Karen Hansen was admitted and graduated with the class of 1978. Every subsequent class has had at least one female student.[354]

Until his death in 1899, Webb paid all operating expenses of the academy. He also transferred properties to the school and left an endowment in his will. The endowment income, along with gifts from foundations, corporations, alumni and other individuals, covers most current operating costs. So the school, whose name was shortened to Webb Institute in 1994, still offers a free education to its one hundred undergraduates.[355]

In the spring of 2018, Webb announced plans for a new academic building designed to blend in with the 106-year-old Pratt mansion. The 29,563-square-foot mostly underground structure with a landscaped roof was being constructed on one of the three grass terraces between the mansion and the sound and is scheduled to open in 2019.[356]

AIRCRAFT MANUFACTURERS LOOK SEAWARD

After the boom years of building military planes during World War II, Long Island's aircraft manufacturers needed to broaden their product lines to remain viable. Building boats proved to be a profitable way to do that.

Grumman Corporation and other companies realized the same materials, machinery and skilled employees that could make warplanes could also make canoes, patrol boats and even experimental submarines.

The most visible and famous of these new products was an aluminum canoe produced by Grumman. These turned out to be a major improvement over their wooden predecessors. They were lighter, almost indestructible and safer because of built-in watertight compartments on either end that kept the canoe from totally sinking.[357]

The inspiration for the aluminum canoe came from a Grumman executive who was portaging a heavy wood and canvas canoe in the Adirondacks in 1944. As he hefted the traditional canoe, company vice president William Hoffman thought about World War II coming to an end and realized that defense contractors would be looking to convert their factories for peacetime production. Hoffman thought that Grumman could make lighter, sturdier aluminum canoes relying on the same materials and metalworking expertise it had used to turn out thousands of Hellcat, Tigercat and Bearcat warplanes.

The company's two top executives, Leroy Grumman and Jake Swirbul, embraced Hoffman's concept. Not long after, seventeen-foot prototypes were being constructed in the employee bowling alley in Bethpage. When

Leroy Grumman in one of his company's famous and ubiquitous aluminum canoes in 1945. *Courtesy of Northrop Grumman Corporation.*

the crafts passed a test in the rapids of the Allagash River in Maine, the company gave the green light to the project. In October 1945, Leroy Grumman announced that the company had invented its first canoe: a thirteen-foot, thirty-eight-pound model that "even a woman can carry." The initial model was displayed in the window of Abercrombie & Fitch sporting goods store in Manhattan. The *New York Times* described it as lighter "than Hiawatha's birchbark vessel...and impervious to either porcupines or termites" thanks to a special aluminum alloy.

Grumman geared up for mass production by tapping twenty-seven-year-old tooling engineer John Achilich to design models of fifteen, seventeen and nineteen feet. He was a logical choice, having built his own wood and cloth kayak as a teenager and worked as a canoeing instructor while studying at Pratt Institute. Achilich, ordered to keep mum about the project, was sent to work alone in a remote office in a hangar at Bethpage Plant 2. Over the next month, the engineer, often working into the night, laid out paper on top of long pieces of thin aluminum to draw the lines for the hull segments. His patented designs were used to make hardwood molds over which sheets of aluminum were stretched on presses to make each half of a canoe. The halves were held together by rivets and extrusions at the seams as well as ribs and seats. "The important thing about the Grumman canoe was that it was so strong," Achilich said in a 2007 interview.

The new product proved to be popular. Grumman sold ninety-four of the watercraft in 1945, and then sales mushroomed to more than ten thousand the following year. The canoes became ubiquitous at summer camps and river and lake rental operations. They sold so well that Grumman built a boat manufacturing plant in Marathon, forty miles south of Syracuse, to free up space in Bethpage for Korean War aircraft production in 1952.

A 1975 Grumman brochure cited sales of more than 300,000 canoes in three decades. Demand peaked in 1974 with sales of 33,000, thanks to the canoe's visibility in the 1972 movie *Deliverance* and concerns about fuel consumption during the mid-1970s energy crisis.

Over the years, the company expanded into several types of aluminum vessels. These included square-backed canoes that could mount an outboard motor, fishing boats, pontoon boats, hovercraft and even canoes rigged for sailing. Aluminum canoe sales eventually slowed to about four thousand a year as plastic and fiberglass models became more popular.

Grumman sold its boat division in 1990 to Outboard Marine Corporation (OMC), a manufacturer of outboard motors. Six years later, that company produced its last Grumman-brand canoe. But only a few months later, four former Grumman and OMC employees and an upstate investor formed Marathon Boat Group Inc. and began producing canoes again at the old Grumman plant. Nine different models of aluminum canoes are still made at the upstate factory located at 1 Grumman Way.[358]

Grumman's 129-foot *Denison*, the world's first oceangoing hydrofoil. *Courtesy of Northrop Grumman Corporation.*

Grumman also received new postwar business from the federal government. In 1957, the company was awarded a contract to build a large hydrofoil boat that would ride on wings above the waves. The company began working on it at the Bethpage plant in 1960 and launched it in Long Island Sound two years later. The 129-foot *Denison* was the world's first oceangoing hydrofoil. Riding on its three foils and propelled by a fourteen-thousand-horsepower engine, the vessel could travel at almost seventy miles an hour. That meant *Denison* could go from Oyster Bay to Newport, Rhode Island, in two hours.

Using what they had learned from building the *Denison*, Grumman engineers designed and constructed an eighty-passenger hydrofoil ferry named *Dolphin* in 1966. A Spanish firm used it as a ferry serving the Canary Islands off the west coast of Africa. Grumman also built the patrol boat USS *Flagstaff* for the navy in 1968 and two missile-equipped patrol boats for the Israeli navy in the early 1980s.[359]

Grumman competitor Republic Engine and Airplane Corporation in East Farmingdale expanded its product line after the war by building an

Republic Engine and Airplane Corporation's experimental *X-1* submarine built for the U.S. Navy after its launch at Jakobson Shipyard in Oyster Bay in 1955. *U.S. Navy, Submarine Force Museum.*

experimental "vest pocket" submarine. It designed and built the fifty-foot-long *X-1* for the U.S. Navy in 1954–55. Weighing twenty-five tons, it carried a crew of four. Its engine was powered by a volatile mixture of kerosene and peroxide that allowed it to travel underwater at ten and a half knots and dive to four hundred feet. It was launched at Jakobson Shipyard in Oyster Bay in September 1955 and underwent a month of sea trials in Long Island Sound before sailing on his own power to the navy submarine base in New London, Connecticut. During the navy's sea trials, the engine failed repeatedly and was modified. Then in May 1957, an explosion blew off the entire bow. The submarine was rebuilt with a conventional diesel-electric motor but remained inactive until 1960, when it began to be used at the U.S. Naval Shipyard in Philadelphia for research. In 1973, USS *X-1* was put on display at a naval station in Maryland. Since 2001, the submersible has been on display outside the U.S. Navy Submarine Force Museum in Groton, Connecticut.[360]

28

ROADSIDE ASSISTANCE ON THE WATER

C aptain Joe Frohnhoefer Jr. of Southold saw an opportunity in 1982 when Congress mandated that non-emergency distress calls be handled by private towing companies rather than the Coast Guard. He envisioned a company that would operate on the water the same way AAA, the American Automobile Association, functioned on the highways: members would be able to call for assistance around the clock and trained employees would respond.

"When the law was passed, I started meeting with independent tow [operators]," Frohnhoefer recalled in an interview. "It was a ragtag group of people with little boats that usually worked on weekends. I saw what we were facing. It was a monumental task, but I decided to take it on."

Frohnhoefer, a former marine police officer and bay constable, took out a $30,000 loan, bought a boat and, under the name Sea Tow, began helping stranded mariners. On September 3, 1983, Sea Tow Services International, headquartered in Southold, began operations.

"I worked with the Coast Guard to develop professionalism in the industry and to work hand in hand with them," Frohnhoefer said. "We more or less started this industry." Sea Tow's major competitor is the Boat Owners Association of the United States (BOAT/US), which runs a marine towing operation for its members.[361]

In 1989, Sea Tow started a sister organization, Sea Spill, to respond to fuel spills. The company moved into a new twenty-thousand-square-foot headquarters in Southold in 2006.

Sea Tow Services International founder Joe Frohnhoefer. *Courtesy of Sea Tow Services International.*

The next year, the nonprofit Sea Tow Foundation was formed to promote safe boating practices and prevent accidents. It operates three primary programs. The Life Jacket Loaner Program, with the help of hundreds of volunteers, has made 44,484 life jackets available to the public to borrow for free from 470 stations at boat ramps, marinas and parks. The Designated Sober Skipper Program asks boaters to "take the pledge" to be sober or designate a sober skipper. And the Beacon Rental Program provides EPIRB emergency locator beacons and personal locator beacons through a partnership with ACR Electronics.

In 2012, the company launched a free mobile app to allow boaters to call for help and get tide and other useful information. That same year, it also set up a free automated radio check system for marine radios that allows boaters to verify that their radios are working without tying up VHF channels used for important communication.

Frohnhoefer died in March 2015; his son, Captain Joe Frohnhoefer III, was named CEO and his daughter, Kristen Frohnhoefer, was named president in October 2015.

As of 2018, the family-run company had more than 110 independently owned franchise locations operating in more than 1,000 ports in the United States, Europe, the Virgin Islands and Puerto Rico. Its nearly 600 employees serve almost 200,000 members and other recreational boaters.[362]

29

LONG ISLAND MARITIME
HISTORY PRESERVED

Much of Long Island's maritime history has been lost over the past few centuries because little thought was given to the old and the emphasis was on the new and improved.

But through luck and the dedication of a few individuals or groups, some critical artifacts of the region's nautical past have survived. Eighteen of the twenty-one lighthouses are still standing; three are museums and four others can be visited at least occasionally (see chapter 11). The Amagansett Life-Saving Station has been restored as a museum (see chapter 16).

And in some cases, when historic boats haven't been saved, museums or nonprofit groups have created replicas. This chapter provides examples of both preserved vessels and those re-created.

CHRISTEEN

The oldest of five remaining New York or Long Island oyster sloops, the fifty-one-foot *Christeen* was constructed in Glenwood Landing in 1883 for William W. Smith of Oyster Bay. The Long Island or New York oyster sloop is a round-bottom centerboard boat with a shallow draft and broad beam. There were once thousands of them working in Long Island Sound, the Great South Bay and Rhode Island coastal waters. Now all that remain are *Christeen, Priscilla* and *Modesty* at the Long Island Maritime Museum in West

Sayville and two in Connecticut, *Hope* at the Maritime Center in Norwalk and *Nellie* at Mystic Seaport.

Smith named his boat, built to pull a dredge that would rake oysters from the bottom of the bay, after his wife. He kept the boat in Oyster Bay for four years. Then it went to a succession of owners in New York, New Jersey and Connecticut and almost disintegrated before returning to where it first sailed. *Christeen* was saved by volunteers on both sides of the sound to become an iconic symbol of Oyster Bay, where it takes groups out for environmental education or just enjoyment.

The story of the sloop's survival and revival began when three friends decided to start a maritime education center for Connecticut schoolchildren. They founded Tradewinds Education Network and bought *Christeen* for $1 in 1989 from the last private owner when the vessel was on the verge of destruction by neglect. They brought it to the Connecticut River Museum in Essex, recruited volunteers and raised funds. The group put almost eight thousand hours of work into the boat and spent $11,000 on materials. They made the boat watertight and painted it above the water line. They installed a new deck and cabin, rebuilt the engine, reinforced the mast and purchased new sails. But with the hull sagging on both ends and other problems still unaddressed as the economy remained in recession, the number of volunteers and available money dried up. The solution turned out to be returning *Christeen* to its original home.

This book's author had written several stories about the sloop for *Newsday* and kept in touch with Ben Clarkson, the head of the Connecticut group. When Clarkson related that the restoration project was foundering, the author suggested he arrange to bring the boat to Oyster Bay for the annual Oyster Festival to generate interest and possibly find people on Long Island to take over the project. He put Clarkson in touch with the head of the event, and *Christeen* was a hit at the 1991 festival.

The sloop was turned over to the Oyster Bay–based Friends of the Bay, which formed a Christeen Restoration Group that later became Christeen Oyster Sloop Preservation Corporation headed by Oyster Bay Town harbormaster Clint Smith. Over eight years, all of the boat's wooden structure except the rear portion of the keel—the lowest timber running the length of the hull—was replaced by volunteers led by professional shipwright David Short working in a shed at the former Jakobson shipyard. Then *Christeen* was relaunched in 1999. Three years later, the restoration group merged into the nonprofit WaterFront Center, an Oyster Bay marine education and recreation facility based at the former shipyard.

The Frank M. Flower & Sons dredge *Ida May*, which was demolished in 2011. A volunteer group has been building a replica in Oyster Bay. *Courtesy of Frank M. Flower & Sons.*

Eleven years after it had been relaunched following the initial restoration, the sloop, now designated as a National Historic Landmark, was hoisted from Oyster Bay for replacement of the rear section of the keel because the last original piece of the hull had begun to rot and leak.

Today, *Christeen*, the unofficial flagship of all the sailing vessels in the harbor, continues to take out groups for school and Scout trips, public sails and private charters.[363]

Ida May

The oyster dredge *Ida May* was launched in 1925 by Frank M. Flower & Sons of Oyster Bay and Bayville and spent almost eight decades scooping up shellfish from the shallow waters of Oyster Bay. The boat, one of the first oyster dredges in the harbor with an engine, was retired in 2003. Then the historic vessel languished on the harbor's southwestern shore for eight years awaiting a restoration that never came together in time. The project had begun, but the boat had deteriorated beyond repair and was demolished in 2011.

That was not the end of the *Ida May* story, however. The same group of volunteers who had restored the oyster sloop *Christeen* decided to create a working replica of the dredge in a shed near where the original spent its last years. The plan was to complete the boat in early 2013 and turn it over to the WaterFront Center, as had been done with *Christeen*, for environmental education, excursions and fishing trips.

But even though singer-songwriter Billy Joel, who has a large home across the harbor in Centre Island and had worked on an oyster dredge in the harbor as a teenager, donated $125,000 to the project and the group has received other donations and grants, funding has been a recurring problem. That has forced work to stop once and slow other times when there was no money to pay shipwright David Short to direct the volunteers.

When the dredge was dismantled in 2011, all that was salvageable was the oak keel and stem—the horizontal backbone for the boat and the vertical timber that formed the leading edge of the bow—along with some hardware and fittings that might be incorporated into the replica.

Even if the original forty-five-foot-long hull could have been restored, the group learned that it would never have passed the Coast Guard inspections for licensing to carry passengers. So the replica will be one foot wider, which will allow the boat to carry forty people and provide more space for educators to show how the craft dredged for oysters.

As of early 2019, the new *Ida May* was about two-thirds complete. The interior structure was almost finished and the rudder fitted. The volunteers had most of the necessary hull planking, and it was drying in the yard so it could be installed. The group was starting work on the pilothouse and hatch covers. And a tree had been acquired and milled to become the mast and boom. But even with substantial 2018 year-end donations, funding was still up in the air. No completion date for the project had been set, but the volunteers are hopeful for a launch in the summer of 2020.[364]

Priscilla and the Long Island Maritime Museum

Priscilla is one of two surviving South Shore oyster sloops out of a fleet that once numbered about five hundred. It was built in Patchogue in 1888 by Elisha Saxton, an early partner of Gil Smith, Long Island's best-known boat designer (see chapter 8). The gaff-rigged craft—the mainsail is supported by a heavy wooden gaff or pole—was built for George

Rhinehart, an oysterman from Lawrence. Rhinehart named his purchase for his new wife and worked the boat in Jamaica Bay and the Rockaways. A series of Connecticut oystermen owned it from 1900 to 1967, when it became a private yacht.

The sixty-foot-long sloop was donated to the Long Island Maritime Museum in West Sayville in 1976. *Priscilla* underwent a complete restoration in 2002–3. Shipwright Joshua Herman trained volunteers who replaced everything but part of the keel and some deck fittings, including the anchor winch and cleats. Designated a National Historic Landmark in 2005, the boat sailed only a few times after the restoration, and only with a museum crew aboard. Additional work was done on the rigging and sails, while a Coast Guard inspection led to the addition of three thousand pounds of lead ballast for added stability. Then the agency approved the museum's request to take out paying passengers, which Priscilla has been doing since 2010.[365]

Priscilla is not the only floating artifact at the museum founded in 1966 on fourteen acres once part of the former Florence and Anson Wales Hard estate. The museum also owns *Modesty*, a thirty-four-foot oyster- and scallop-dredging sloop built in 1923 and thought to be the last commercial sailing work boat built on Long Island. It is being stored in a barn pending funding for restoration. Also in the fleet is *Charlotte*, a twenty-six-foot tugboat built around 1880, and *Alice Victoria*, a forty-three-foot bay boat built in 1906.

The boats are not the only attractions at the museum. The former estate garage now houses display galleries and a library. The Frank F. Penney Boat Shop, where volunteers restore old boats and build replicas, was once the laundry building for the Brooklyn Hotel in Center Moriches. When the hotel burned down in 1907, Penney rescued the building for use at his boatyard on Senix Creek. In 1978, the boat shop was floated by barge to the museum. The William Rudolph Oyster House, another National Historic Landmark, is an example of the oyster culling houses that once dominated the South Shore. Built in 1909, it was used by Rudolph to process and distribute oysters. Originally located on Shore Road in West Sayville, it was relocated to the museum in 1975 and now houses historical displays. The Bayman's Cottage is an 1890 structure built for Mr. and Mrs. Leonard Beebe at 45 West Avenue in West Sayville and relocated to the museum in 1982.[366]

Bayles Boat Shop

The shop at the Long Island Seaport and Eco Center, part of the Port Jefferson Village Center, is located on Port Jefferson Harbor on the former site of the Bayles Shipyard that operated from 1797 to 1921. The shop was built in 2006 using traditional framing methods. It is one of several locations on Long Island where volunteers restore historic boats or build replicas of them. The project started in 1995. The volunteers gather several mornings a week to work on old and new power and sailing vessels.[367]

Elvira

It took a dozen years of restoration by volunteers, but in the summer of 2018, *Elvira*, a sailboat constructed by famed Patchogue boat builder Gil Smith (see chapter 8) in 1906, was relaunched for a new life.

Smith constructed the red- and cream-colored *Elvira* for Harry A. Walton of Bellport. One of Smith's last works, it won Bellport Bay Yacht Club's inaugural boat race in August 1906. At one time, P-Class sloops were one of the largest racing classes of boats to sail on the Great South Bay. Smith built about a dozen P-Class sloops in the early 1900s. "This is the only one that has survived and can sail," said Ralph Maust, president of the nonprofit Carmans River Maritime Center of Brookhaven hamlet, which did the restoration.

Brookhaven hamlet resident Bob Starke acquired *Elvira* from his father, who had purchased it around 1935. By the end of the twentieth century, the boat had been out of commission for a decade after a collision with a jetty. In 1999, Starke donated the boat to the Post-Morrow Foundation, the maritime center's parent organization, hoping it would be repaired and one day sail again.

"Almost the whole boat has been rebuilt," Maust said. "The planking is original to the boat, but everything else—the interior framework and the deck—was rebuilt." The volunteers supervised by shipwright Joshua Herman put in 2,500 hours of work. The thirty-eight-foot sloop has also been listed in the National Register of Historic Places.[368]

There are numerous other Long Island institutions and nonprofit groups that have gathered and preserved artifacts and historic documents. They range geographically and thematically from the American Merchant

Marine Museum in Kings Point to the Montauk Point Lighthouse. In between, history buffs can enjoy sites such as the East Hampton Town Marine Museum in Amagansett and the East End Classic Boat Society, which builds replica boats behind the museum, the Cold Spring Harbor Whaling Museum and many others. They—and this book—are all part of the ongoing effort to ensure Long Island's maritime history is not forgotten.

NOTES

Chapter 1

1. Shodell, *Cross Currents*, 17.
2. Strong, *Algonquian Peoples*, 41; Stone, *Shinnecock Indians*, 32.
3. Lippman, "Forgotten Contest."
4. Bookbinder, *Long Island*, 23.
5 Stone, *Shinnecock Indians*, 34.

Chapter 2

6. Lippman, "Forgotten Contest"; Stoff, *From Canoes to Cruisers*, 15; Wick, "Stranded in a Strange Land"; Wick, "Property of the Netherlands"; Weigold, *American Mediterranean*, 4.

Chapter 3

7. Strong, *Algonquian Peoples*, 41; Lippman, "Forgotten Contest"; Matthiessen, *Men's Lives*, 11; Stoff, *From Canoes to Cruisers*, 11–13.
8. Stone, *Shinnecock Indians*, 32; Dayan, *Whaling*, 7.
9. Dayan, *Whaling*, 7; Strong, "Indian Whalers."
10. Strong, "Indian Whalers"; Stone, *Shinnecock Indians*, 34.

11. Stone, *Shinnecock Indians*, 231.

12. Dayan, *Whaling*, 14, 16; Stoff, *From Canoes to Cruisers*, 17.

13. Dayan, *Whaling*, 16; Nuccio, "Of Whales"; Stone, *Shinnecock Indians*, 231; Schmitt, *Mark Well*, 8.

14. Dayan, *Whaling*, 16.

15. Schmitt, *Mark Well*, 8; Stoff, *From Canoes to Cruisers*, 17.

16. Stone, *Shinnecock Indians*, 231–32; Matheson, *Men's Lives*, 14.

17. Stone, *Shinnecock Indians*, 231–32.

18. Dayan, *Whaling*, 7.

19. Ibid.

20. Ibid., 7, 14, 29.

21. Strong, "Indian Whalers"; Stone, *Shinnecock Indians*, 233; Lippman, "Forgotten Contest"; Stoff, *From Canoes to Cruisers*, 11–13.

22. Schmitt, *Mark Well*, 45.

23. Ibid., 49.

24. Stoff, *From Canoes to Cruisers*, 17.

25. Wick, "In Search of Whales"; Dayan, *Whaling*, 8.

26. Turano, "Papers of William Cooper."

27. Wick, "In Search of Whales"; Dayan, *Whaling*, 9.

28. Dayan, *Whaling*, 9; Matthiessen, *Men's Lives*, 16.

29. New Bedford Whaling Museum, Inventory; *Friend* (Honolulu, HI), "Japan."

30. Bleyer, "Cold Welcome"; James, "Freed Slave's Southampton Property."

31. James, "Freed Slave's Southampton Property"; Euler, "Pyrrhus Concer Home."

32. Wiggin, "Maritime History"; Dayan, *Whaling*, 117.

33. Wiggin, "Maritime History."

34. Ibid.

35. Ibid.

36. Schmitt, *Mark Well*, 8–11.

37. Ibid., 13, 23–24; Watson, *Houses for Science*, 184, 190.

38. Schmitt, *Mark Well*, 24.

39. Ibid., 39, 44, 85–89, 94–96, 125.

40. Ibid., 8–9, 124–25; MacKay, Rossano and Traynor, *Between Ocean*, 84–85; Dayan, *Whaling*, 33, 47, 117; Stoff, *From Canoes to Cruisers*, 35, 37.

41. Schmitt, de Jong and Winter, *Thomas Welcome Roys*, 18–19, 23.

42. Ibid., 2, 22, 26, 28, 197; *Newsday* staff, "Milestones in Transportation," 388.

43. Schmitt, de Jong and Winter, *Thomas Welcome Roys*, 33, 50.

44. Ibid., 57, 59; Wallace, "Rare Catch."

45. Schmitt, de Jong and Winter, *Thomas Welcome Roys*, 64, 66–67, 80–81, 181, 198.

46. Ibid., 71.

47. Ibid., 67, 197; Stoff, *From Canoes to Cruisers*, 35, 37; Dayan, *Whaling*, 8.

48. Schmitt, de Jong and Winter, *Thomas Welcome Roys*, ix, x, 98.

49. Ibid., 81.

50. Ibid., 86.

51. Ibid., ix, 86, 197–99.

52. Wick, "In Search of Whales."

53. Ibid.

54. Ibid.

55. Schmitt, *Mark Well*, 59–60.

56. Wick, "In Search of Whales"; Wiggin, "Maritime History."

57. Hanc, "Long Island Spotlights."

58. Ibid.

59. Ibid.

60. Ibid.

61. Ibid.

62. MacKay, *She Went*, 56; Druett and Wallace, *Sailing Circle*, 36–39.

63. MacKay, *She Went*, 55.

64. Ibid., 57; Druett and Wallace, *Sailing Circle*, 36–39.

65. MacKay, *She Went*, 13, 16, 33, 82; Bleyer, "Seafaring Women."

66. Bleyer, "Wife Copes."

67. Ibid.

68. Dayan, *Whaling*, 8.

69. Wiggin, "Maritime History"; Dayan, *Whaling*, 117.

70. MacKay, Rossano and Traynor, *Between Ocean*, 84–85; Dayan, *Whaling*, 33, 47, 117; Schmitt, *Mark Well*, 126.

71. Dayan, *Whaling*, 117; Matthiessen, *Men's Lives*, 16.

72. Matthiessen, *Men's Lives*, 17.

73. Roth, *Sag Harbor*, 18.

Chapter 4

74. Matthiessen, *Men's Lives*, 11–12, 15.

75. Ibid.; Stoff, *From Canoes to Cruisers*, 67.

76. Research by Southold Town Historian Amy Folk; Wiggin, "Oil & Fertilizer."

77. Research by Southold Town Historian Amy Folk.

78. Ibid.; Wiggin, "Oil & Fertilizer"; Bolster, *Mortal Sea*, 171.

79. Wiggin, "Oil & Fertilizer."

80. Research by Southold Town Historian Amy Folk; Stoff, *From Canoes to Cruisers*, 49–51.

81. Research by Southold Town Historian Amy Folk.

82. Ibid.; Corwin and Corwin, *Greenport Yesterday and Today*, 218; Wiggin, "Oil & Fertilizer."

83. Corwin and Corwin, *Greenport Yesterday and Today*, 219; Wiggin, "Oil & Fertilizer."

84. Wiggin, "Oil & Fertilizer."

85. Ibid.; Geus, *From Sea to Sea*, 176; research by Southold Town Historian Amy Folk.

86. Shodell, *Cross Currents*, 9; Stoff, *From Canoes to Cruisers*, 67.

87. Matthiessen, *Men's Lives*, 16.

88. Stoff, *From Canoes to Cruisers*, 67.

89. Matthiessen, *Men's Lives*, 24.

90. Geus, *From Sea to Sea*, 173.

91. Stoff, *From Canoes to Cruisers*, 67.

92. Matthiessen, *Men's Lives*, 26, 39.

93. Ibid., 162–164.

94. Griffith, "LI Fishing Families."

Chapter 5

95. Stoff, *From Canoes to Cruisers*, 63–65.

96. Hunt, *Long Island and the Civil War*, 56.

97. Stoff, *From Canoes to Cruisers*, 63–65.

98. Ibid.

99. Ibid.

100. Bleyer, "Oyster Wars."

101. Stoff, *From Canoes to Cruisers*, 63–65; Bleyer, "Oyster Wars."

102. Bleyer, "Oyster Wars."

103. Ibid.

104. Ibid.

105. Stoff, *From Canoes to Cruisers*, 63–65; Bleyer, "Oyster Wars."

106. Nuccio, "Shell Fishing"; Coburn, "Glory Days."

107. Bleyer, "The Doxsee."

108. Stephens, *Seawanhaka Corinthian Yacht Club*, xvi; Bleyer, "Legacy."

109. Shodell, *Cross Currents*, 9, 17.
110. Bleyer, "Oyster Wars"; Bleyer, "Legacy"; Olson, "Shellfish Firm Faces Lawsuit."
111. Wiggin, "History of the Greenport."
112. Harrington, "Huge Scallop Harvest"; statistics from the New York State Department of Environmental Conservation.
113. Schneider, "Tale of Lobstering."
114. Solomon, *On the Bay*, 6, 28.
115. Bleyer, "Bay Windows."
116. Solomon, *On the Bay*, 6, 20.
117. Bleyer, "Bay Windows."
118. Dazio, "Shelling Out"; Hampton, "Grant Boosts"; Hampton, "Board Passes"; Merritt, "Catching a Rising Tide."

Chapter 6

119. Stoff, *From Canoes to Cruisers*, 15.
120. Bookbinder, *Long Island*, 72; Huntington Historical Society, "Van Wyck-Leffers Tide Mill," http://huntingtonhistoricalsociety.org/van-wyck-lefferts-tide-mill; Nassau County, "Saddle Rock Grist Mill," nassaucountyny.gov/2947/Saddle-Rock-Grist-Mill.
121. Bleyer, "Feversham."
122. *Newsday* staff, "Milestones in Transportation"; Preservation Long Island, preservationlongisland.org.
123. Rossano, "To Market."
124. Ibid.
125. Griswold, *Manor*, 64–66.
126. Stoff, *From Canoes to Cruisers*, 53; Bookbinder, *Long Island*, 96–98.

Chapter 7

127. Stoff, *From Canoes to Cruisers*, 19; Wick, "Legend of Capt. Kidd."

Chapter 8

128. Welch, *Island's Trade*, 1.

129. Ibid., ix, 11–12, 14, 18.

130. Stoff, *From Canoes to Cruisers*, 45; Bookbinder, *Long Island*, 96–98; Welch, *Island's Trade*, 4; Bleyer, "Shipshape in Suffolk."

131. Welch, *Island's Trade*, x–xi.

132. Ibid., 18.

133. Rossano, "Prosperity on the Ways."

134. Ibid.

135. Ibid.

136. Shipbuilding History, "Jakobson Shipyard, Oyster Bay, NY," http://shipbuildinghistory.com/shipyards/small/jakobson.htm; Jakobson Shipyard records held by Oyster Bay Town Historian John Hammond; McQuiston, "State Will Buy."

137. Brookhaven Town Records, vol. 1, 1662–1679, book II, page 124, entry July 24, 1662.

138. Minuse, "Shipbuilding."

139. Ibid., Welch, *Island's Trade*, 2, 31; Welles, *Port Jefferson*, 8–11.

140. Welch, *Island's Trade*, 18; Stoff, *From Canoes to Cruisers*, 47; Welles, *Port Jefferson*, 17.

141. Welch, *Island's Trade*, 18–20; Welles, *Port Jefferson*, 41–45; Stoff, *From Canoes to Cruisers*, 73.

142. Welles, *Port Jefferson*, 41–45; Stoff, *From Canoes to Cruisers*, 73.

143. Welch, *Island's Trade*, 2–3; Stoff, *From Canoes to Cruisers*, 45.

144. Northport Historical Society exhibit.

145. Welch, *Island's Trade*, 19–20.

146. Wiggin, "Shipbuilding in Greenport."

147. Welch, *Island's Trade*, 3.

148. Wiggin, "Shipbuilding in Greenport."

149. Welch, *Island's Trade*, 18–19.

150. Wiggin, "Greenport Builds"; information from Steve Clarke of Greenport Yacht & Ship Building Co.

151. Bleyer, "Gil Smith"; Suffolk County Historical Society, "Gil Smith"; Wooden Boatworks, "Gilbert Monroe Smith," woodenboatworks.com/index.php/designers/yacht/Smith.

152. Dinn, *Boats by Purdy*, 13, 20, 25–27, 31, 64, 73–75, 91, 93, 96, 100, 107–8; Moore, *Yachts in a Hurry*, 78, 80–82.

153. Bleyer, "Staying Afloat"; Long Island Traditions boatbuilding exhibit.

154. Long Island Traditions boatbuilding exhibit.
155. Ibid.; author interview with Fred Scopinich.
156. Long Island Traditions boatbuilding exhibit; Steiger Craft, steigercraft.com.

Chapter 9

157. Branson, Fleming and Folk, *World Unto Itself*, 31–33.
158. Zaykowski, *Sag Harbor*, 57.
159. De Wan, "Whaleboat Warfare."
160. Ibid.; Grasso, *American Revolution*, 50–51.
161. Griffin, *Lost British Forts*, 115–17; De Wan, "Whaleboat Warfare"; Pam Johnson, "A Revolutionary Effort: Reynolds Helps 6th CT Commemorate 'Meigs' Raid," Zip 06, May 16, 2018, www.zip06.com/profile/20180516/a-revolutionary-effort-reynolds-helps-6th-ct-commemorate-x2018meigsx2019-raidx2019.
162. Griffin, *Lost British Forts*, 85–88; De Wan, "Whaleboat Warfare."
163. Griffin, *Lost British Forts*, 49–56; De Wan, "Whaleboat Warfare"; Grasso, *American Revolution*, 50–51.
164. Griffin, *Lost British Forts*, 93–99; De Wan, "Whaleboat Warfare"; Bayles, *Early Years*, 25; Luke and Venables, *Long Island*, 49; Onderdonk, *Revolutionary Incidents*, 99.
165. Griffin, *Lost British Forts*, 79–84; De Wan, "Whaleboat Warfare"; Harris, *Battle of Fort Slongo*, 5–7, 9–11; *Documents of the Assembly*, 293; Bayles, *Early Years*, 25.
166. Bleyer, "Warship Defeated"; Schmitt and Schmid, *H.M.S. Culloden*, 42–46; Aqua Explorers, aquaexplorers.com.
167. Griffin, *Lost British Forts*, 59–62.
168. De Wan, "Long Island Exodus"; interview with Oyster Bay Town Historian John Hammond.

Chapter 10

169. Information from Beverly Tyler, historian of the Three Village Historical Society.
170. Ibid.; De Wan, "Washington's Eyes"; Rose, *Washington's Spies*, 132–54.
171. De Wan, "Ruse." Note that the popular AMC television series on the spy ring, *Turn*, takes considerable liberty with the facts.

Chapter 11

172. Research by Robert Müller, U.S. Lighthouse Society.
173. Osmers, *On Eagle's Beak*, 323–25; Bleyer, "Beautiful Beacons"; Bleyer, "Lighthouses of Long Island"; Müller, *New York State Lighthouses*, 116–18; Müller, *Long Island's Lighthouses*, 232.
174. Bleyer, "Beautiful Beacons"; Bleyer, "Lighthouses of Long Island"; Müller, *Long Island's Lighthouses*, 77, 89.
175. Lighthouse Friends, lighthousefriends.com; Bleyer, "Beautiful Beacons"; Bleyer, "Lighthouses of Long Island"; Müller, *Long Island's Lighthouses*, 164, 167–68; Branson, *World Unto Itself*, 116.
176. Bleyer, "Beautiful Beacons"; Bleyer, "Lighthouses of Long Island"; Müller, *Long Island's Lighthouses*, 33–34.
177. Müller, *New York State Lighthouses*, 98; Müller, *Long Island's Lighthouses*, 93–94; Bleyer, "Beautiful Beacons"; Bleyer, "Lighthouses of Long Island."
178. Bleyer, *Fire Island Lighthouse*, 99, 115–17; Müller, *New York State Lighthouses*, 127.
179. Müller, *New York State Lighthouses*, 108; Bleyer, "Beautiful Beacons"; Bleyer, "Lighthouses of Long Island"; Müller, *Long Island's Lighthouses*, 143, 162.
180. Bleyer, "Beautiful Beacons"; Bleyer, "Lighthouses of Long Island"; Müller, *Long Island's Lighthouses*, 251, 261; Peraino, "Architects Chosen."
181. Bleyer, "Beautiful Beacons"; Bleyer, "Lighthouses of Long Island"; Müller, *New York State Lighthouses*, 112; Müller, *Long Island's Lighthouses*, 211, 213.
182. Bleyer, "Beautiful Beacons"; Bleyer, "Lighthouses of Long Island"; Merritt, "Long Island's Islands"; Hamilton, *Lights & Legends*, 27.
183. Kuperschmid, "Ghosts of Gardiner's"; Müller, *Long Island's Lighthouses*, 243–50.
184. Bleyer, "Beautiful Beacons"; Bleyer, "Lighthouses of Long Island"; Müller, *Long Island's Lighthouses*, 62; Hamilton, *Lights & Legends*, 46.
185. Bleyer, "Beautiful Beacons"; Bleyer, "Lighthouses of Long Island"; Müller, *Long Island's Lighthouses*, 113, 117–18.
186. Bleyer, "Beautiful Beacons"; Bleyer, "Lighthouses of Long Island"; Müller, *New York State Lighthouses*, 121–22; Müller, *Long Island's Lighthouses*, 276.
187. Müller, *New York State Lighthouses*, 103; Bleyer, "Lighthouses of Long Island"; Bleyer, "New Keeper"; Müller, *Long Island's Lighthouses*, 129–30, 132.

188. Müller, *Long Island's Lighthouses*, 214, 217, 222.

189. Bleyer, "Beautiful Beacons"; Bleyer, "Lighthouses of Long Island"; Save Stepping Stones Lighthouse, steppingstoneslight.com.

190. Bleyer, "Beautiful Beacons"; Bleyer, "Lighthouses of Long Island"; Müller, *Long Island's Lighthouses*, 190; New London Maritime Society, nlmaritimesociety.org.

191. Müller, *New York State Lighthouses*, 92; Müller, *Long Island's Lighthouses*, 56, 59; Bleyer, "Lighthouses of Long Island"; Hamilton, "Cold Spring Harbor Light"; Bachand, "Cold Spring Harbor Lighthouse."

192. Müller, *New York State Lighthouses*, 104–7; Müller, *Long Island's Lighthouses*, 140; Bleyer, "Beautiful Beacons"; Bleyer, "Lighthouses of Long Island."

193. Bleyer, "Beautiful Beacons"; Bleyer, "Lighthouses of Long Island"; Huntington Lighthouse Preservation Society, huntingtonlighthouse.org; Bleyer, "Preservationists Band"; Bleyer, "Lighthouse Leased"; Morris, "Renovation."

Chapter 12

194. Bleyer, "War on the Waters"; Wick, "Sag Harbor's Heyday."

195. Bleyer, "War on the Waters"; Southold Historical Society, "War of 1812," www.southoldhistoricalsociety.org/lh-war-of-1812-display.

196. Bleyer, "War on the Waters."

197. Ibid.

198. Ibid.

199. U.S. Coast Guard, www.uscg.mil.

200. Squire, "Tale of the Cutter."

201. Southold Historical Society, "War of 1812"; Rattray, *Ship Ashore!*, 44–46.

202. Bleyer, "War on the Waters"; *East Hampton Star* staff, "Wreck of H.M.S. *Sylph*."

Chapter 13

203. Hammond, *Oyster Bay Remembered*, 313–14.

204. Bleyer, "Water World"; Stoff, *From Canoes to Cruisers*, 59.

205. Weigold, *American Mediterranean*, 35–36.

206. Dunbaugh, *Long Island Sound Steamboats*, 2.

207. Ibid.

208. Brouwer, *Steamboats*, 8–9; Dunbaugh, *Long Island Sound Steamboats*, 2; Weigold, *American Mediterranean*, 37.

209. Dunbaugh, *Night Boat*, 27; Weigold, *American Mediterranean*, 38–39.

210. Brouwer, *Steamboats*, 8–9; Dunbaugh, *Long Island Sound Steamboats*, 2; Weigold, *American Mediterranean*, 37.

211. Dunbaugh, *Long Island Sound Steamboats*, 2, 4; Weigold, *American Mediterranean*, 39.

212. Dunbaugh, *Long Island Sound Steamboats*, 4; Weigold, *American Mediterranean*, 40.

213. Dunbaugh, *Long Island Sound Steamboats*, 4.

214. Bleyer, "Wreck of the *Lexington*"; Weigold, *Long Island Sound*, 41–42; Field, *Wrecks and Rescues*, 29; Dunbaugh, *Long Island Sound Steamboats*, 4.

215. Grohman, "Daniel and His Date"; Weigold, *American Mediterranean*, 41; *Sailor's Magazine*, "Tolling Bell."

216. Dunbaugh, *Long Island Sound Steamboats*, 4; Dunbaugh, *Night Boat*, 104–6; Brouwer, *Steamboats*, 8–9.

217. Dunbaugh, *Long Island Sound Steamboats*, 9; Dunbaugh, *Night Boat*, 181–82.

218. Dunbaugh, *Long Island Sound Steamboats*, 2.

219. Brouwer, *Steamboats*, 8–9.

220. Dunbaugh, *Long Island Sound Steamboats*, 13, 16.

221. Brouwer, *Steamboats*, 8–9; Dunbaugh, *Long Island Sound Steamboats*, 17.

222. Hammond, *Oyster Bay Remembered*, 239, 313.

223. Stoff, *From Canoes to Cruisers*, 59–61; Mundus, "Starboard Tack"; Dunbaugh, *Long Island Sound Steamboats*, 11.

224. Dunbaugh, *Long Island Sound Steamboats*, 7.

225. Bleyer, "Rye Cliff Ferry."

226. *Bridgeport & Port Jefferson*, 6–8, 10, 14–16; Bridgeport & Port Jefferson Steamboat Company, "History," 88844ferry.com/AboutUs/History.aspx; information from the Bridgeport & Port Jefferson Steamboat Company.

227. Cross Sound Ferry Services, "History of Achievements."

228. Shodell, *Port Washington*, 67; Walton, *Cold Spring Harbor*, 32–36.

229. Blidner, "Ferry Smooth Service"; information from Fire Island Ferries Inc.

230. Wiggin, "Beebe McLellan"; information from the North Ferry Company.

231. Information from the South Ferry Company.

Chapter 14

232. Stoff, *From Canoes to Cruisers*, 39–41; Geus, *From Sea to Sea*, 162.
233. Field, *Wrecks and Rescues*, 27; Bleyer, *Fire Island Lighthouse*, 15.
234. Braynard, *S.S. Savannah*, 199–204; Grohman, *Claimed by the Sea*, 13–21; Bleyer, *Fire Island Lighthouse*, 17, 19.
235. Mattson, *Water and Ice*, 58–61, 64, 66, 70, 88–92, 96–101, 106–7; Field, *Wrecks and Rescues*, 144.
236. Mattson, *Water and Ice*, 138, 157, 164, 170, 179–81, 183–88, 190–98, 201–2, 205, 227–28, 232, 239; Field, *Wrecks and Rescues*, 144; Nuccio, "*Bristol*"; Whitman, *Complete Poetry*, 111, 696.
237. Rattray, *Ship Ashore!*, 31–32; Field, *Wrecks and Rescues*, 123–26; Bleyer, *Fire Island Lighthouse*, 28.
238. Stone, *Shinnecock Indians*, 367–93; Field, *Wrecks and Rescues*, 46–49; Geus, *From Sea to Sea*, 162; Nuccio, "More than Brave."
239. Grohman, *Claimed by the Sea*, 62–70; Bleyer, "Claimed by the Sea"; Ward Melville Heritage Organization, "Hercules Pavilion," wmho.org/attractions/hercules-pavilion.
240. Field, *Wrecks and Rescues*, 117–22; Rattray, *Ship Ashore!*, 145–50; Grohman, *Claimed by the Sea*, 87–105.
241. Kaasman, *Oregon*, 7, 77, 174; Grohman, *Claimed by the Sea*, 71–86; Bleyer, *Fire Island Lighthouse*, 52.
242. Grohman, *Claimed by the Sea*, 166–83; Bleyer, "Claimed by the Sea."

Chapter 15

243. De Wan, "Captives of the *Amistad*," 183.
244. The remains of *Clotilda*, which was scuttled and burned after the voyage, were discovered by an Alabama reporter who revealed his discovery in early 2018; Alabama, AL.com.
245. Brown, "Divergent Foes"; History Close at Hand, historycloseathand.com; History Channel, history.com.

Chapter 16

246. Field, *Wrecks and Rescues*, foreword, 2; Mattson, *Water and Ice*, 254–55; Bleyer, "Lifeline for Sailors."

247. Bleyer, "Lifeline for Sailors."
248. Noble, *Legacy*, 4–5; Gonzalez, *Storms, Ships & Surfmen*, 11–12; Field, *Wrecks and Rescues*, foreword, 2; Bleyer, "Lifeline for Sailors."
249. Field, *Wrecks and Rescues*, foreword; Bleyer, "Lifeline for Sailors"; Stoff, *From Canoes to Cruisers*, 43.
250. Field, *Wrecks and Rescues*, 100; Bleyer, "Lifeline for Sailors."
251. Field, *Wrecks and Rescues*, 17–19.
252. Keatts, *Shipwrecks & Lighthouses*, 28; Geus, *From Sea to Sea*, 168–69, 171; "Restoration of Amagansett Life-Saving Station"; Field, *Wrecks and Rescues*, 51.
253. Field, *Wrecks and Rescues*, 8; Wiggin, "Beebe McLellan Surf Boats."

Chapter 17

254. Hunt and Bleyer, *Long Island*, 78, 85–86; Spann, *Gotham at War*, 158.

Chapter 18

255. Zaykowski, *Sag Harbor*, 266–67.
256. Bleyer, "Submarines in LI"; Bleyer, "Rising Out."
257. Stoff, *From Canoes to Cruisers*, 71.

Chapter 19

258. Stoff, *From Canoes to Cruisers*, 8; Rafferty, *Guardian of the Sound*, xi.
259. Ibid., xv.
260. Ibid.
261. Ibid., vi.
262. Rafferty, *Guardian of the Sound*, xvi; Stoff, *From Canoes to Cruisers*, 81; Kuperschmid, "Ghosts of Gardiner's"; Müller, *Long Island's Lighthouses*, 154.
263. Bramson, *World Unto Itself*, 112.
264. Ibid.
265. Bramson, Fleming and Folk, "Coastal Forts"; Bramson, *World Unto Itself*, 112.

266. Bramson, *World Unto Itself*, 113, 116; New York State Military Museum, "Fort Michie," dmna.ny.gov/forts/fortsM_P/michieFort.htm.
267. Bramson, *World Unto Itself*, 141–45, 147, 194, 197–98, 201, 203; Bramson, Fleming and Folk, "Coastal Forts."
268. Rafferty, *Guardian of the Sound*, ix.
269. Ibid., vi.
270. Ibid., x.
271. Ibid.
272. Ibid., vi.
273. Ibid., vi, xix.
274. Ibid., vii, xviii.
275. Ibid., vii.
276. Ibid.
277. Ibid.
278. Bramson, *World Unto Itself*, 198.
279. Rafferty, *Guardian of the Sound*, vii.
280. Ibid.
281. Kuperschmid, "Ghosts of Gardiner's"; Bramson, Fleming and Folk, "Coastal Forts."
282. Bramson, Fleming and Folk, "Coastal Forts."
283. Camp Hero, "Time Line," camphero.net; U.S. Army Corps of Engineers, "Fact Sheet—Camp Hero," www.nan.usace.army.mil/Media/Fact-Sheets/Fact-Sheet-Article-View/Article/626470/fact-sheet-camp-hero; Stoff, *From Canoes to Cruisers*, 81.

Chapter 20

284. Needham, "Theodore Roosevelt."
285. Roosevelt, "Outdoors and Indoors," October 25, 1913.
286. Bleyer, *Sagamore Hill*, 46–47.
287. Ibid., 56–57, 85.
288. Hammond, *Oyster Bay Remembered*, 111–12.
289. Bleyer, *Sagamore Hill*, 15–19; Reckner, "Fleet Triumphant."
290. Grohman, *Presidential Plunge*, 58–62, 70.

Chapter 21

291. Gentile, *U.S.S. San Diego*, 55–65; Bleyer, "Sinking of the *San Diego*"; Hampton Roads Naval Museum, "Remembering USS *San Diego* at Christmastime," http://hamptonroadsnavalmuseum.blogspot.com/2014/12/remembering-uss-san-diego-at.html.
292. Bleyer, "Sinking of the *San Diego*"; Aqua Explorers, aquaexplorers.com.
293. Welles, *Port Jefferson*, 41–45; Stoff, *From Canoes to Cruisers*, 73; Welch, *Long Island*, 19–20.

Chapter 22

294. Stoff, *Long Island Airports*, 7, 23–34.
295. Kroplick, "North Hempstead," 78.
296. Ibid., 77.
297. Welch, *Long Island*, 28–31.
298. Stoff, *Long Island Airports*, 35–36, 52.

Chapter 23

299. Stephens, *Seawanhaka Corinthian Yacht Club*, 3–5.
300. Ibid., 7, 20.
301. Ibid., 7, 9–10.
302. Ibid., 15; Sewanhaka Corinthian Yacht Club, "History of the Club," seawanhaka.org/About/History.
303. Stephens, *Seawanhaka Corinthian Yacht Club*, 15–20.
304. Ibid., xvi–xvii, 20–21, 129, 138.
305. Ibid., 103–4.
306. Ibid., 195–96.
307. Ibid., 198; Sewanhaka Corinthian Yacht Club, "History of the Club."
308. Sewanhaka Corinthian Yacht Club, "History of the Club"; Stephens, *Seawanhaka Corinthian Yacht Club*, 21.
309. Newcomb, *Lloyd's Register*; MacKay, *Great Yachts*, 7–8; Manhasset Bay Yacht Club, "History," manhassetbayyc.org/About/History; Sayville Yacht Club, sayvilleyachtclub.org; Bleyer, "Knickerbocker Club."
310. MacKay, *Great Yachts*, 7–8; Reynolds, "New York Yacht Club."
311. Parkinson, *Seawanhaka Corinthian Yacht Club*, 62.

312. Moore, *Yachts in a Hurry*, 34; Bleyer, "Historian Chronicles."

313. MacKay, *Great Yachts*, 8.

314. Moore, *Yachts in a Hurry*, 7–8.

315. Ibid.

316. Ibid., 23, 33.

317. Ibid., 23–24, 26, 35.

318. MacKay, *Great Yachts*, 7.

319. Moore, *Yachts in a Hurry*, 9.

320. Ibid., 10.

321. Ibid.

322. MacKay, *Great Yachts*, 7–8; Moore, *Yachts in a Hurry*, 11, 23.

323. Moore, *Yachts in a Hurry*, 156, 159.

324. MacKay, *Great Yachts*, 7–8; Bleyer, "Knickerbocker Club."

325. Around Long Island Regatta, alir.org.

326. WaterFront Center, thewaterfrontcenter.org.

327. Herreshoff Marine Museum, www.herreshoff.org; *Newsday* staff, "Milestones in Transportation"; "Capt. Hank Haff Is Dead," *New York Times*, July 1, 1906.

328. Village of Greenport, "History," villageofgreenport.org/history-maritime-greenport-village.php; Mundus, "Starboard Tack."

329. Bleyer, "Training Sailing Champs"; Dawn Riley, "Biography," dawnriley.com/biography.

330. MacKay, *Great Yachts*, 8.

331. "Powerboats Compete in Freeport Grand Prix"; "5th Annual Freeport Grand Prix Set for August"; "Speedboat Regatta Slated for Sunday"; nationalpowerboat.com/around-long-island-2.htm.

332. Sorrentino, "Battle on the Bay Races."

Chapter 24

333. Bleyer, "Rumrunners Run."

334. Stoff, *From Canoes to Cruisers*, 79.

335. Olly, "Long Island During Prohibition"; Koetzner, "Rum Runner's Adventures."

336. Long Island Traditions boatbuilders' exhibit; Olly, "Long Island During Prohibition."

337. Olly, "Long Island During Prohibition."

338. Aqua Explorers, aquaexplorers.com.

339. Solomon, *On the Bay*, 24.

340. Grohman, *Runner Aground*, 12, 15–17, 33–35, 45, 78; Upright, *Times and Tides*, 46–48; "Rum Ship," *New York Times*, February 21, 1927; "Wrecked Rum," *New York Times*, February 22, 1927; "Wrecked Schooner," *New York Times*, February 27, 1927; "Davy Jones's," *New York Times*, March 27, 1927; "Owners of Stranded Ship," *Oyster Bay Guardian*, February 26, 1927.

341. Olly, "Long Island During Prohibition."

342. Bleyer, "Rumrunners Run"; Olly, "Long Island During Prohibition"; Koetzer, "Rum Runner's Adventures."

343. Stoff, *From Canoes to Cruisers*, 79.

Chapter 25

344. Bachand, *Northeast Lights*, 251.

345. Stoff, *From Canoes to Cruisers*, 87.

346. Osmers, *American Gibraltar*, 60–66.

347. Bleyer, "70-Year-Old Cutter"; Mundus, "All American."

348. Wiggin, "Greenport Builds"; information from Steve Clarke of Greenport Yacht & Ship Building Co.

349. Jakobson Shipyard records held by Oyster Bay Town Historian John Hammond; NavSource Naval History, navsource.org; McQuiston, "State Will Buy"; Long Island Traditions boatbuilders exhibit; Moore, *Yachts in a Hurry*, 78, 80–82.

350. Dobbs, *Saboteurs*, 91–106, 108, 125–26, 141–43, 145–46, 181–82, 264, 273; Federal Bureau of Investigation, "Nazi Saboteurs and George Dasch," www.fbi.gov/history/famous-cases/nazi-saboteurs-and-george-dasch; Wick, "Nazi 'Invasion' of LI"; Bleyer, "Military Way."

351. Aqua Explorers, aquaexplorers.com.

Chapter 26

352. Merchant Marine Academy, *Place in History*; Cruikshank, *In Peace*, 44, 46, 47, 76, 79, 85, 93, 99–100, 151, 157–58, 161; Bleyer, "Kings Point Story."

353. Kelly, *Webb Institute*, 7; Dunbaugh, *Centennial History*, 79–80.

354. Dunbaugh, *Centennial History*, 135, 137.

355. Webb Institute, webb.edu.

356. Olson, "Small College."

Chapter 27

357. Stoff, *From Canoes to Cruisers*, 89.
358. Striegel, "Paddling a Canoe"; Blasl, "John H. Achilich."
359. Stoff, *From Canoes to Cruisers*, 89.
360. Douglas, "Farmingdale's Submarine."

Chapter 28

361. "Former Marine Starts," *Entrepreneur Magazine*, July 26, 2013.
362. Information from Sea Tow Services International.

Chapter 29

363. Bleyer, "Making It Shipshape"; Bleyer, "Historic Sloop"; Bleyer, "New Look"; information from the WaterFront Center.
364. Bleyer, "Keeping History"; Bleyer, "Fundraising for Ship"; information from Christeen Oyster Sloop Preservation Corporation.
365. Bleyer, "Sailing Past"; Bleyer, "History Takes Sail."
366. Long Island Maritime Museum, limaritime.org/exhibits.html; information from the Long Island Maritime Museum.
367. Long Island Traditions boatbuilding exhibit.
368. Hampton, "Recouped Sloop"; information from Carmans River Maritime Center.

BIBLIOGRAPHY

Applebome, Peter. "The Recession Takes Down a Yacht Club." *New York Times*, February 11, 2009.

Bachand, Robert G. "Cold Spring Harbor Lighthouse." *Long Island Forum*, November 1, 1990.

———. "Fire Island Lightship." *The Keeper's Log*, Summer 2000.

———. *Northeast Lights: Lighthouses and Lightships.* Norwalk, CT: Sea Sports Publications, 1989.

Bayles, Thomas R. *The Early Years in Brookhaven Town.* Middle Island, NY: Town of Brookhaven, 1962.

Blasl, Courtney. "John H. Achilich, 94." *Riverhead Local*, February 12, 2014.

Bleyer, Bill. "Bay Windows." *Soundings*, February 2016.

———. "Beautiful Beacons—The Lighthouses of Long Island." *Newsday*, May 25, 1986.

———. "Claimed by the Sea." In *Long Island: Our Story*, 185. Melville, NY: Newsday, 1998.

———. "A Cold Welcome in Japan." In *Long Island: Our Story*, 172. Melville, NY: Newsday, 1998.

———. "Doxsee Sea Clam Company." *Long Island Boating World*, September 2016.

———. "The Doxsee Sea Clam Company." In *Long Island: Our Story*, 220. Melville, NY: Newsday, 1998.

———. "Farming Takes Root." In *Long Island: Our Story*, 194. Melville, NY: Newsday, 1998.

———. "Feversham: Colonial LI's Bustling Port." *Long Island Boating World*, August 2015.

———. *Fire Island Lighthouse: Long Island's Welcoming Beacon.* Charleston, SC: The History Press, 2017.

———. "Fundraising for Ship Replica Lags." *Newsday*, December 20, 2011.

———. "Gil Smith, Maker of Sleek Sailboats." *Newsday*, April 19, 1998.

———. "Historian Chronicles Gold Coast Yachting Heyday." *Long Island Boating World*, September 2014.

———. "Historic Sloop out of Slump." *Newsday*, September 26, 1991.

———. "History Takes Sail. Museum to Welcome Public Aboard 122-Year-Old Sailboat." *Newsday*, May 16, 2010.

———. "Keeping History AFLOAT." *Newsday*, November 20, 2011.

———. "The Kings Point Story." *Newsday*, February 24, 2008.

———. "Knickerbocker Club Goes Up for Auction." *Soundings*, February 2010.

———. "The Legacy of 'Mister Oyster.'" *Newsday*, October 4, 1992.

———. "A Lifeline for Sailors." In *Long Island: Our Story*, 184. Melville, NY: Newsday, 1998.

———. "Lighthouse Leased to Preservationists." *Newsday*, November 7, 1988.

———. "Lighthouses of Long Island." In *Long Island: Our Story*, 184. Melville, NY: Newsday, 1998.

———. "Making It Shipshape: Old Oyster Boat Refitted to Teach Young." *Newsday*, October 9, 1990.

———. "The Military Way." *Newsday*, November 18, 2001.

———. "New Keeper for Bug Light's Light." *Newsday*, September 18, 1991.

———. "New Look for Oyster Sloop." *Newsday*, October 13, 2010.

———. "The Oyster Was Their World." In *Long Island: Our Story*, 220 Melville, NY: Newsday, 1998.

———. "Preservationists Band to Rescue Lighthouse." *Newsday*, November 11, 1985.

———. "Rising Out of History's Depths." *Newsday*, March 29, 2000.

———. "Rumrunners Run Around LI." In *Long Island: Our Story*, 279. Melville, NY: Newsday, 1998.

———. "Rye Cliff Ferry." *Long Island Boating World*, March 2013.

———. "Sailing Past a Centennial." *Newsday*, April 20, 1988.

———. "Seafaring Women in the Age of Sail." *Newsday*, June 29, 1995.

———. "70-Year-Old Cutter in Need of 'Friends.'" *Soundings*, April 2008.

———. "Shipshape in Suffolk." In *Long Island: Our Story*, 271. Melville, NY: Newsday, 1998.

———. "The Sinking of the *San Diego*." In *Long Island: Our Story*, 271. Melville, NY: Newsday, 1998.

———. "Staying Afloat. Boatyards Hark to a Vanishing Era—But Feel Squeeze of Recession, Sandy." *Newsday*, June 23, 2013.

———. "Submarines in LI Waters." In *Long Island: Our Story*, 251. Melville, NY: Newsday, 1998.

———. "Training Sailing Champs." *Newsday*, September 14, 2014.

———. "War on the Waters." In *Long Island: Our Story*, 166. Melville, NY: Newsday, 1998.

———. "A Warship Defeated by a Nor'easter." In *Long Island: Our Story*, 185. Melville, NY: Newsday, 1998.

———. "The Water World Begins to Pick Up Steam." In *Long Island: Our Story*, 182. Melville, NY: Newsday, 1998.

———. "A Wife Copes on a Whaling Ship." In *Long Island: Our Story*, 171. Melville, NY: Newsday, 1998.

———. "The Wreck of the *Lexington*." In *Long Island: Our Story*, 185. Melville, NY: Newsday, 1998.

Blidner, Rachelle. "A Ferry Smooth Service." *Newsday*, April 29, 2018.

Bolster, W. Jeffrey. *The Mortal Sea.* Cambridge, MA: Harvard University Press, 2012.

Bookbinder, Bernie. *Long Island: People and Places Past and Present.* New York: Harry N. Abrams Inc., 1983.

Bramson, Ruth Ann, Geoffrey K. Fleming and Amy Kasuga Folk. *A World Unto Itself: The Remarkable History of Plum Island, New York.* Southold, NY: Southold Historical Society, 2014.

Braynard, Frank O. *S.S. Savannah: The Elegant Steam Ship.* Athens: University of Georgia Press, 1963.

The Bridgeport & Port Jefferson Steamboat Company. Port Jefferson, NY: Bridgeport & Port Jefferson Steamboat Company, 1983.

Brookhaven Town Records, vol. 1, 1662–1679. Book II.

Brouwer, Norman J. *Steamboats on Long Island Sound.* Charleston, SC: Arcadia Publishing, 2014.

Brown, Joye. "Divergent Foes of Slavery." In *Long Island: Our Story*, 200. Melville, NY: Newsday, 1998.

Coburn, Jesse. "Glory Days of the Baymen." *Newsday*, June 12, 2018.

Corwin, Elsie Knapp, and Frederick Langton Corwin. *Greenport Yesterday and Today and the Diary of a Country Newspaper.* Greenport, NY: privately published and printed by the *Suffolk Times*, 1972.

Cruikshank, Jeffrey L., and Chloë G. Klein. *In Peace and War.* New York: John Wiley & Sons Inc., 2008.

Dayan, Nomi. *Whaling on Long Island.* Charleston, SC: Arcadia Publishing, 2016.

Dazio, Stephanie. "Shelling Out $400G for Hatchery." *Newsday*, June 27, 2018.

De Wan, George. "Captives of the *Amistad*." In *Long Island: Our Story*, 183. Melville, NY: Newsday, 1998.

———. "A Long Island Exodus." In *Long Island: Our Story*, 152. Melville, NY: Newsday, 1998.

———. "A Ruse Saves the French Fleet." In *Long Island: Our Story*, 136. Melville, NY: Newsday, 1998.

———. "Washington's Eyes and Ears." In *Long Island: Our Story*, 137. Melville, NY: Newsday, 1998.

———. "Whaleboat Warfare." In *Long Island: Our Story*, 142–43. Melville, NY: Newsday, 1998.

Dinn, Alan E. *Boats by Purdy.* St. Michael's, MD: Tiller Publishing, 2003.

Dobbs, Michael. *The Saboteurs: The Nazi Raid on America.* New York: Alfred A. Knopf, 2004.

Documents of the Assembly of the State of New York 141st Session 1918. Albany: J.B. Lyon Company, 1918.

Douglas, Leroy. "Farmingdale's Submarine: The Fairchild X-1." *Nassau County Historical Society Journal* 69 (2014).

Druett, Joan, ed. *She Was a Sister Sailor.* Mystic, CT: Mystic Seaport Museum, 1970.

Druett, Joan, and Mary Anne Wallace. *The Sailing Circle: 19th Century Seafaring Women from New York.* Setauket, NY: Three Village Historical Society, 1997.

Dunbaugh, Edwin L. *A Centennial History of Webb Institute of Naval Architecture.* Glen Cove, NY: Webb Institute of Naval Architecture, 1994.

———. *Long Island Sound Steamboats.* Roslyn, NY: Nassau County Museum of Fine Art, 1984.

———. *Night Boat to New England: 1815–1900.* New York: Greenwood Press, 1992.

East Hampton Star staff. "The Wreck of H.M.S *Sylph*." *East Hampton Star*, October 15, 1998.

Entrepreneur Magazine. "Former Marine Starts International Franchise Helping Stranded Boats." July 26, 2013.

Euler, Laura. "Pyrrhus Concer Home to Be Rebuilt in Southampton Village Soon." Hamptons Curbed, October 19, 2016. https://hamptons.curbed.com/2016/10/19/13331066/pyrrhus-concer-home-to-be-rebuilt-in-southampton-village-soon.

Felknor, Bruce L., ed. *The U.S. Merchant Marine at War, 1775–1945*. Annapolis, MD: Naval Institute Press, 1998.

Field, Van R. *Wrecks and Rescues on Long Island*. Patchogue, NY: Searles Graphics, 1997.

Fischler, Marcelle S. "Bon Voyage to a Gilded Club." *New York Times*, July 26, 2012.

Fleming, Geoffrey K., and Amy Kasuga Folk. *Munnawhatteaug: The Last Days of the Menhaden Industry on Eastern Long Island*. Southold, NY: Southold Historical Society, 2011.

Freeport-Baldwin Leader. "5th Annual Freeport Grand Prix Set for August." July 12, 1990.

Friend (Honolulu, HI). "Japan." February 2, 1846.

Gentile, Gary. *U.S.S San Diego: The Last Armored Cruiser*. Philadelphia: Gary Gentile Productions, 1989.

Geus, Averill Dayton. *From Sea to Sea*. West Kennebunk, ME: Phoenix Publishing, 1999.

Gonzalez, Ellice B. *Storms, Ships & Surfmen*. New York: Eastern Acorn Research Service, 1982.

Grasso, Joanne S. *The American Revolution on Long Island*. Charleston, SC: The History Press, 2016.

Griffin, David M. *Lost British Forts of Long Island*. Charleston, SC: The History Press, 2017.

Griffith, Janelle. "LI Fishing Families Adapt to Survive." *Newsday*, July 30, 2018.

Griswold, Mac. *The Manor*. New York: Farrar, Straus and Giroux, 2013.

Grohman, Adam M. *Claimed by the Sea: Long Island Shipwrecks*. New York: Underwater Historical Research Society, 2008.

———. "Daniel and His Date with the Devil Delayed." *Long Island Boating World*, November–December 2016.

———. *Presidential Plunge: Theodore Roosevelt, the Plunger Submarine & The United States Navy*. Self-published, 2009.

———. *Runner Aground: A History of the Schooner William T. Bell*. Self-published, 2006.

Hagedorn, Hermann. *The Roosevelt Family of Sagamore Hill*. New York: McMillan Company, 1954.

Hamilton, Harlan. "Cold Spring Harbor Light." *Long Island Boating World*, November–December 1997.

———. *Lights & Legends*. Stamford, CT: Wescott Cove Publishing, 1987.

Hammond, John E. *Oyster Bay Remembered*. Huntington, NY: Maple Hill Press, 2002.

Hampton, Dion J. "Board Passes $400G Bond for Hatchery." *Newsday*, June 22, 2018.

———. "Grant Boosts Shellfish Hatchery." *Newsday*, July 3, 2018.

———. "Recouped Sloop." *Newsday*, July 11, 2018.

Hanc, John. "Long Island Spotlights People of Color in Whaling History." *Newsday*, February 7, 2016.

Harrington, Mark. "Huge Scallop Harvest, Growth in Oyster Farming Boost East End." *Newsday*, December 1, 2017.

Harris, Brad. *The Battle of Fort Slongo, 1781.* Fort Salonga, NY: Fort Salonga Association, 2015.

"History of Achievements 1975 to Present." Undated document compiled by Cross Sound Ferry Services Inc. and provided by the company.

Hunt, Harrison, and Bill Bleyer. *Long Island and the Civil War.* Charleston, SC: The History Press, 2015.

James, Will. "Freed Slave's Southampton Property Searched for Artifacts." *Newsday*, June 4, 2016.

Kaasman, Herb "Cap." *Oregon: Greyhound of the Atlantic.* Navesink, NJ: Old Walrus Productions, 1993.

Karppi, Walter G. "Teddy Roosevelt and the Plunger." *The Freeholder* (Oyster Bay Historical Society), Summer 2003.

Keatts, Henry, and George Farr. *Shipwrecks & Lighthouses of Eastern Long Island.* Eastport, NY: Fathom Press, 2002.

Kelly, Douglas R. *Webb Institute: 125 Years of Excellence.* Glen Cove, NY: Webb Institute, 2014.

Koetzer, Virginia. "Rum Runner's Adventures." *Long Island Boating World*, January 2017.

Kroplick, Howard. *North Hempstead.* Charleston, SC: Arcadia Publishing, 2014.

Kuperschmid, David. "Ghosts of Gardiner's Point." *East Hampton Star*, June 9, 2016.

Leader. "Powerboats Compete in Freeport Grand Prix." May 26, 1988.

Lippman, Andrew. "The Forgotten Contest between Colonists and American Indians for Command of the Atlantic." *Slate*, November 24, 2015.

Luke, Myron, and Robert W. Venables. *Long Island in the American Revolution.* Albany: New York State American Revolution Bicentennial Commission, 1976.

MacKay, Anne, ed. *She Went A-Whaling.* Orient, NY: Oyster Ponds Historical Society, 1993.

MacKay, Robert B. *Great Yachts of Long Island's North Shore.* Charleston, SC: Arcadia Publishing, 2014.

MacKay, Robert B., Geoffrey L. Rossano and Carol A. Traynor, *Between Ocean and Empire*. Northridge, CA: Windsor Publications, 1985.

Matthiessen, Peter. *Men's Lives*. New York: Random House, 1986.

Mattson, Arthur S. *Water and Ice: The Tragic Wrecks of the* Bristol *and the* Mexico *on the South Shore of Long Island*. Lynbrook, NY: Lynbrook Historical Books, 2009.

McQuiston, John T. "State Will Buy Old Shipyard for Oyster Bay Waterfront." *New York Times*, March 15, 1997.

Merritt, Jim. "Catching a Rising Tide." *Newsday*, August 13, 2017.

———. "Long Island's Islands." *Newsday*, July 3, 2018.

Minuse, William B. "Shipbuilding in the Three Village Area." Manuscript, March 1955. Contained in the Emma S. Clark Memorial Library, Long Island Collection. L.I. 623.822 MINASBarcode 06279003518226.

Moore, C. Philip. *Yachts in a Hurry*. New York: W.W. Norton & Company, 1994.

Morris, Deborah S. "A Renovation to Beam About." *Newsday*, July 3, 2018.

Müller, Robert G. *Long Island's Lighthouses Past and Present*. Patchogue, NY: Long Island Chapter of the U.S. Lighthouse Society, 2004.

———. *New York State Lighthouses*. Charleston, SC: Arcadia Publishing, 2005.

Mundus, Pat. "All American: 1937 Alden Cutter Zaida III." *Soundings*, March 17, 2016. https://www.soundingsonline.com/boats/all-american-1937-alden-cutter-zaida-iii.

———. "Starboard Tack." *East Hampton Star*, July 16, 1998.

Needham, Henry Beach. "Theodore Roosevelt as a Country Gentleman." *Country Calendar*, October 1905.

New Bedford Whaling Museum. Inventory of the Cooper Family Papers in the New Bedford Whaling Museum Research Library. https://www.whalingmuseum.org/explore/library/finding-aids/mss85.

Newcomb, James F. *Lloyd's Register of American Yachts, 1927*. London: Lloyd's of London, 1927.

Newsday. "Speedboat Regatta Slated for Sunday." August 8, 1946.

Newsday staff. "Milestones in Transportation." In *Long Island: Our Story*, 388–89. Melville, NY: Newsday, 1998.

New York Times. "Capt. Hank Haff Is Dead." July 1, 1906.

———. "Davy Jones's Locker Loses a Lot of Booze." March 27, 1927.

———. "Rum Ship Wrecked, Townsfolk Save Crew, Then Brave Raging Sea to Share in Liquor." February 21, 1927.

———. "Wrecked Rum Craft Yields 250 More Kegs." February 22, 1927.

———. "Wrecked Schooner Yields More Liquor." February 27, 1927.

Noble, Dennis L. *A Legacy: The United States Life-Saving Service.* Washington, D.C.: U.S. Coast Guard Historian's Office, 1990.

Nuccio, Mark C. "The *Bristol*, The *Mexico*, and The *Poet.*" *Long Island Boating World*, May 2017.

———. "More than Brave—The Wreck of the *Circassian.*" *Long Island Boating World*, April, 2017.

———. "Of Whales, Colonists and Native Americans." *Long Island Boating World*, January 2018.

———. "Shell Fishing: A Story of Bounty to Bust." *Long Island Boating World*, February 2017.

Olly, Jonathan. "Long Island During Prohibition, 1920–1933." *Long Island History Journal*, 2017.

Olsen, David. "Shellfish Firm Faces Lawsuit." *Newsday*, April 10, 2018.

———. "Small College with Big Plans." *Newsday*, May 4, 2018.

———. "Within Their Rights." *Newsday*, August 23, 2017.

Onderdonk, Henry, Jr. *Revolutionary Incidents of Suffolk and Kings Counties.* Port Washington, NY: Ira J. Friedman, Kennikat Press, 1970. (First published 1849.)

Osmers, Henry. *American Gibraltar.* Denver, CO: Outskirts Press, 2011.

———. *On Eagle's Beak.* Denver, CO: Outskirts Press, 2008.

Oyster Bay Guardian. "Owners of Stranded Ship at Bayville Fail to Claim Her." February 26, 1927.

Parkinson, John, Jr. *The Seawanhaka Corinthian Yacht Club: The Early Twentieth Century.* New York: Clarke & Way, 1965.

Peconic Bay Shopper. "Famous Boat Built in Greenport." April 2015.

Peraino, Chris. "Architects Chosen to Renovate Cedar Island Lighthouse in Sag Harbor." *Southampton Press*, August 15, 2017.

A Place in History. Kings Point, NY: U.S. Merchant Marine Academy, 2006.

Radune, Richard A. *Sound Rising: Long Island Sound at the Forefront of America's Struggle for Independence.* Branford, CT: Research in Time Publications, 2011.

Rafferty, Pierce, and John Wilton. *Guardian of the Sound: A Pictorial History of Fort H.G. Wright, Fishers Island, N.Y.* New York: Mount Mercer Press, 1998.

Rattray, Jeanette Edwards. *Ship Ashore!* New York: Coward-McCann Inc., 1955.

Reckner, James R. "The Fleet Triumphant." *Theodore Roosevelt Association Journal*, Summer 2008.

Reynolds, Richard J. "New York Yacht Club Station 10." *Long Island Forum*, Summer 1997.

Roosevelt, Theodore. "Outdoors and Indoors." *Outlook*, October 25, 1913.

Rose, Alexander. *Washington's Spies.* New York: Bantam Dell, 2006.

Ross, Tucker Burns. *Sag Harbor.* Charleston, SC: Arcadia Publishing, 2018.

Rossano, Geoffrey L. "Prosperity on the Ways: Shipbuilding in Colonial Oyster Bay, 1745–1775." *Long Island Historical Journal* 2, no. 1 (Fall 1989): 21–28.

———. "To Market, to Market—Oyster Bay and the International Economy in the Mid-18th Eighteenth Century." In *Evoking a Sense of Place: Long Island Studies*, edited by Joann P. Krieg. Madison, WI: Heart of the Lakes Publishing, 1988.

Sailor's Magazine. "The Tolling Bell." January 1947.

Schmitt, Frederick P. *Mark Well the Whale!* Cold Spring Harbor, NY: Whaling Museum Society Inc., 1986.

Schmitt, Frederick P., Cornelis de Jong and Frank H. Winter. *Thomas Welcome Roys: America's Pioneer of Modern Whaling.* Charlottesville: University Press of Virginia, 1980.

Schmitt, Frederick P., and Donald E. Schmid. *H.M.S. Culloden.* Mystic, CT: Marine Historical Association, 1961.

Schneider, Craig. "A Tale of Lobstering on Long Island." *Newsday*, July 16, 2018.

Shodell, Elly. *Cross Currents.* Port Washington, NY: Port Washington Public Library, 1993.

———. *Port Washington.* Charleston, SC: Arcadia Publishing, 2009.

Solomon, Nancy, and Paul Bentel. *On the Bay: Bay Houses and Maritime Culture on Long Island's Marshlands.* Syosset, NY: Friends for Long Island's Heritage, 2011.

Sorrentino, Michael. "Battle on the Bay Races Coming to Shorefront." *Patch*, August 20, 2010.

Spann, Edward K. *Gotham at War.* Wilmington, DE: SR Books, 2002.

Squire, Paul. "The Tale of the Cutter *Eagle.*" *Riverhead News-Review*, May 25, 2014.

Stephens, W.P. *The Seawanhaka Corinthian Yacht Club: Origins and Early History 1871–1896.* New York: Seawanhaka Corinthian Yacht Club, 1963.

Stoff, Joshua. *From Canoes to Cruisers: The Maritime Heritage of Long Island.* Interlochen, NY: Empire State Books, 1994.

———. *Long Island Airports.* Charleston, SC: Arcadia Publishing, 2004.

Stone, Gaynell, ed. *The Shinnecock Indians: A Culture History.* Lexington, MA: Ginn Custom Publishing, 1983.

Striegel, Lawrence. "Paddling a Canoe to Success." *Newsday*, 2007.

Strong, John A. *The Algonquian Peoples of Long Island from Earliest Times to 1700.* Interlaken, NY: Empire State Books, 1997.

———. "Indian Whalers on Long Island, 1669–1746." *Long Island History Journal* 25, no. 1 (2016).

Suffolk County Historical Society. "Gil Smith, Master Boatbuilder." *Register* 12, no. 2 (1986): 38–50.

Turano, Francis. "The Papers of William Cooper (1785–1857), Sag Harbor Whale Boat Builder." *Long Island Historical Journal* 25, no. 1 (2016).

Upright, Carlton. *The Times and Tides of Bayville, Long Island, NY.* Bayville, NY: Village of Bayville, 1969.

U.S. Lighthouse Society News. "Restoration of Amagansett Life-Saving Station Now Complete." May 10, 2017.

Vincitorio, Gaetano L. "The Revolutionary War and Its Aftermath in Suffolk County, Long Island." *Long Island Historical Journal* 7, no. 1 (September 1994).

Wallace, George. "Rare Catch for Cold Spring Harbor Whaling Museum." *Oyster Bay Guardian,* April 6, 2018.

Walton, Terry. *Cold Spring Harbor.* Cold Spring Harbor, NY: Whaling Museum Society, 1999.

Watson, Elizabeth L. *Houses for Science.* Cold Spring Harbor, NY: Cold Spring Harbor Laboratory Press, 1991.

Weigold, Marilyn E. *The American Mediterranean: An Environmental, Economic and Social History of Long Island Sound.* Port Washington, NY: Kennik Press, 1974.

———. *The Long Island Sound: A History of Its People, Places and Environment.* New York: New York University Press, 2004.

Welch, Richard F. *An Island's Trade: Nineteenth-Century Shipbuilding on Long Island.* Mystic, CT: Mystic Seaport Museum, 1993.

———. *Long Island and World War I.* Charleston, SC: The History Press, 2018.

Welles, Gordon, and William Proios. *Port Jefferson—Story of a Village.* Port Jefferson, NY: Historical Society of Greater Port Jefferson, 1977.

Whitman, Walt. *Complete Poetry and Collected Prose Works.* New York: Literary Classics of the United States, 1982.

Wick, Steve. "In Search of Whales." In *Long Island: Our Story,* 168–70. Melville, NY: Newsday, 1998.

———. "The Legend of Capt. Kidd." In *Long Island: Our Story,* 85. Melville, NY: Newsday, 1998.

———. "The Nazi 'Invasion' of LI." In *Long Island: Our Story,* 313. Melville, NY: Newsday, 1998.

————. "Property of the Netherlands." In *Long Island: Our Story*, 45. Melville, NY: Newsday, 1998.

————. "Sag Harbor's Heyday." In *Long Island: Our Story*, 163. Melville, NY: Newsday, 1998.

————. "Stranded in a Strange Land." In *Long Island: Our Story*, 163. Melville, NY: Newsday, 1998.

Wiggin, Merlon E. "Beebe McLellan Surf Boats." *Peconic Bay Shopper*, September 2005.

————. "Greenport Builds Wooden Ships for World War II." Parts 1, 2 and 3. *Peconic Bay Shopper*, October and November 2005 and February 2006.

————. "History of the Greenport Area's Oyster Industry." Parts 1 and 2. *Peconic Bay Shopper*, June and August 2002.

————. "Maritime History of the North Fork of Eastern Long Island, NY: Whaling." *Peconic Bay Shopper*, November 1998.

————. "Oil & Fertilizer from the Sea." Parts 1, 2 and 6. *Peconic Bay Shopper*, November and December 2004 and May 2005.

————. "Shipbuilding in Greenport." *Peconic Bay Shopper*, August 2004.

Zaykowski, Dorothy Ingersoll. *Sag Harbor: The Story of an American Beauty.* Sag Harbor, NY: Sag Harbor Historical Society, 1991.

Websites

Alabama, AL.com.

America Scoop, america-scoop.com.

Aqua Explorers, aquaexplorers.com.

Around Long Island Regatta, alir.org.

Bramson, Ruth Ann, Geoffrey K. Fleming and Amy K. Folk. "The Coastal Forts of Eastern Long Island." Southold Historical Society, http://www.southoldhistoricalsociety.org/coastal-forts.

Bridgeport & Port Jefferson Steamboat Company, 88844ferry.com.

Camp Hero, camphero.net.

Coast Defense Study Group. "Harbor Defenses of Long Island Sound." cdsg.org/fort-michie-great-gull-island-ny-april-2006.

Dawn Riley, dawnriley.com.

Federal Bureau of Investigation, fbi.gov.

Greater Patchogue Historical Society, greaterpatchoguehistoricalsociety.com.

Hampton Roads Naval Museum, hamptonroadsnavalmuseum.blogspot.com.

Hamptons Curbed, hamptons.curbed.com.

Herreshoff Marine Museum, herreshoff.org.

History Channel, history.com.

History Close at Hand, historycloseathand.com.

Huntington Historical Society, huntingtonhistoricalsociety.org.

Huntington Lighthouse Preservation Society, huntingtonlighthouse.org.

Lighthouse Friends, lighthousefriends.com.

Long Island Maritime Museum, limaritime.org.

Manhasset Bay Yacht Club, manhassetbayyc.org.

Nassau County, nassaucountyny.gov.

NavSource Naval History, navsource.org.

New London Maritime Society Custom House Maritime Museum, nlmaritimesociety.org.

New York State Military Museum, dmna.ny.gov.

Preservation Long Island, PreservationLongIsland.org.

Save Stepping Stones Lighthouse, steppingstoneslight.com.

Sayville Yacht Club, sayvilleyachtclub.org.

Sewanhaka Corinthian Yacht Club, https://seawanhaka.org.

Shipbuilding History, http://shipbuildinghistory.com.

Southold Historical Society. "The War of 1812." southoldhistoricalsociety.org/lh-war-of-1812-display.

Steiger Craft, steigercraft.com.

U.S. Army Corps of Engineers, nan.usace.army.mil.

U.S. Coast Guard, www.uscg.mil.

Village of Greenport, villageofgreenport.org.

Ward Melville Heritage Organization, wmho.org.

WaterFront Center, thewaterfrontcenter.org.

Webb Institute, webb.edu.

Wooden Boatworks, woodenboatworks.com.

Wikipedia. "Mercator Cooper." Last modified January 22, 2019. https://en.wikipedia.org/wiki/Mercator_Cooper.

Zip 06, zip06.com.

Miscellaneous

An early Sperry gyroscope, Box 3, Folder 10, Elmer Sperry Photograph Collection (1985.257), Hagley Museum & Library, Wilmington, DE 19807.

Jakobson Shipyard records in the collection of Oyster Bay Town Historian John Hammond.

INDEX

ABOUT THE AUTHOR

Copyright 2016 by Audrey C. Tiernan.

B ill Bleyer was a prizewinning staff writer for *Newsday*, the Long Island daily newspaper, for thirty-three years before retiring in 2014 to write books and freelance for the newspaper and magazines.

He is coauthor, with Harrison Hunt, of *Long Island and the Civil War* (The History Press, 2015). He is the author of *Sagamore Hill: Theodore Roosevelt's Summer White House* (The History Press, 2016) and *Fire Island Lighthouse: Long Island's Welcoming Beacon* (The History Press, 2017).

He contributed a chapter to the anthology *Harbor Voices: New York Harbor Tugs, Ferries, People, Places & More*, published in 2008, and he was a contributor and editor of the Bayville history book published by Arcadia in 2009.

The Long Island native has written extensively about history for newspapers and magazines. In 1997–98, he was one of four *Newsday* staff writers assigned full-time to *Long Island: Our Story*, a year-long daily history of Long Island that resulted in three books and filled hundreds of pages in the newspaper.

His work has been published in *Civil War News*, *Naval History*, *Sea History*, *Lighthouse Digest* and numerous other magazines and in the *New York Times*, *Chicago Sun-Times*, the *Toronto Star* and other newspapers.

Prior to joining *Newsday*, Bleyer worked for six years at the *Courier-News* in Bridgewater, New Jersey, as an editor and reporter. He began his career as editor of the *Oyster Bay Guardian* for a year.

Bleyer graduated Phi Beta Kappa with highest honors in economics from Hofstra University, where he has been an adjunct professor teaching journalism and economics. He earned a master's degree in urban studies at Queens College of the City University of New York. He is an adjunct professor at Webb Institute, the naval architecture college in Glen Cove, New York.

An avid sailor, diver and kayaker, he lives in Bayville, Long Island.